The Nuclear Arms Race — Control or Catastrophe?

The Nuclear Arms Race — Control or Catastrophe?

Edited by
Frank Barnaby
Geoffrey Thomas

Proceedings of the General Section of the
British Association for the Advancement of Science 1981

St. Martins Press, New York

ISBN 0-312-57974-8

Library of Congress Cataloging in Publication Data
Main entry under title:

The Nuclear arms race.

    1. Atomic warfare—Congresses.   2. Deterrence
(Strategy)—Congresses.   3. Strategic forces—Con-
gresses.   4. Atomic weapons and disarmament—Congresses.
I. Barnaby, Frank, 1927-   .   II. Thomas Geoffrey
(Geoffrey P.)   III. British Association for the Ad-
vancement of Science. General Section.
UF767.N77   1982   355'.0217   81-21282
ISBN 0-312-57974-8   AACR2

CONTENTS

1. INTRODUCTION

Frank Barnaby and Geoffrey Thomas

The papers which follow were all presented to the General Section of the British Association for the Advancement of Science at its Annual Meeting in September 1981. The Meeting marked the 150th Anniversary of the Association and was held at York, where the Association first met in 1831.

The Association, which in its early years quickly established itself as the national forum for the presentation and discussion of scientific advances, also developed as a meeting-point between scientist and layman, between professional and public. Whilst other platforms have been established for practitioners to talk to other professionals within the same scientific discipline, the Association has remained as probably the only gathering where scientists from many different disciplines can meet together and can present their ideas to interested laymen. The notion of the British Association also as 'the parliament of science' emerged very early in its history, and remains a useful one in reflecting on many of its activities.

The Association has sixteen sections which embrace most fields of the natural and social sciences. The General Section which was established in 1954 differs from these in that each year it takes a theme which crosses disciplinary boundaries, and is often concerned with social implications of scientific developments. In pursuing this sort of theme the Section has carried on the work of the Division of Social and International Relations of Science which it absorbed in 1959. The Division had been launched in the late 1930s, largely through the efforts of Richard Gregory, then editor of *Nature*, and attracted a very distinguished group of enthusiasts including J. D. Bernal, H. G. Wells, Ritchie Calder, Lancelot

Hogben and Julian Huxley. One of the most notable conferences arranged by the DSIRS was the 1941 International Conference on 'Science and the World Order'.

The General Section, in choosing its theme for the 1981 Meeting, sought to establish a forum where scientists and others could discuss the crucially important and increasingly worrying developments in the nuclear arms race. The papers reprinted in this volume were presented to large audiences at York, and attracted a good deal of attention in the media. Although practical constraints prevented comprehensive coverage of all aspects of the issue, varying viewpoints were represented, and a great deal of factual information was made available.

In order that this collection of papers should be produced as soon after the British Association's meeting as possible, we did not ask the authors substantially to reshape their contributions for purposes of publication, although most of the chapters contain rather more material than was presented at York. Neither have we thought it wise to try to impose a uniformity of style which might mask the character of the various contributions.

The papers in summary

The President of the General Section for 1981, Professor Frank Barnaby, presents in his opening paper a review of the current state of nuclear arsenals, and of the massive overkill capabilities of the superpowers and other nuclear states. He argues that as military science drives the nuclear spiral ever upwards, and as nuclear policies change from deterrence to nuclear war-fighting, so also does the probability of nuclear conflict — almost inevitably global conflict — increase.

Dr David Owen, welcoming the return of the nuclear arms issue to the agenda of public debate, argues that calls for unilateral nuclear disarmament are unrealistic at present in the absence of alternative strategies for balancing NATO and Warsaw Pact forces. He advocates a strengthening of NATO conventional forces which could allow a nuclear 'no first strike' agreement to be arrived at followed by negotiations towards a multilateral reduction in nuclear arsenals. For deterrence to be effective, Dr Owen stresses the need for arms control and disarmament to be put at the centre of international political activity.

Mr E. P. Thompson adopts a very different stance. Condemning theories of deterrence as the 'astrology of the nuclear age' he argues that the retention of nuclear weapons, menacing in themselves and deeply symbolic of mutually threatening attitudes, blocks any prospect of the dialogues which could lead to the making of peace. 'Deterrence', he says, 'enters deeply into the structure, the economy and the culture of both blocs', making nuclear war probable in our life-times. He calls for scientists and others to go ahead of politicians in the resumption of every possible mode of discourse to break down the unnatural opposition of the blocs.

Professor John Erickson distinguishes notions of deterrence through punishment (US theory) and deterrence through denial (Soviet theory), the latter aiming to deny the enemy army the advantage of striking first as well as to reduce his prospect of military gain. Deterrence by denial has a pronounced military bias; it presupposes an unremittingly hostile adversary and is based on a deep-seated sense of vulnerability. Professor Erickson explains how Soviet deterrence theory thus rejects mutual assured destruction and leaves no option should deterrence fail.

Professor Egbert Boeker, using the development of laser physics as an example, discusses the contributions of science and scientists to human welfare on the one hand, and to human destructive power on the other. Pointing to a typical discussion, in the European Physical Society, he decries the discouragement of open debate of contentious issues within the scientific community. He urges the acceptability of military research only if it fits into an unambiguously defensive context.

While the nuclear stockpiles still exist, the awesome consequences of possible nuclear conflict have to be faced. Professor Joseph Rotblat, discussing the physical and medical effects of nuclear weapons, points to their different modes of destruction (blast, heat, radiation and fall-out) and to how relatively unpredictable these are. His conclusion is that most statements about the effects of nuclear weapons underestimate the consequences of radiation.

Mr Sidney Butler reviews the work of the Home Office scientists charged with advising on the civil defence measures which might be taken to mitigate the effect of a nuclear attack. Short- and long-term effects and the percentage of the population likely to survive are discussed, in the light of the suggested effectiveness of the three main measures (warning, shelter and dispersal) which influence survival levels. He argues that sensible home defence precautions are necessary on humanitarian grounds and worthwhile for Great Britain in present circumstances. He estimates that for a representative (200 megatons) nuclear attack on the country, at least half the population could survive.

Professor George Rathjens stresses the folly of basing ideas of nuclear conflict on notions of limited damage, let alone of victory. Mutual assured destruction, he says, is not a matter of doctrine, but an accurate description of the present capabilities of the superpowers. He cites the likely devastating effects of full-scale nuclear attacks on densely populated areas, from which 'there is no defence'. He goes on to argue that a Soviet first-strike against US strategic targets is not a likely prospect, given the uncertainties in the responses it would elicit; and should not therefore be shaping US strategic thinking. Given the sheer unpredictability of adversary behaviour, Professor Rathjens also argues that scenarios limiting any potential European nuclear conflict are worthless.

Mr Nicholas Sims analyses the present gloomy prospects for nuclear disarmament as pursued through diplomatic channels. He points first to the gulf between, on the one hand, governments which accord absolute priority to dealing with nuclear weapons, and on the other, those which refuse to discuss nuclear disarmament separately from conventional arms reductions. A second major difficulty is whether nuclear disarmament is seen as the proper concern of nuclear-weapon states only, or of the world as a whole. Although he makes suggestions which might reduce these tensions, Mr Sims concludes that progress, if any, down the diplomatic road to nuclear disarmament will be painfully slow and hard-won with no alternative routes in prospect.

Dr Nigel Young considers the role of public opinion in relation to the control or reversal of the nuclear arms race against the background of transnational non-governmental movements and their traditions — pacific, internationalist, etc. He also discusses the evolution of secular anti-militarist attitudes to date and concludes that if the multifarious peace movements can unite to establish a mass movement then public opinion may succeed in averting the nuclear threat where governments have hitherto failed.

Professor John Humphrey analyses the crucial involvement of the scientist in the nuclear arms race, explicable in terms of the availability of well-paid jobs, the challenging nature of the problems, official approval and the spice of secrecy. He urges the professional bodies of science to elaborate ways in which scientists who wish to leave military research could be usefully employed in other sectors of the economy. He also suggests that scientific societies should undertake part of the responsibilities for the verification of arms control and disarmament treaties.

Acknowledgements

We extend our enormous thanks to the individual authors and to all those whose help has made this volume possible. It is offered in all humility as a contribution to what is undoubtedly the most urgent and important discussion of our times.

2. NUCLEAR CONFLICT: A GLOBAL PROSPECT?

Frank Barnaby

Five countries — the USA, the USSR, the UK, France, and China — are known to have nuclear weapons. Some believe that other countries — like Israel and South Africa — also have them but the evidence for this is inconclusive. What is certain, however, is that, of the nuclear-weapon powers, the nuclear arsenals of the USA and the USSR are enormous (see Tables 1 and 2). In comparison, the other arsenals are pygmies (see Table 3). Whereas the superpowers deploy several tens of thousands of nuclear warheads, the British, French, and Chinese arsenals contain a total of a thousand or so nuclear weapons. Even though each of these smaller nuclear forces could wreak unimaginable damage, we will concentrate in this chapter on the American and Soviet nuclear arsenals simply because they are so huge that they totally dominate the others.

But before we discuss these aresenals in detail, we will describe the basic types of nuclear weapons which exist. The improvements being made in nuclear-weapon systems will then be explained and the consequences of them discussed. It will be suggested that the new nuclear military technologies themselves increase the probability of a nuclear world war. The possible ways in which such a war may occur are briefly described.

Types of nuclear weapons

Atomic bombs. The most basic nuclear weapon is the fission bomb (or A-bomb). A fission chain reaction is used to produce a large amount of energy in a very short time — roughly a millionth of a second — and, therefore, a very powerful explosion.

Table 1   US strategic delivery capability (mid-1981)

Vehicle	Number of delivery vehicles deployed	Number of warheads per delivery vehicle	Total delivery capability (number of warheads)	Total yield per delivery vehicle (Mt)	Total delivery capability (Mt)	Estimated CEP (m)
MIRVed vehicles						
Minuteman III	450	3	1350	0.51	230	300
Minuteman III (Mk 12A)	100	3	300	1.05	105	200
Poseidon C-3[a]	320	10[b]	3200	0.4	128	500
Trident C-4[d]	200	8	1600	0.8	160	500
Sub-total	1070		6450		623	
Non-MIRVed vehicles						
B-52 (SRAMS + bombs)	150[c]	12[d]	1800	5.6	840	180
B-52 (bombs)	190[c]	4[d]	760	4	760	180
Titan II	53	1	53	9	477	1300
Minuteman II	450	1	450	1.5	675	400
Polaris A-3[a]	80	3	240	0.6	58	900
Sub-total	923		3303		2780	
TOTAL	1993		9753[e]		3423	

[a] SLBM
[b] Average figure
[c] Including heavy bombers in storage, etc. there are 573 strategic bombers.
[d] Operational loading. Maximum loading per aircraft may be eleven bombs, each of about one megaton.
[e] Of these, 7033 are independently targetable warheads on ballistic missiles (2153 on ICBMs and 4880 on SLBMs.) Ballistic missiles carry 53% of the megatonnage, 43% on ICBMs and 10% on SLBMs, and bombers carry 47%.

Table 2 Soviet strategic missile delivery capability (mid-1981)

Vehicle	Number of delivery vehicles deployed	Number of warheads per delivery vehicle	Total delivery capability (number of warheads)	Total yield per delivery vehicle (Mt)	Total delivery capability (Mt)	Estimated CEP (m)
MIRVed vehicles						
SS-17	150	4	600	2	300	300–600
SS-18	308	8	2464	5	1540	300–600
SS-19	360	6	2160	3	1080	330–450
SS-N-18[a]	192	3	576	0.6	115	550–1000
Sub-total	1010		5800		3035	
Non-MIRVed vehicles						
SS-11	230	1	230	1	230	1000–1800
SS-11 (MRV)	290	3	870	0.6	174	
SS-13	60	1	60	1	60	
SS-N-5[a]	18	1	18	1	18	
SS-N-6[a]	166	1	166	1	166	1000–2500
SS-N-6[a] (MRV)	272	3	816	0.6	163	1400
SS-NX-17[a]	12	1	12	1	12	500
SS-N-8[a]	290	1	290	1	290	1000–1500
Sub-total	1338		2462		1113	
TOTAL	2348		8262[b]		4148	

a SLBM

b Of these, 7138 are independently targetable (5804 on ICBMs and 1334 on SLBMs). ICBMs carry 81% of the total megatonnage, and SLBMs carry the remaining 19%.

Table 3   The strategic nuclear forces of other powers[a]

Weapon	First deployed	Maximum range[b] (km)	No. of re-entry vehicles	Yield	Number deployed
FRANCE					
IRBM S-2[c]	1971	3000	1	150 *kt*	18
SLBM M-20[d]	1977	3000	1	1 *Mt*	80
Aircraft Mirage IV-A	1964	3000	1 nuclear weapon per aircraft		33
BRITAIN					
SLBM Polaris A-3[e]	1967	4600	3	200 *kt*	64
Aircraft Vulcan B-2[f]	1960	6500	2 nuclear weapons per aircraft		48
CHINA					
MRBM CSS-1	1966	about 1200	1	about 20 *kt*	about 40

IRBM CSS-2	1971	about 3000	1	about 1 Mt	about 50
ICBM CSS-3g	1978	about 6000	1	about 3 Mt	about 2
Aircraft Tu-16	1968	about 3500	1 nuclear weapon per aircraft		about 75

MRBM: medium range ballistic missile

IRBM: intermediate range ballistic missile

ICBM: intercontinental ballistic missile

SLBM: submarine launched ballistic missile

kt: kiloton

Mt: megaton

a The total nuclear-weapon stockpiles are larger than is implied here because of reserves and tactical nuclear weapons. China probably has about 300 or 400 nuclear weapons, and France and the UK roughly the same. Fighter aircraft could be used to deliver tactical nuclear weapons. France has 32 PLUTON ground-to-ground missiles, each of which carries a warhead with a yield of about 20 kt and has a range of 120 km.

b For aircraft the operational range which would allow the aircraft to reach the target and return to base is less than a half of the maximum range.

c Being replaced with the S-3, which has the same range but a 1.2 Mt warhead.

d Carried on 5 nuclear submarines, each having 16 SLBMs. One more strategic nuclear submarine is being built. The M-4 SLBM, carrying 6 or 7 multiple independently targetable re-entry vehicles each with a yield of 150 kt, is being developed. The M-4 will have a range of 4000 kilometers.

e Carried on 4 nuclear submarines, each having 16 SLBMs. The British may replace their Polaris submarines with Trident submarines.

f These aircraft will probably soon be retired.

g An ICBM, the CSS-4, has been tested to a range of about 12.000 km. It will probably soon be deployed.

The fission occurs in a heavy material — specifically uranium or plutonium. The atomic bombs built so far have used the isotopes uranium-235 or plutonium-239 as the fissile material[1]. A fission occurs when a neutron enters a nucleus of an atom of one of these materials, which then breaks up, or undergoes fission. When a fission occurs a large amount of energy is released, the original nucleus is split into two radioactive nuclei (the fission products), and two or three neutrons are released. These neutrons can be used to produce a self-sustaining chain reaction. A chain reaction will take place if at least one of the neutrons released in each fission causes the fission of another heavy nucleus.

There exists a critical mass of uranium-235 and plutonium-239 — the smallest amount of the material in which a self-sustaining chain reaction (and hence a nuclear explosion) will take place. The critical mass depends on the nuclear properties of the material used for the fission (whether, for example, it is uranium-235 or plutonium-239), the density of the material (the higher the density the shorter the average distance travelled by a neutron before causing another fission and therefore the smaller the critical mass), the purity of the material (if materials other than fissile ones are present some neutrons may be captured by their nuclei instead of causing fission), and the physical surroundings of the material (if, for example, the material is surrounded by a medium like natural uranium, which reflects neutrons back into the material, some of the neutrons may be used for fission which would otherwise have been lost, thus reducing the critical mass).

The critical mass of, for example, a bare sphere of pure plutonium-239 metal in its densest phase would be about 10 kilograms, about the size of a small grapefruit. Using a technique called implosion, in which conventional explosive lenses are used to compress a slightly less than critical mass to a mass which is slightly greater than critical, a nuclear explosion could be achieved with less than 2 kilograms of plutonium-239. (A 2-kilogram sphere of plutonium-239 would have a radius of about 2.8 cm, smaller than a tennis ball.)

In a nuclear explosion exceedingly high temperatures (hundreds of millions of degrees Celsius) and exceedingly high pressures (hundreds of millions of bar) build up extremely rapidly (in about one-half of a millionth of a second, corresponding to the time taken for about 55 generations of fission). The mass of the fissile material expands, therefore, at very fast speeds (initially at a speed of about 1000 kilometres a second). In much less than a millionth of a second, the size and density of the mass of fissile material becomes less than critical and the chain reaction stops. The designer of a nuclear weapon must aim at keeping the fissile material together, against its tendency to fly apart, long enough to get sufficient generations of fission to produce an explosion strong enough for his purpose.

In the atomic bomb which destroyed Nagasaki, about 8 kilograms of plutonium (which contained more than 90 per cent plutonium-239) were used, in the form of two gold-clad hemispheres of plutonium metal. The plutonium was surrounded by a tamper which had two functions. Firstly, to reflect back into the plutonium some of the neutrons which escaped through the surface of the core, allowing some reduction in the mass of plutonium needed for a nuclear explosion. Secondly, and more importantly, because the tamper was made of a heavy material, its inertia helped hold together the plutonium during the explosion to contain the disintegration of the fissile material and obtain greater efficiency.

The plutonium core was surrounded by chemical explosives arranged as explosive lenses focused on the centre of the plutonium sphere. When these lenses were detonated the sphere was compressed uniformly, by the implosion. The compression increased the density of the plutonium so that the sub-critical mass was made super-critical.

The final component in the Nagasaki bomb was the 'initiator', used to initiate the fission reaction in the plutonium at precisely the right moment during the explosion of the chemical explosive lenses. The initiator consisted of a hollow sphere placed at the centre of the plutonium core. Inside the initiator was some polonium and berrylium, two elements which produce neutrons when intimately mixed. The two substances were placed separately on opposite sides of the initiator. Explosive lenses were focused onto the surface of the initiator. At the moment of implosion the initiator was crushed, the berrylium and polonium mixed and a pulse of neutrons given off when the plutonium was super-critical.

The complete detonation of 1 kilogram of plutonium would produce an explosion equivalent to that of about 20 000 tons of TNT. The 8 kilograms of plutonium in the Nagasaki bomb produced an explosion equivalent to that of 22 000 tons of TNT. Its efficiency was, therefore, only about 10 per cent.

A major problem in designing this type of nuclear weapon for maximum efficiency is to prevent the chain reaction from being started before the greatest achievable super-criticality is reached, an eventuality called pre-initiation. If this occurs it will reduce the explosive power, or the yield, of the explosion and will also make the yield uncertain.

Pre-initiation is most likely to be caused by a neutron from spontaneous fission — fission that occurs without the stimulus of an external neutron — in the fissionable material. In 8 kilograms of plutonium-239 the average time between spontaneous fissions is only about three millionths of a second. The assembly of a plutonium bomb must, therefore, be rapid; implosion is necessary for such microsecond precision. In uranium, however, the average time between spontaneous fissions is much greater and so a gun method can be used to assemble a critical mass in a nuclear weapon.

In the Hiroshima bomb, for example, a sub-critical mass of uranium-235 was fired down a 'cannon barrel' into another sub-critical mass of uranium-235 placed in front of the 'muzzle'. When the two masses came together they formed a super-critical mass which exploded.

About 60 kilograms of uranium-235 were used in the Hiroshima bomb (of which about 700 grams underwent fission). The average time between spontaneous fissions was about one-fiftieth of a second — adequate for the gun technique. The yield of the Hiroshima bomb was equivalent to that of about 12 500 tons of TNT.

Although designs based on the Hiroshima and Nagasaki bombs might still be used by countries beginning a nuclear-weapon programme, they are crude compared with current

American and Soviet nuclear warheads. The Nagasaki bomb, for example, was about 3 m long, 1.5 m wide, and weighed about 4 500 kilograms. A modern American warhead weighs about 100 kilograms and has an explosive power of about 350 000 tons of TNT. Yield-to-weight ratios, the standard measure of the efficiency of a bomb, have gone from about 5 000 for the Nagasaki bomb to about 3.5 million for today's best nuclear warheads. The latter figure is, in fact, close to the theoretical maximum attainable. Another indication of the sophistication of modern nuclear warheads is that they can be packed into 8-inch nuclear artillery shells.

H-bombs. The next significant advance in nuclear warhead design after the Nagasaki bomb was the 'boosted weapon', in which fusion was used to obtain nuclear explosions with yields in the 100 000 ton (100-kiloton) range. The maximum explosive yield achievable by pure fission weapons is limited to a few tens of kilotons because the chain reaction can, in practice, be sustained for only a relatively short time.

The fusion process is the opposite to that of fission. In fusion, light nuclei are formed (fused) into heavier ones. In nuclear weapons the heavier isotopes of hydrogen — deuterium and tritium — are fused together to form helium. The reaction produces energy and is accompanied by the emission of neutrons. There is no critical mass for the fusion process and, therefore, in principle there is no limit to the explosive yield of fusion weapons — or H-bombs as they are often called.

Fission is relatively easy to start: one neutron of any speed will initiate a chain reaction in a critical mass of fissile material (such as uranium-235 or plutonium-239). But fusion is possible only if the component nuclei are given a high enough energy to overcome the repulsive electric force between them due to their like positive charges. In the H-bomb this energy is provided by raising the temperature of the fusion material. Hence H-bombs are also called thermonuclear weapons.

In order to make the deuterium–tritium fusion reaction work, a temperature of a hundred million degrees Celsius or so is required. This can be provided only by an A-bomb in which such a temperature is achieved at the moment of the explosion. An H-bomb, therefore, consists of a fission stage (the A-bomb which acts as a trigger), and a fusion stage (in which hydrogen is ignited by the heat produced by the trigger).

The energy released from an H-bomb comes from the fission trigger and the fusion material. But if the fusion weapon is surrounded by a shell of uranium-238 the high energy neutrons produced in the fusion process will cause additional fissions in the uranium shell (low-energy neutrons do not cause uranium-238 to undergo fission). This technique can be used to enhance considerably the explosive power of an H-bomb. Such a weapon is called a fission-fusion-fission device. On average, about a half of the yield from a typical thermonuclear weapon will come from fission and the other half from fusion.

H-bombs are much more difficult to design than A-bombs. The problem is to prevent the A-bomb trigger from blowing the whole weapon apart before enough fusion material has been ignited to give the required explosive yield. Sufficient energy has to be delivered to the fusion material to start the thermonuclear reaction in a time much shorter than the time it takes for the explosion to occur. This requires the energy to be delivered with a speed approaching the speed of light[2]. It is this requirement that makes the design of an H-bomb much more sophisticated than that of an A-bomb.

H-bombs of very large yields have been exploded. For example, the Soviet Union exploded one in 1962 with a yield equal to that of 58 million tons of TNT (megatons), equivalent to about 3000 Nagasaki bombs. Such huge bombs, however, make little sense. The largest city would be completely devastated by an H-bomb of 10 megatons or so.

The Soviet and American strategic nuclear arsenals

Current operational nuclear weapons have a vast range of explosive power, varying between 100 tons and at least 25 000 000 tons of TNT equivalent. (In practice, the minimum yield of a nuclear weapon is about 0.1 ton. This is because the chemical explosive needed for the implosion lens weighs at least about 100 kilograms. In principle, any amount of fission energy could be added to this yield. About 100 kilograms is also, of course, the minimum physical weight of a nuclear weapon. Some modern nuclear warheads, in fact, weigh little more than 100 kilograms.) To put these numbers into some sort of perspective, all of the bombs dropped in the eight most violent years of the Vietnam war totalled only about 4 million tons. *A single American B-52 strategic nuclear bomber can carry more explosive power than that used in all the wars in history.*

American *strategic* nuclear forces carry about 9800 nuclear warheads, with a total explosive power equivalent to that of about 3400 million tonnes of high explosive (see Table 4). Soviet strategic nuclear forces could deliver about 7000 nuclear warheads, with a total explosive power equivalent to that of about 4200 million tons of high explosive (Table 4). In the tactical nuclear arsenals there are probably about 35 000 nuclear warheads — about 20 000 American and about 15 000 Soviet — each on average several times more powerful than the Hiroshima bomb. These add another 4500 or so million tons of high-explosive equivalent to make a grand total of about 12 000 million tons — the equivalent of about 1 million Hiroshima bombs, or about 3 tons of TNT for every man, woman and child on earth.

Strategic nuclear weapons are deployed on intercontinental ballistic missiles (ICBMs), submarine-launched ballistic missiles (SLBMs), and strategic bombers. Soviet and American ICBMs have ranges of about 11 000 km, modern SLBMs have ranges of about 7000 km, and strategic bombers have ranges of about 12 000 km. Range is the main distinguishing feature between strategic and tactical nuclear weapons, the former having long (intercontinental) ranges.

Some ballistic missiles carry multiple warheads. Modern multiple warheads are independently targetable on targets hundreds of kilometres apart. These are called multiple independently targetable re-entry vehicles or MIRVs.

Strategic bombers carry free-fall nuclear bombs and air-to-ground missiles fitted with nuclear warheads. The most modern of these missiles is the American air-launched

Table 4   Nuclear arsenals

			Warheads	Megatons
USA				
	Strategic	ICBM	2153	1487
		SLBM	5040	336
		Bombers	2560	1600
		Total	9753	3423
	Tactical	Howitzers		
		Artillery shells		
		Missiles		
		Bombs		
		Land-mines		
		Torpedoes		
		Etc		
		Total	~20 000	~2600
USSR				
	Strategic	ICBM	6384	3384
		SLBM	1878	764
		Total	8262	4148
	Tactical	(As USA)	~15 000	~1900
Grand Total			~53 000	~12 000
UK + France + China				
	Strategic and tactical		1000	Few hundred

cruise missile (ALCM) which can fly over a range of about 2500 km.

The United States now has 1653 ballistic missiles (1053 ICBMs and 600 SLBMs) of which 1070 (550 ICBMs and 520 SLBMs) are fitted with MIRVs. Some 340 B-52s are operational as long-range strategic bombers.

The Soviet Union has deployed 2348 ballistic missiles (1398 ICBMs and 950 SLBMs), of which about 1010 (818 ICBMs and 192 SLBMs) are MIRVed. About 150 of its long-range bombers are probably assigned strategic roles.

Tactical nuclear weapons are deployed in a wide variety of systems, including howitzer and artillery shells, ground-to-ground ballistic missiles, free-fall bombs, air-to-ground missiles, anti-aircraft missiles, atomic demolition munitions (land mines), submarine-launched cruise missiles, submarine-launched ballistic missiles, torpedoes, naval mines and anti-submarine rockets. Land-based systems have ranges varying from about 12 km (artillery shells) to a few thousand km (intermediate range ballistic missiles). The explosive power of these warheads varies from about 100 tons to about a megaton.

The USA deploys tactical nuclear weapons in Western Europe, Asia, and the United States, and with the Atlantic and Pacific fleets. The USSR deploys its tactical nuclear weapons in Eastern Europe, in the Western USSR, and East of the Urals.

Future developments in the nuclear arsenals

Although, according to present plans, there will be significant increases in the number of warheads in the Soviet and American arsenals over the next few years, mainly because of the deployment of more MIRVed ICBMs and SLBMs and cruise missiles, the most important developments in nuclear weapons in the foreseeable future will be qualitative improvements. There are so many nuclear weapons in the arsenals that any further increases in numbers will, in any case, make no sense, from a military or from any other point of view. This has been true for many years now.

The most important qualitative advances in nuclear weapons are those which improve the accuracy and reliability of nuclear weapon systems.

Modernization of US and Soviet strategic nuclear weapons. The accuracy of a nuclear warhead is normally measured by its circular error probable (CEP), the radius of the circle centred on the target within which half of a large number of warheads, fired at the target, will fall. In both the USA and the USSR, the CEPs of ICBMs and SLBMs are being continually improved. In the USA, for example, improvements are being made in the computer of the NS-20 guidance system in the Minuteman III ICBMs, involving better mathematical descriptions of the in-flight performances of the inertial platform and accelerometers, and better pre-launch calibration of the gyroscopes and accelerometers. With these guidance improvements, the CEP of the Minuteman III

Table 5   Probable US strategic delivery capability in 1985

Vehicle	Number of vehicles deployed	Number of warheads per delivery vehicle	Total delivery capability (*number of warheads*)	Total yield per delivery vehicle (*Mt*)	Total delivery capability (*Mt*)	CEP (*m*)
MIRVed vehicles						
Minuteman III (Mk 12)	236	3	708	0.51	120	200
Minuteman III (Mk 12A)	300	3	900	1	300	200
Poseidon C-3[d]	336	10[b]	3 360	0.4	134	500
Trident I[a]	160	8	1 280	0.8	128	500
Trident II[a]	168	8	1 344	0.8	134	500
B-52 with ALCM	120	20	2 400	4	480	150
Sub-total	1 320		9 992		1 296	

Non-MIRVed vehicles

B-52 (SRAM, bombs)	150	12[c]	1800	5.6	840	180
B-52 (bombs)	76	4[c]	304	4	304	180
Titan II	53	1	53	9	477	1300
Minuteman II	450	1	450	1.2	540	400
Polaris[a]	80	3	240	0.66	53	900
Sub-total	809		2847		2214	
Total	2129		12 839[d]		3510	

CEP: Circular error probability   ALCM: air launched cruise missile   SRAM: short range attack missile

[a] SLBM
[b] Average
[c] Operational. Maximum loading per aircraft may be eleven bombs, each of about one megaton.
[d] Of these, 8175 are independently targetable warheads on ballistic missiles (2111 on ICBMs, and 6864 on SLBMs). Ballistic missiles carry 54% of the total megatonnage, 41% on ICBMs and 13% on SLBMs.

will probably decrease from about 350 to about 200 metres (see Table 5). At the same time the Mark-12 re-entry vehicle and the W62 170-kiloton nuclear warhead are being replaced with the Mark-12A re-entry vehicle and the W78 350-kiloton nuclear warhead. The plan is to put the new warheads on 300 of the existing 550 Minuteman III missiles. The Mark-12A will have roughly the same weight, size, radar cross-section and aerodynamic characteristics as the Mark-12.

Mark-12A warheads with the higher accuracy will be able to destroy Soviet ICBMs in silos hardened to about 1500 psi (pounds per square inch) with a probability of about 57 per cent for one shot and about 95 per cent for two shots. Superior arming and fusing devices will provide more control over the height at which the warhead is exploded and, hence, the damage done.

The upgraded land-based ICBM force will significantly increase US nuclear war-fighting capabilities. These will be further increased by the MX missile system, now under development.

The MX system includes both a new ICBM and a related basing scheme. The guidance for the MX missile will probably be based on the advanced inertial reference sphere (AIRS), an 'all-attitude' system which can correct for movements of the missile along the ground before it is launched. A CEP of about 100 m should be achieved with this system. If the MX warhead is provided with terminal guidance, using a laser or radar system to guide the warhead on to its target, CEPs of a few tens of metres may be possible.

No decision has yet been made about the yield and other characteristics of the MX warhead but each missile will probably carry ten warheads.

The launch-weight of the MX will probably be about 86 000 kg, about 2.4 times more than that of the Minuteman III, and the throw-weight about 3500 kg. The three MX booster stages will use advanced solid propellants, very light motor cases, and advanced nozzles to produce nearly twice the propulsion efficiency of the Minuteman.

The MX missile, by design, could fit into the existing Minuteman silos. But, if deployed, a mobile basing system will probably be used. The first missiles will probably be operational in 1986.

The most formidable Soviet ICBM is the SS-18, or the RS-20 in Soviet terminology (see Table 6). This is thought currently to have a CEP of about 500 m. This accuracy will probably improve to about 250 m within a few years. Each SS-18 warhead probably has an explosive power equivalent to about 500 kilotons. With the higher accuracy, the warhead will have about the same silo-destruction capability as the new US Minuteman III warhead.

The USSR also has the SS-19 ICBM (the RS-18). This is thought to be more accurate than the SS-18 and to be equipped with a similar warhead. Some of both the SS-18s and -19s are MIRVed. So far, a total of 668 SS-18s and -19s have been deployed. If these are MIRVed to the extent allowed by the SALT II Treaty, they are equipped with a total of about 4500 warheads. The other Soviet MIRVed ICBM, the SS-17 (or RS-16), has been tested with four warheads. So far, about 150 SS-17s have been deployed. According to US sources, the USSR is developing at least two new types of ICBM.

The Soviet MIRVed strategic missile force is clearly an increasing threat to the 1000-strong US Minuteman ICBM force as the accuracy and reliability of the Soviet warheads are improved and their number increases.

Strategic nuclear submarines. The quality of strategic nuclear submarines and the ballistic missiles they carry is also being continuously improved. In the USA, for example, the present Polaris and Poseidon strategic nuclear submarine force is being augmented, and may eventually be replaced, by Trident submarines. The Polaris submarines now operating will be phased out by the end of 1982. Thirty-one Poseidon submarines are now operating.

Trident submarines will be equipped with a new SLBM, the Trident I, the successor of the Poseidon C-3 SLBM. Yet another SLBM, the Trident II, is currently being developed for eventual deployment on Trident submarines.

In the meantime, the Trident I missiles will also be deployed on Poseidon submarines. The first of 12 Poseidons

Table 6 Probable maximum Soviet strategic delivery capability in 1985

Vehicle	Number of vehicles deployed	Number of warheads per delivery vehicle	Total delivery capability (*number of warheads*)	Total yield per delivery vehicle (*Mt*)	Total delivery capability (*Mt*)
MIRVed vehicles					
SS-17	200	4	800	2	400
SS-18	308	10	3080	5	1540
SS-19	312	6	1872	3	936
SS-N-18[a]	176	7	1232	1.4	246
New MIRVed SLBM	180	14[b]	2520[b]	2.8	504
Sub-total	1176		9504		3626
Non-MIRVed vehicles					
SS-11 (MRV)	60	3	180	0.6	36
New ICBM	300	1	300		[d]
SS-N-6 (MRV)[a]	352	3	1056	0.6	211
SS-N-8[a]	268	1	268	1	268
Sub-total	980		1804		515
Total	2156		11308[c]		4141–8641[d]

[a] SLBM.
[b] Maximum allowed.
[c] Of these, 10 484 are independently targetable warheads (6112 on ICBMs and 4372 on SLBMs).
[d] If the new ICBM has a 15 megaton warhead the total megatonnage will be 8641.

to be modified to carry Trident I missiles went to sea in October 1979; the others should be ready by 1984.

The first Trident submarine, the *USS Ohio* became operational in 1981. According to current plans, at least 8 Trident submarines (these have already been ordered) will become operational during the 1980s. But the ultimate size of the Trident fleet has yet to be decided.

The Trident displaces 18 700 tons when submerged. Its enormous size can be judged from the facts that it is twice as large as a Polaris/Poseidon submarine, which has a submerged displacement of about 8300 tons, and is as large as the new British through-deck cruiser (displacement 19 500 tons).

Each Trident will carry twenty-four SLBMs. The Trident I SLBM is designed to have a maximum range of 7400 km when equipped with eight 100-kiloton MIRVed warheads. Even longer ranges can be achieved if the missile has a smaller payload. The Poseidon SLBM, which it replaces, can carry up to fourteen 40-kiloton MIRVed warheads, but has a maximum range of only 4600 km. With the longer-range missile, Trident submarines will be able to operate in many times more ocean area and still remain within range of its targets. The long-range missiles will also allow Trident submarines to operate closer to US shores and still reach their targets, giving the submarines greater protection against Soviet anti-submarine warfare (ASW) activities.

Trident I, a two-stage solid propellant rocket, is provided with a stellar-aided inertial guidance system to provide course corrections. The CEP of the Trident SLBM is probably about 500 m at a maximum range, whereas that of the Poseidon SLBM is about 550 m, and that of the Polaris I SLBM is about 900 m. The development and deployment of mid-course guidance techniques for SLBMs and the more accurate navigation of missile submarines will steadily increase the accuracy of the missiles.

SLBM warheads may eventually be fitted with terminal guidance, using radar, laser or some other device to guide them onto their targets after re-entry into the earth's atmosphere. This could give CEPs of a few tens of metres. SLBMs will then be so accurate as to cease to be only deterrence weapons aimed at enemy cities, and will become nuclear war-fighting weapons.

The most modern Soviet SLBM is the 7400 km range SS-N-18, equipped with three 200-kt MIRVs. So far, 192 SS-N-18s have been put to sea, 16 on each of 12 Delta-class submarines, the most modern Soviet strategic nuclear submarines. The other main Soviet SLBM is the SS-N-8, with a range of 8000 km and a single 1-Mt warhead. Two hundred and ninety SS-N-8s are deployed on 22 Delta-class submarines.

The USSR also operates about 30 Yankee-class strategic nuclear submarines, each carrying 16 SS-N-6 SLBMs, a 3000 km range missile carrying either a 1-Mt warhead or two 200-kt warheads. In all, the USSR has 950 SLBMs, 192 of them MIRVed.

The USSR is developing a new ballistic-missile firing submarine — the Typhoon — which is apparently even bigger than the American Trident. A new SLBM, the SS-NX-20, is also under development, presumably for deployment on the Typhoon.

Soviet SLBMs are less accurate than are US ones. The SS-N-6 is thought to have a CEP of about 1000 m. But one can expect that the accuracy of Soviet SLBMs will be steadily improved and that more Soviet MIRVed SLBMs will be deployed.

Current US ballistic missiles carry 7033 independently targetable warheads. Of these missile warheads, 4880 are sea-based. US ballistic missiles have a total explosive yield of about 1820 Mt, of which about 330 Mt are carried by SLBMs. US sea-based strategic nuclear forces account, therefore, for about 70 per cent of the missile warheads. If all US strategic warheads, on bombers and missiles, are included, the sea-based forces account for about 50 per cent of the number.

Almost all Soviet strategic nuclear warheads are deployed on ballistic missiles; the USSR operates no more than 150 strategic bombers and there is no evidence that they are assigned an intercontinental role. There are said to be about 7140 independently targetable Soviet missile warheads. Of these, about 1300, or 20 per cent, are probably carried by SLBMs, while the rest are on ICBMs. The SLBM warheads probably have a total explosive yield of about 770 Mt out of a total missile megatonnage of about 4100 Mt. According to US sources, the Soviet Union normally has only about one-seventh of its strategic submarines (about ten boats) at sea at any one time. The land-based ICBM force is, at present, therefore, by far the most important component of the Soviet strategic nuclear arsenal.

Cruise missile. The US strategic bomber force, the third component of America's strategic triad, will be modernized by equipping B-52 strategic bombers with air-launched cruise missiles (ALCMs). The ALCM is a small, long-range, subsonic, very accurate, nuclear-armed, winged vehicle. ALCMs can be launched against Soviet targets by bombers penetrating Soviet defences or from outside Soviet territory.

According to current plans, ALCMs should become operational in December 1982, when the first B-52G squadron is loaded with cruise missiles under the aircraft's wings. Full operational capability is planned for 1990, when all 151 B-52G aircraft will be loaded, each with 12 ALCMs under the wings and 8 in the bomb bays. ALCMs will about double the number of nuclear weapons these aircraft carry.

New tactical nuclear weapons. Many of the 7000 or so tactical nuclear weapons in NATO countries in Western Europe were put there during the late 1950s and early 1960s. Since nuclear weapons have a lifetime of about 20 years, these are about due for replacement. In the meantime, new types of nuclear weapons have been developed and the plan is to replace the old nuclear weapons with some of these new types.

Among the new types planned for NATO are Pershing II missiles and ground-launched cruise missiles. These weapons are so accurate as to be perceived as nuclear war-fighting weapons. In December 1979, NATO decided to deploy 108 Pershing IIs and 464 cruise missiles, starting at the end of 1983.

Although less accurate than the American weapons, the Soviet SS-20 intermediate-range ballistic missile — a new type of Soviet tactical nuclear weapon — is accurate enough, or will soon be made so, to be regarded as a nuclear war-fighting weapon, given the large explosive yield of its war-head. About 250 were deployed in mid-1981, about 60 per cent targetted on Western Europe and the rest targetted on China.

The SS-20. The Soviet SS-20, a two-stage mobile missile, was first deployed in 1977. The missile carries three MIRVs. With these warheads its range is said to be about 5000 km.

The yield of each SS-20 warhead is estimated by Western sources to be between 150 and 500 kilotons and the CEP is said to be about 400 m.

The Pershing II Missile. The Pershing II missile will replace the Pershing I missile, first deployed in 1962.

Pershing II will use the same rocket components as Pershing I. But there the similarity ends. Pershing II will be provided with a formidable new guidance system called RADAG. In the terminal phase of the trajectory, when the warhead is getting close to the target, a video radar scans the target area and the image is compared with a reference image stored in the computer carried by the warhead before the missile able to penetrate a significant distance into the USSR: vanes which guide the warhead onto the target with accuracy unprecedented for a ballistic missile with a range of about 1700 km. The CEP of Pershing II is about 45 m.

Pershing II has double the range of Pershing I (750 km) because it has new rocket motors and uses a new highly efficient solid fuel. The missile is the only NATO ballistic missile able to penetrate a signficant distance into the USSR: it could, for example, reach Moscow from the Federal Republic of Germany.

The Ground-launched Cruise Missile (GLCM). The GLCMs to be deployed in Europe will carry light-weight 200-kt nuclear warheads. These missiles are not only very accurate, with CEPs of about 40 m, but, although flying at sub-sonic speeds, are relatively invulnerable, having a very small radar cross-section.

The replacement of existing tactical nuclear weapons with new types is likely to reduce somewhat the total number deployed but the reduction is unlikely to be very significant. Over the next few years, the number deployed in NATO countries in Western Europe may, for example, decrease from about 7000 to about 6000. A similar reduction may occur on the Warsaw Pact side.

The increasing probability of a nuclear world war

As we have seen, the world's arsenals contain tens of thousands of nuclear weapons, probably topping 50 000. The total explosive power of these weapons is equivalent to about one million Hiroshima bombs. If all, or a significant portion of them were used, the consequences would be beyond imagination (see Table 7).

All the major cities in the Northern Hemisphere, where most nuclear warheads are aimed, would be destroyed (on average, *each* is targeted by the equivalent of some 2000 Hiroshima bombs). Most of the urban population there would be killed by blast and fire, the rural population by radiation from fallout. Many millions of people in the Southern Hemisphere would be killed by radiation. And the disaster would not end even there. The unpredictable (and, therefore, normally ignored) long-term effects might well include changes in the global climate, severe genetic damage and depletion of the ozone layer that protects life on earth from excessive ultraviolet radiation. No scientist can convincingly assure us that human life would survive a nuclear world war.

Utterly catastrophic though a nuclear world war would be, its probability is steadily increasing. Symptoms of the current drift to a nuclear world war include the recent propaganda campaign to try to convince us that nuclear war may not be so bad after all, that limited nuclear wars are not only possible but may in some circumstances even be militarily effective, that civil defence measures could reduce casualties to an 'acceptable' level, that essential industry should be protected against nuclear blast, that the Warsaw Treaty Organization will soon militarily overwhelm NATO (and,

Table 7   Consequences of a nuclear world war

Short-term and medium-term effects
*   *All cities in the northern hemisphere would be destroyed (on average, each is targetted with the equivalent of 200 Hiroshima bombs)
*   *The bulk of the urban population would be killed by radiation
*   *Tens of millions would be killed in the southern hemisphere by radiation

Long-term (unpredictable) effects
*   *A change in the global climate
*   *A reduction of the ozone layer
*   *Genetic effects of radiation

Long-term consequences
*   *The northern hemisphere would be reduced to a stone age economy
*   *Third world economies would suffer greatly
*   *Humankind may not survive a nuclear world war

---

no doubt, the opposite is said in the East), and so on. The current hawkish mood seems to be worldwide, or at least to extend throughout official circles in most of the Northern Hemisphere.

There are a number of reasons for the drift to war. The most obvious are related to international politics. Others are connected with advances in military technology.

The escalation of a regional conflict to a general nuclear war is perhaps the most likely way in which a nuclear world war would start (see Table 8); more likely than a direct nuclear attack by one superpower on the other, although the danger of its starting by accident or miscalculation is ever present. A local conflict in, say, a Third World region (like the Persian Gulf) might begin as a conventional war and then escalate to a limited nuclear war, using the nuclear weapons of the local powers. This could in turn escalate to a general nuclear war involving the superpowers (see Table 9), especially if the superpowers supplied the conventional weapons for the original conflict. And that is why both the international arms trade, now totally out of control, and nuclear-weapon proliferation are so dangerous.

Table 8 How a nuclear war may start

---

* A deliberate decision by a great power
* Escalation of a conventional war
* Mechanical failure or malfunction of a nuclear-weapon system
* An error by humans or computers controlling the nuclear alert and firing systems
* Irrational behaviour by those controlling nuclear weapons
* The acquisition and use of nuclear weapons by irresponsible governments
* The use of nuclear weapons by terrorists

Table 9 Escalation of a third world conflict to a nuclear world war

---

* A future third world war (one starts, on average, every three months) begins as a conventional war
* This escalates to a nuclear war, using nuclear weapons made locally
* The war then spreads to Europe
* This begins with conventional weapons and then escalates to a tactical nuclear war
* Finally, this escalates to an all-out nuclear world war

We seem to be on the threshold of a new round of nuclear-weapon proliferation, with Pakistan the next probable nuclear power. The widening access to nuclear-weapon technology goes hand in hand with the spread of peaceful nuclear technology, itself a spin-off from military programmes. The more nuclear reactors there are generating electricity around the world, the greater will be the number of countries acquiring the skills and the capability to produce the fissile material to make nuclear weapons. And as the number of countries with nuclear weapons increases, the probability of nuclear war will increase.

International politics (particularly those related to the intensifying East-West competition for scarce raw materials) will greatly increase the probability of a nuclear world war, but military technology will increase it even more. The most significant technological reason is that military scientists are developing weapons which will seem more suitable for *fighting* than for *deterring* a nuclear war: very accurate and reliable ballistic missiles with warheads that can be aimed at smaller and, therefore, many more military targets than in the past. In other words, the day is coming when one country might hope to destroy its enemy's nuclear retaliatory capability by striking first.

In this context, a first strike does not mean the ability to destroy totally the other side's strategic nuclear forces in a surprise attack. What it does mean is that the attacker *perceives* that he can destroy enough of the enemy's retaliatory forces in a surprise attack to reduce the casualties he receives in a retaliatory strike to a number he regards as 'acceptable' for a given political goal. In his calculations the attacker is likely to make assumptions about the performance of his own and the enemy's nuclear forces which suit his arguments. Specifically, military calculations are likely to be based mainly on estimates of prompt deaths and ignore the uncertain long term effects of a nuclear war which may well be far more lethal than the early effects. (Also the sociological and psychological consequences of a total loss of all social and technical services, even though extremely serious, are likely to be ignored.) Remember that, in times of crisis, political leaders listen to their military chiefs rather than their scientific advisors.

The lingering death of nuclear deterrence, based on mutual assured destruction, and the birth of nuclear war-fighting strategies, are now more or less common knowledge. The public's awareness largely stems from the publicity surrounding the White House leaks of top-secret Presidential Directive 59, as part of ex-President Carter's election campaign.

Moves to a nuclear war-fighting strategy by the USA are, however, not new. They have been going on for seven years or so. And there is every reason to believe that the Soviet Union is following the USA in refining a nuclear war-fighting policy. The main reason why political leaders are changing their nuclear policies is the development of new nuclear war-fighting weapons by military scientists. Once available, weapons are usually deployed, and policies have to be modified to justify (i.e. rationalise) the deployment.

Nuclear deterrence depends on the belief that the enemy will not attack pre-emptively if he knows that most of his people and industry will be destroyed in retaliation. Cities are the hostages to deterrence. If the enemy stops fearing that his cities are at risk nuclear deterrence no longer works. This will happen if accurate and reliable missile warheads are deployed.

Remember that deterrence is essentially a matter of psychology. What the enemy believes is all-important. It is, therefore, impossible to maintain a policy of nuclear deterrence with accurate weapons simply because the enemy will assume, willy nilly, that the other side's warheads are targetted on his military forces and not on his cities. Accuracy, in other words, kills deterrence. Nuclear war-fighting, based on the destruction of hostile military forces, will then become the only credible and, therefore, feasible policy.

As already described, within the forseeable future, military scientists will achieve missile accuracies close to the theoretical limit, at least for land-based intercontinental ballistic missiles. We can also expect the accuracy of submarine-launched ballistic missiles to be improved as the position of strategic nuclear submarines is more accurately determined and as mid-course guidance is deployed on the missiles.

With terminal guidance (the key to very high accuracy), submarine-launched ballistic missiles will be as accurate as land-based ones. When all strategic nuclear warheads are accurate enough to threaten even the most hardened military targets the policy of nuclear deterrence will be finally dead. This will probably happen during the 1980s.

Nuclear war-fighting perceptions are being strengthened by a whole range of first-strike technologies. The most dangerous are those related to anti-submarine warfare. Now that land-based ballistic missiles are vulnerable to a first (i.e. pre-emptive) strike by hostile land-based missiles, nuclear deterrence depends solely on the continuing invulnerability of strategic submarines.

If one side could severely limit the damage that the other side's strategic nuclear submarines could do in a retaliatory strike, then the temptation to make an all-out first strike would become well nigh irresistible. Nevertheless, both the Soviets and the Americans are devoting large research and development resources to anti-submarine warfare techniques. It is probably only a matter of time before these efforts succeed enough to greatly increase the danger of a nuclear world war, particularly during a period of severe international tension. In fact, if strategic nuclear submarines do become vulnerable, a first strike may be seen as desirable and even essential to prevent the enemy from himself acquiring a first-strike capability.

The fact that the superpowers continue working so energetically on anti-submarine warfare shows that they are unable to control military science and technology even though this activity is jeopardising their policy of nuclear deterrence: a policy the leaderships desperately want to maintain.

Other first-strike technologies currently being developed or deployed include: navigational systems, providing unprecedented three-dimensional accuracies; anti-satellite warfare systems; ballistic missile defence systems; early-warning-of-attack systems; command, control, communications, and intelligence systems; and reconnaissance systems.

The path from the Hiroshima bomb to a nuclear world war brought on by the characteristics of nuclear weapons themselves may, given the enormous scientific effort put into it, be a technological inevitability. Today, nearly half a million scientists work only on military research and development; about 40 per cent of all scientists employed on research. If only physicists and engineering scientists are counted, the percentage is well over 50. Two-fifths of world research and development expenditure, about $50 000 million a year, is devoted to military research and development.

The large group of scientists who rely entirely on military money for support is, of course, a powerful political lobby. Moreover, vast bureaucracies have grown up in the great powers to deal with military matters. (As many civilians are paid out of military budgets as there are troops in uniform.) Academics and bureaucrats join with the military and defence industries to form an academic–bureaucratic–military–industrial complex intent on maintaining and increasing military budgets and agitating for the use of every conceivable technological advance for military purposes. This complex has so much political power as to be almost politically irresistible. In fact, the nuclear arms race is now totally out of the control of political leaders. *And this is as true in the Soviet Union as it is in the USA.* The uncontrolled nuclear arms race is without doubt the greatest single threat to our survival.

This is not to deny that great efforts have been made to control military technology and to stop the nuclear arms race between the Americans and the Russians. Since World War II many of the world's most brilliant people have been actively involved in these efforts. No other problem has received so much attention in the United Nations and other international forums. Whole libraries have been written on the subject. Yet, because of the enormous political influence of those groups that continually press for greater military efforts, nuclear and other arms races go on just as fast as human skill in the American and Soviet societies allows. We are being driven toward nuclear world war by the sheer momentum of military technology.

The main, perhaps the only, hope for the future is that the public will learn the facts in time and that an aroused public opinion will force reluctant politicians to stop the nuclear arms race and reduce armaments. I am convinced that political leaders, left to themselves, will not be able to prevent a nuclear holocaust.

The main driving force of a political leader is to ensure his re-election, or to remain in power. At present, the political leaders of the great powers are convinced that they will be thrown out of office if they oppose the demands of the academic-bureaucratic-military-industrial complexes. What we must do is mobilise public opinion (and, here, the scientific community is obviously a key element) sufficiently to convince the political leaders that they will not be re-elected or stay in power *unless they stop the nuclear arms race.* The force of public opinion must, in other words, exceed the influence of the militaristic groups in society.

I am convinced that if the public knew the truth about the dangers of the nuclear arms race, and the increasing threat of nuclear war, it would insist that political leaders stop this insanity. We will avoid nuclear disaster only if the public protests in time.

References

1. The total amount of highly-enriched uranium produced for nuclear weapons since World War II is roughly 1500 tons. To get this material about 2.5 million tons of natural uranium have been mined and processed. In addition, about 200 tons of plutonium have been produced worldwide for nuclear weapons.
2. Professor J. Rotblat has described the technique used thus:

   The solution to the problem lies in the fact that at the very high temperature of the fission trigger most of the energy is emitted in the form of X-rays. These X-rays, travelling with the speed of light, radiate out from the centre and on reaching the tamper (surrounding the fusion material) are absorbed in it and then immediately re-emitted in the form of softer X-rays. By an appropriate configuration of the trigger and the fusion material it is possible to ensure that the X-rays reach the latter almost instantaneously. If the fusion material is subdivided into small portions, each surrounded with a thin absorber made of a heavy metal, the bulk of the fusion material will simultaneously receive enough energy to start the thermonuclear reaction before the explosion disperses the whole assembly. (*Nuclear Radiation in Warfare* (London: Taylor and Francis, 1981).

Source material. The data in this paper was mainly taken from *World Armaments and Disarmament: SIPRI Yearbook 1981* (London: Taylor and Francis, 1981).

3. EFFECTIVE DETERRENCE

David Owen

The security of our nation as judged by our ability to survive, and be free is one of the supreme responsibilities of every political leader. How individuals or parties measure up to that responsibility is a key issue on which the electorate determines their vote. Security is a complex area for political debate, and for too long its complexity has been used as an excuse to avoid and obfuscate public discussion. One of the benefits of the current public argument on the merits of 'unilateral' or 'multilateral' disarmament is that at last the central issues of security and disarmament are being subjected to welcome critical assessment. They are becoming once again, as in the days of the League of Nations in the 1920s and early 1930s, political subjects, engaging all members of Parliament. For the electoral implications, if nothing else, force a concern which has hitherto been largely confined to Prime Ministers and Foreign Secretaries, and at times sadly been given far too low a priority, even by them. Debate must not be stifled, for the conventional wisdoms are frequently as mistaken as their critics.

National security where there is a defined enemy has two elements, deterrence and defence. Deterrence is to convince an enemy that the burdens and risks of any attack far outweigh any possible gains. Defence is to reduce the likely burdens and risks if any enemy attacks, deterrence having failed. Deterrence aims at changing the intentions of the enemy, making it less likely they will decide to act. Defence aims at reducing the effectiveness of the enemy if they decide to act. Defensive and deterrent strategies must therefore interlink and there is a complex interplay with any offensive strategies. In the pre-nuclear days, the armed forces using tanks, ships, aircraft and conventional weapons developed strategies which were often unclear as to whether they were being used in a deterrent role or in an offensive role.

This interchangeability of roles was initially challenged by the introduction of nuclear weapons. The weapons were so devastating, the consequences of their use so appalling, that it was possible to envisage a purely deterrent force. The concept was one of mutually assured destruction. Then as the technology of nuclear warfare developed, with miniaturisation of the warheads, multiple independently-targetted re-entry vehicles and pinpoint accuracy from 4000 miles, with nuclear mines, nuclear depth charges and short-range battlefield nuclear weapons, some saw nuclear deterrence as being merged with conventional deterrence. Nuclear weapons began to be part of the arsenal of war. Fortunately, concerned public opinion began to question whether there are any limits to what is acceptable in war. What are the precedents?

In April 1972 most of the world signed a ban on all biological weapons and agreed to destroy existing stocks, one of the few actual measures of disarmament as distinct from arms control. The use of gas in the trenches in the 1914–18 war evoked considerable public concern and led to the Geneva Protocol on Gas Warfare of 1925. The Allied saturation bombing of German cities in the 1939–45 War aroused some public feeling since many people were affected and it involved civilians as well as combatants, but the bombing continued and did not influence the eventual decision to use the atom bomb. Hiroshima and Nagasaki had an impact, though at the time this was blunted by the knowledge of the conditions of German and Japanese prisoners of war and the 40–50 million lives lost in the War. A hopeful sign is that medical doctors including the British Medical Association are looking afresh at the implications, and Japanese doctors have been documenting the revulsion aroused by nuclear weapons[1].

Public anxiety over nuclear weapons since Hiroshima has come in two waves, in the 1950s with the first CND campaign, and now again in the 1980s. It has many ingredients, not least despair over progress on disarmament. Some allege that the consequences of nuclear weapons are so morally outrageous that it is immoral to even threaten their use when the threat, to be credible, must carry a readiness to act and risk an uncontrolled escalation. Some argue that there is no morality to killing of any kind and therefore none in war. In this sense the arguments of the pacifist have an absoluteness that no argument can easily confound, and deserve respect. Religious thought has through the ages tried to wrestle with the moral dilemma of war and many compromises have evolved over time, some even to be blessed. But there has always been a sense that there is some undefined limit to the extent of the compromise. To many, nuclear weapons cross that threshold, and they rightly demand verifiable reductions by multilateral negotiations.

A non-nuclear defence strategy

Those who advocate a non-nuclear defence strategy in terms of morality or practicality must rebut the argument that nuclear deterrence is the only way of preventing a war with nuclear weapons. If it is possible to show that there is any other way of preventing nuclear weapons being used, while other countries still possess them, then there is no possible justification for their retention. Arguments based on money and manpower ought to have little consequence when weighed against the horror of nuclear weapons. So we must first ask, is there a way of convincing the Soviet Union, for that is the only country at present that can be defined as an enemy which has nuclear weapons, that the burdens and risks of mounting a military attack in Western Europe outweigh any possible gains, and that political blackmail with nuclear weapons carries no credibility?

Firstly, to be certain of holding over a few days, let alone weeks, a Warsaw Pact surprise conventional military attack, few would deny that NATO needs on the ground in Western Europe more men, tanks, aircraft and weapons. Ever since 1947, in part because of the fact the the United States possessed nuclear weapons, the Western European democracies have not been prepared to financially support expensive conventional military budgets. Somewhat surprisingly so far, both the US and Canada have continued to base forward forces in Europe but not in such numbers that they can be described as anything more than a crucial contribution to a conventional delaying force, not by any stretch of the imagination a conventional holding force. The Warsaw Pact Forces, on the other hand, are clearly strong enough to sustain a NATO conventional attack. It is this acknowledged imbalance of conventional forces which has meant that the US, France and Britain have never been prepared to sign a 'no first use' nuclear weapons agreement. We are not confident that our conventional defence can stop a Warsaw Pact attack and we felt it necessary to say that if attacked in overwhelming numbers, we reserve the right to threaten the first use of nuclear weapons against a Warsaw Pact which has nuclear weapons. This is the crucial link that could lead to nuclear war, and needs to be re-examined. Until the non-nuclear strategists face up to this issue of Western conventional forces inferiority, their non-nuclear strategy lacks all credibility. Sweden at least has recognised that issue in its own way by spending more per head on defence than most other European countries while remaining neutral and rejecting nuclear weapons.

For the sake of argument, let us accept that the Western democracies are ready to finance, equip and assemble on the ground, a credible holding defensive force. Even then we should not forget Field Marshal Lord Carver's warning about believing that conventional warfare is a comparatively harmless affair — one reason why some West German strategists accept even the risks of NATO's current tactical nuclear weapon deterrent strategy for their territory.

The Yom Kippur War of 1973 reminded us of the purely military effects of modern warfare. In a contest that lasted less than three weeks, with limited forces in a limited area, both sides lost about half of their tanks and a quarter of their aircraft. To provide sufficient material to last out a prolonged major conventional war demands immensely expensive industrial effort, and its use would bring about a deveastation in the area of operations.[2]

Some non-nuclear strategists sidestep arguments over Western conventional forces by saying that the Soviet Union has no intention of crossing the by now agreed East/West frontier in Europe; that Hungary in 1956, Czechoslovakia in 1968, and the threat of invasion to Poland in 1980–1 was within their own direct sphere of influence; that even Afghanistan was in the grey area of Soviet influence and not comparable in any way to an attack on Western Europe. Honest unilateralists find such rationalisations no substitute for a strong conventional defence strategy. But few non-nuclear strategists argue that governments should pay more for a conventional defence capability. This issue has not begun to be faced, but even if it is, the non-nuclear strategist must face other problems, besides increasing the conventional defence effort. Unless they can negotiate more than reductions in existing Warsaw Pact nuclear arms, they must argue through the implications of a NATO giving up all nuclear weapons, even if the Soviet Union continues to maintain its nuclear weapon systems. Despite having developed a substitute conventional holding force capable of deterring a conventional attack, they need to convince people that the Warsaw Pact would never threaten to use their nuclear weapons, even when they knew that NATO had no nuclear weapons with which to retaliate. It is incredible to argue that at some forseeable date, public opinion in Eastern Europe will force a nuclear change, but in the meantime the Western democracies should unilaterally abandon nuclear deterrence. It would certainly be better to have a conventional deterent strategy of sufficient credibility to be in a position to be able to sign a 'no first use' of nuclear weapons agreement. Buttressed by a battlefield nuclear-free zone, this should be a stated negotiating objective for the Mutual Balanced Force Reduction talks in Vienna. To unilaterally abandon the ability to threaten a second strike nuclear response, however, is a decision to quite awesome dimensions. It goes against all past experience of how political leaders or nations actually act.

The Soviet Union, which has had conventional superiority since 1945, felt obliged to build nuclear weapons to counter the US possession of nuclear weapons. The Chinese Government responded similarly, despite its large conventional forces, to the Soviets' ability to make nuclear weapons. The Pakistan Government has felt obliged to build its own nuclear weapons following the Indian nuclear explosion, despite having conventional forces that have in the past held a reasonable balance when fighting India, despite being a smaller country. The wish to retain a balance of force goes deep into the nature of man and nations. There is a justified fear of creating an imbalance in forces, for history shows that this is often the trigger for war.

We need to give as much weight to the behavioural sciences when we consider deterrence, as we do to the technological and productive sciences. It was Basil Liddell Hart, before the Second World War, who said, 'if you wish for peace, understand war', and to 'limit the danger of war, unlimited patience is needed'[3]. The main problem of a unilateralist strategy is that it does not try to understand war, and by its impatience it can provoke war.

An effective deterrent

In searching for a stable deterrent strategy, NATO and the Warsaw Pact should set as their first objective a negotiated conventional force balance which would allow the negotiation of a 'limited no first use' of nuclear weapons treaty. The Soviet Union pays lip service in the UN to such a declaration while still deploying weapons systems and exercising their forces on the basis of a battlefield nuclear exchange. A Treaty establishing a nuclear-free zone and by negotiating away all battlefield nuclear weapons could make a crucial contribution to delaying any decisions over nuclear war fighting. A Treaty could provide a formal warning procedure before a major conventional attack triggered a nuclear response. It is a fact that military strategists in both the Warsaw Pact and NATO believe that nuclear weapons would be used in any war in Europe and that both sides expect to win such a war. But fortunately there is a strong scientific and military opinion on both sides that has never accepted that nuclear weapons are an instrument for waging war, opposes weapons like the neutron bomb because they lower the nuclear threshold, and feel battlefield nuclear weapons are dangerous and should be abandoned[4]. Enhanced radiation weapons are specifically designed to compensate for a perceived inferiority in conventional tank warfare. Their proponents see them as a deterrent to a surprise tank attack; their opponents rightly fear more their potential for escalating nuclear war. The criticism should not be concentrated on the weapon itself but on the battlefield nuclear war-fighting strategy of both East and West that encourages the deployment of neutron bombs.

Fortunately politicians on both sides are also sceptical of the concept of a battlefield nuclear exchange because of the problems associated with command and control. One argument that led to the deployment of battlefield weapons was that it was not credible to base a deterrent strategy on countering a deep conventional armed thrust in the central front with the launching of strategic ballistic missiles aimed at the US or Soviet Union. This had some validity in the days when it was impossible to target ballistic missiles with pinpoint accuracy in a tactical sense. Now, if it was felt necessary to respond in or close to the battlefield area, this could be done by submarine-based weapons systems or various land-based missile systems. So the abandonment of battlefield nuclear weapons does not mean that the option of a tactical battlefield response is foreclosed. This is one of the reasons why it is possible to believe that the negotiations over theatre nuclear weapons could succeed if they are linked to the SALT process. The SS20 is not vital for the Warsaw Pact's tactical or strategic nuclear strategy, any more than Cruise missiles are vital for NATO's. It is an aspect of the arms race that has its roots in the military's wish to always have a comprehensive range of weaponry. There is no need to deploy European land-based Cruise missiles for their own sake, if major Soviet reductions are negotiated instead. A specifically Euro-strategic balance has never been necessary if there is a stable overall nuclear balance. The balance is not a purely mechanistic matter, nor just an arithmetical missile count; it should be a rounded assessment of overall capability that embraces conventional weapons and even involves general economic and political factors. The Soviet Union sustains the Warsaw Pact, not just because of its dominant relationship with the other East European countries, but because its territory adjoins theirs and it is part of continental Europe. As yet there is no sign that Poland, Hungary or East Germany have any impact at all on Soviet nuclear strategy. It is possible that eventually they will, and the European Nuclear Disarmament movement is correct to try and influence opinion in Eastern Europe, but there is likely to be more progress on issues like trades union rights than on nuclear policy for many years ahead. Europe is still very deeply divided, as the Polish situation demonstrates every day, and it will take a long time to erode the Soviet stranglehold. It will require a subtle and determined Western attitude to help us do so and a dialogue of partners in NATO where US perceptions have to be married with the differing perceptions of her European partners. The alliance no longer gives the US automatic authority; something President Carter understood and President Reagan initially did not understand.

The US is separated from Western Europe by the Atlantic. This geographical asymmetry presents unique problems for NATO. It has haunted the Vienna force reduction negotiations, since the reinforcement capability of the Soviet-based forces far surpasses that of US-based forces, even if one makes allowance for the Soviet need to guard their Chinese border. There is also an ever-present, though understated, anxiety on the part of the West German Government about the credibility to be attached to the resolve of a US President to use nuclear weapons, even if faced by the Soviet forces overrunning NATO forces in Germany. To demonstrate that resolve, the maintenance of US military personnel in Europe in a conventional role has always been judged essential on the basis that no President would dare to stand by while thousands of US servicemen were sacrificed. But European doubts remain even so, and the fear of US inaction and the need for a specifically European counter-threat over nuclear blackmail, however inferior it may be to that of the United States, lies behind the UK and French decisions to become and remain nuclear weapon states. It also perhaps explains the wish of some Europeans to see US Cruise missiles deployed on the ground in Europe. The Western nuclear deterrent posture is marginally but importantly strengthened by three centres of decision-making and there is a sense in which the decision-making of the United States is circumscribed by the knowledge that France and Britain can make their own assessment of a threat to their national security that may not always be the same as that of the US. Similarly, the decision-making of the Soviet Union is circumscribed by the French, British and Chinese nuclear bombs, and even by India and Pakistan when they become nuclear weapon states.

The decision of France or Britain or both to give up their nuclear weapons would not affect the Soviet or US arsenals. Nor would it ensure that either country avoided nuclear weapons being used on their territories. France has always been an extension of the European battlefield, Britain a strategic military island that would have to be towed away into the Southern Atlantic before it would be inviolate. A non-nuclear Britain would be just as subject to nuclear blackmail and possibly to nuclear attack.

The effectiveness of the NATO deterrent, as for the Warsaw Pact deterrent, depends critically on its conventional component first, and secondly on its having an invulnerable second strike nuclear offensive component. If both these components could be assured, then the whole range of intermediate nuclear weapons could be negotiated away. Provided the political will existed, even some risks could be safely taken to withdraw these weapons systems in a step-like change.

What would make the deterrent ineffective would be if the conventional imbalance of forces continued and if the vulnerability of second strike forces increased. If battlefield nuclear weapons were unilaterally withdrawn or if the number of US forces stationed in Europe were unilaterally reduced, or if France or Britain unilaterally gave up their own weapons systems, there would be only a reduction in the effectiveness of the deterrent.

What is needed is for politicians deliberately to work for the threshold at which they would contemplate using nuclear weapons to be continually raised, and for a balanced reduction in the quantity of nuclear weaponry. To reduce the quality of nuclear weapons is not always a contribution to peace.

For example, to avoid the launch on warning strategy, nations need to be certain that their second strike weapons systems are of a quality that will render them invulnerable.

Perhaps we can all gain, whether we give a primacy to negotiations or to protestation, by recalling the common-sense advice of Basil Liddell Hart.

> There is no panacea for peace that can be written out in a formula like a doctor's prescription. But one can set down a series of practical points — elementary principles drawn from the sum of human experience in all times. Study war, and learn from its history. Keep strong, if possible. In any case, keep cool. Have unlimited patience. Never corner an opponent, and always assist him to save his face. Put yourself in his shoes — so as to see things through his eyes. Avoid self-righteousness like the devil — nothing is so self-blinding. Cure yourself of two commonly fatal delusions — the idea of victory and the idea that war cannot be limited.[5]

What is needed for effective deterrence is to put arms control and disarmament at the centre of international political activity and start to demonstrate to the people of the world that verifiable agreements can be achieved to make the world a safer and more secure place to live in.

There are two dangerous misconceptions which have done much to stimulate concern about nuclear deterrence. Firstly, the folly of stressing the significance of measures to protect civilian populations against thermo-nuclear war. Governments must do something to protect their citizens, but to pretend that civil defence can add to the deterrent effect of nuclear weapons is an absurdity; and to pretend that it is anything more than a palliative for the population is a cruel deception. Secondly, the folly of planning for a nuclear war fighting strategy. Governments must plan for limiting nuclear way if by inadvertence or design nuclear weapons are ever used, but to set nuclear weapons within a seamless robe of defence decision-making is to increase massively the risk that nuclear weapons will be used again. At Hiroshima the inscription on the memorial is 'Rest in peace, for the mistake will not be repeated'. Effective deterrence means that the mistake will never be repeated.

References

1. *Hiroshima and Nagasaki: The Physical, Medical, and Social Effects of the Atomic Bombings* (Basic Books, New York).
2. *New Statesman* (15 August, 1980).
3. Basil Liddell Hart, *Deterrent or Defence* (Stevens & Sons Limited).
4. David Owen, MP, 'Negotiate and Survive' in his book *Face the Future*, Jonathan Cape and in paperback (OUP, 1981).
5. Basil Liddell Hart, op. cit.

4. DETERRENCE AND ADDICTION

Edward Thompson

I will not take up the time of this conference expounding upon my own views as to the immorality, or even the insanity, of the weaponry which is legitimated by the theory of deterrence. My views on this are sufficiently known. Similar views have been expressed by many others. They have recently been articulated, with greater authority and greater eloquence than I can command, by Mr George F. Kennan; as for example: 'To my mind, the nuclear bomb is the most useless weapon ever invented. It can be employed to no constructive purpose. It is not even an effective defense against itself.'[1]

Immoral or insane, the weapons are now here, in superabundance. They condition our behaviour and our expectations in innumerable ways. The consequences of their use defy our imagination. But, at the same time, the dismantling of all this weaponry, down to the last nuclear land-mine, by the mutual agreement of both blocs, and of other proliferating parties, would require such a total redirection of strategy, resources, ideologies, diplomacies — such an unprecedented investment in agitation, negotiation, and conversion — that this exhausts our imagination also. In confronting this threat to civilisation we are, in the end, confronting ourselves; we turn away from the mirror, exhausted and self-defeated. We will pass the problem on, unresolved, to the next generation or the generation that follows. If any generation does.

The theory of deterrence

This is, essentially, the political meaning of contemporary deterrence theory. In its pure form, that of MAD, or Mutual Assured Destruction, it proposes that war between the superpowers and their allies may be indefinitely postponed because nuclear weapons make any alternative unthinkable or unacceptable. I emphasize 'postponement'. The theory does not propose the victory of one 'side' over the other 'side', neither does it propose the resolution of those differences between the two parties which might, purportedly, bring them to war. On the contrary, by maintaining each party in a posture of menace to the other, it fixes indefinitely the tension which makes the resolution of differences improbable. It transfixes diplomacies and ideologies into a twilight state; while postponing war it postpones also the resolution of peace.

This would be so even if we were to succeed in reducing weaponry to a level of minimal deterrence: let us say six delivery-systems on each side. (In fact, as I will argue later, one major constituent of the meaning of nuclear weapons is *symbolic*; and a reduction to this level would signal so great a symbolic victory for rationality that the threat of the remaining weapons would be increasingly fictitious and the space for political resolutions would enlarge.) But we are not reducing weaponry. Over the past two decades this has been steadily increasing, not only in gross destructive power — as Mr Kennan has said, 'levels of redundancy of such grotesque dimensions as to defy rational understanding' — but also in the quality and accuracy of delivery-systems. Hence the theory of deterrence now legitimates, not Mutual Assured Destruction, but Mutual Aggravated Destruction. And to the degree that menace is aggravated with each year, the resolution of differences by means short of war becomes less probable. There is no longer an even-handed postponement both of war and of peace; terminal war becomes more likely, the terminus of peace recedes from any agenda.

Is such a consequence inherent in the premises of the theory itself? On the one hand, it can be argued that this need not necessarily be so. A rigidly-enforced state of minimal deterrence, policed by some international authority, need not be subject to the law of aggravation. On the other hand, it has been argued, persuasively, that deterrence is inherently addictive, and hence must lead to aggravation. In 1979, shortly before his death, Professor Gregory Bateson, a member of the Board of Regents of the University of California, addressed his fellow Regents with the plea that the University renounce any part in the research and development of nuclear weapons. Employing analogies from biological systems as transferred to social psychology, he argued that

the short-time deterrent effect is achieved at the expense of long-time cumulative change. The actions which today postpone disaster result in an increase in strength on *both* sides of the competitive system to ensure a greater instability and greater destruction if and when the explosion occurs. It is this fact of cumulative change from one act of threat to the next that gives the system the quality of *addiction*.

Bateson reminds us that we are not just dealing with weapons, in a medium of pure theory, where one threat balances and cancels out the other. These weapons operate in the medium of politics, ideology and strategy; they are perceived as menacing and are intended to be so; they induce fear and they simultaneously enhance and frustrate feelings of aggression. Nor need aggravation pursue a steady linear advancement: in the vocabulary of mathematical catastrophe theory, civilisation may already be tipping over upon the overhanging cusp between fear and aggression.

This is really enough, and more than enough, about deterrence as theory. It is in truth a pitiful, light-weight theory. It is espoused, in its pristine purity, only by a handful of monkish celibates, retired within the walls of centres of Strategic Studies. It cannot endure any intercourse with the actual world. It is at heart a very simple, and simple-minded, idea, which occurred to the first cave-men when they got hold of clubs. (It is this very simplicity which gives to it a certain populist plausibility.) If I have a club, that will deter him from clobbering me. The thought has gone on, through armies and empires, dreadnaughts and gas; all that a historian can say is that sometimes it has worked for a while, and sometimes it has not, but always in the end it has broken down. All that is new about it now is that the clubs of today, the technology of destruction, are so im-'mense as to defy any rational exercise. It is this which made an old (and massively-disproved) theory appear plausible once more, for a while. It seemed, for a time, that the new weapons were so terrible that they could be employed, not to fight, but to *avert* war.

Deterrence as rationalization. But it is not an *operative* theory: that is, it does not direct any nation's behaviour. It appears always as a gloss, as an *ex post facto* apologia, as a theoretical legitimation of actions which are taken for quite different reasons. The first atomic weapons were not developed because some theorist invented deterrence, and *then* scientists were commissioned to invent a bomb. The bombs were invented to blast the German and Japanese antagonists into submission. The US Strategic Air Command was then established, in 1946, not to deter Soviet nuclear attack, but to threaten a United States first strike against Russia. Thermonuclear weapons were not developed to deter anyone, but to demonstrate United States military superiority, and because it seemed to be a sweet new device worth developing. It was only *after* the Soviet Union also developed thermonuclear weapons that the theory of deterrence came into vogue, and on both sides. But if the theory had been operative, instead of cosmetic, that is where the development of such weaponry would have come to a fixed point of rest. Of course it did not. Development — aggravated menace — has gone on and on. It has been led, in almost every case, by the United States, and the Soviet Union has never passed up an opportunity to answer or match each development. Maybe (but I find the whole argument about balance, when we are in these regions of grotesque overkill, to be absurd) in this or that particular of delivery-systems the Soviet Union is now ahead.

This was not done by a theory. If the theory, in its pure

form, has ever had any operative force, it has perhaps been on the Russian side, at the time when they were developing their first megarockets capable of delivering weapons onto United States territory. Khruschev is the nearest we can get to a philosopher king of deterrence. But since his time the theory has long been admixed with more powerful, and operative, interests and inertias. If Soviet military theory today dispenses with repeated incantations about deterrence, this may be because Soviet strategists have less need to bear in mind the cosmetic, public-relations functions of·theory.

There is now a substantial literature on the weapons-system complex as an effective *interest*, some of which was forcibly drawn to our attention by Lord Zuckerman in a remarkable lecture last year. I do not mean to rehearse it. There has never been a stationary state of mutual deterrence; instead there has been a ceaseless pursuit for advantage *within* that state. The operative pressures have come both from the regions of politics and ideology, and from the inertial thrust towards research and development — sometimes known as 'technology creep' — within the military-industrial complexes of the opposed powers. Deterrence theory did not give us Poseidon and Polaris, the SS-20, the cruise missiles, the neutron bomb. These were given to us by the alchemists in the research laboratories, the arms lobbyists, the alarmist leader-writers and populist politicians, and by the inter-service competition of the military élites. Deterrence theory came in afterwards, to excuse all these things.

In doing so it has become ever less credible, and more spattered with the impurities of the real actors. The Awful yet Sublime doctrine of MAD has given way to sub-doctrines which clearly pursue strategic or tactical advantage; which spell out scenarios in which nuclear wars become thinkable once again: first and *second* strike capacity, counterforce, flexible response, notions of limited nuclear war. Each one of these theories demands more, and more accurate, and more technically sweet, weapons in order to deter not what does exist but what might, in theory, exist on the other side in future. In most cases these weapons are already under development, and are in search of a theory to excuse them. And in all cases they actually hasten the response of the other side — that is the answering weapons which they were, supposedly, to deter.

Deterrence as ideology. We know, as a well-established point of method, that it is more possible to *dis*prove a theory than to prove it. But few of us would wish to see the theory of deterrence disproved, in a definitive manner, for the satisfaction (if we remained alive) of having won an argument. There are, however, other ways of demonstrating that a theory is suspect. One may examine its intellectual credentials, enquire what kind of a theory it is, and to which discipline it belongs.

When a theory can be employed (as this theory is) to endorse *every* new development in strategy and in weaponry — when one knows, in advance, that this will be done — then one has every reason to suppose that one is dealing with ideology, with the apologetics of power. This may appear as unfair to certain distinguished practitioners, who employ the theory with subtlety and who effect distinctions between strategies and between weapons. But what impresses here is the subtlety of the practitioner, not of the theory; there is no fire-break of any *theoretical* kind between the concepts employed in the scholarly strategic journals and the same concepts vulgarised in *Hansard* or in the popular press.

Deterrence theory in fact covers an immense intellectual spectrum. In its most debased, populist form it is sheer humbug. It has even spawned itself as a noun, descriptive of *our* thermonuclear weaponry (but rarely of theirs): 'the deterrent'. There cannot be *a* deterrent. It may be possible to justify the deployment of a weapon capable of effecting the extermination of multitudes within *a theory* of deterrence. But to speak of '*a* deterrent' is to ascribe the intentions (or purported intentions) of the users to the weapon itself, as part of its inherent quality. Yet that weapon will remain the same weapon, even if the intentions of the users change: or if terrorists were to capture it and carry it off for other uses. Those who refer to 'our deterrent' or 'the British deterrent' are guilty of the pathetic fallacy, which, while pardonable in the lines of poets, is something worse than pathetic in the mouths of politicians and military experts. For this usage pre-empts enquiry by attributing normative qualities — and highly desirable normative qualities at that — to this thing in the very same instant as the thing itself is indicated. 'Deterrence' (ideology on every side insists) is a good strategy; our statesmen must be good guys whose intentions cannot be questioned — even if our side does happen to reserve to itself the right of first nuclear strike; therefore the strategy and the good intentions can slither off onto the weaponry itself. If we are reassured in every moment of usage, in the prescribed vocabulary of public discourse, that weapons are only 'deterrents', then the more we have of them the better.

I am sorry to labour the point. I am sorry that it is necessary to do so. But these little points of vocabulary and usage add to the inertial thrust which is carrying us towards the Final Solution. Any politician who refers to '*the* deterrent' is either so slapdash in his logic that he merits our suspicion, or he is dealing knowingly in humbug.

At the other end of the intellectual spectrum — but employing the same family of concepts — are the specialist, prestigious, and well-funded academic think-tanks and periodicals. Not all that has gone on in these has always been rubbish. Serious empirical work has been done, especially in the heyday of the arms control community in the United States during the negotiation of the two SALT treaties. The more recent lurch into ideology has been signalled by the withdrawal of many reputable scholars of an older generation. For it is from an older generation of strategists, arms controllers, scientific advisors, and diplomats — among them Kennan, York, Scoville, Warnke, La Rocque, and Lords Mountbatten and Zuckerman — that some of the most sombre warnings about our present predicament have come.

My own first acquaintance with the vocabulary of deterrence theory is relatively recent. I was unfamiliar with its terms and permutations when my eye alighted, in astonishment, upon a letter from Professor Michael Howard in the correspondence columns of *The Times*[2]. I promptly poured out the vials of my polemic upon Professor Howard's head, unaware that my wrath should have been directed at the general theory of deterrence, with its curiously hermetic vocabulary, limited to posture and worst-case expectations: a vocabulary not invented by Professor Howard, and which consorts uneasily with his richer historical and military studies.

Professor Howard considers that my polemic (*Protest and Survive*[3]) misrepresented his views. I still consider that his letter was open to the reading which I gave it, in most (but not in all) respects. The premises of deterrence theory in which it had been couched (perhaps in an effort to influence authorities who attend to no other premises) are nihilist, and they merited exposure as such. But in attributing to Mr Howard all the sins of deterrence theory — a theory to which he has given only qualified acceptance — I did him an injustice. I can scarcely repair that injustice now, but I can signal, with respect, that he has repaired it himself in an article which marks out his own distaste for deterrence theory (in its reigning versions) and the great distance which lies between it and his own more flexible historical enquiries. Professor Howard quotes from Clausewitz,

> War is only a branch of political activity; it is in no sense autonomous . . . It cannot be divorced from political life — and whenever this occurs in our thinking about war, the many links that connect the two elements are destroyed, and we are left with something that is pointless and devoid of sense.

And Professor Howard himself continues:

> When I read the flood of scenarios in strategic journals about first-strike capabilities, counterforce or counter-vailing strategies, flexibile response, escalation dominance and the rest of the postulates of nuclear theology, I ask myself in bewilderment: this war they are describing, *what is it about*? The defence of Western Europe? Access to the Gulf? The protection of Japan? If so, why is this goal not mentioned, and why is the strategy not related to the progress of the conflict in these regions? But if it is not related to this kind of specific object, what are we talking about? Has not the bulk of American

thinking been exactly what Clausewitz described — something that, because it is divorced from any political context, is 'pointless and devoid of sense'?[4]

Deterrence as scholasticism. Since my first brush with Professor Howard, my own acquaintance with the kind of pure deterrence theory which he has identified as 'theology' has become closer. And I must argue that much of the work of its reigning specialists has become intellectually disreputable, and ought not to be supported by any university. Those who have not studied the specialist treatises and periodicals may sample the character of the work in the Winter 1981 number of *Daedalus*, published (alas) by the American Academy of Arts and Sciences, and devoted to 'United States Defense Policy in the 1980s'.[5]

I read this special issue with attention and growing amazement. I found it to be (in the majority of its articles) a barbaric utterance, and in its sum a signal that civilization is already defeated beyond remedy.

Indeed, this defeat is *assumed*, as a first premise of the discourse. It is assumed that two great blocs are in a state of permanent war (restrained only by something called 'deterrence') and will, forever, remain so. The expertise of the authors — and they were selected for their acknowledged expèrtise — is contained within an infantile political view of the world, derived, I suppose, from too much early reading of Tolkein's *Lord of the Rings*. The evil kingdom of Mordor lies there, and there it ever will lie, while on our side lies the nice republic of Eriador, inhabited by confused liberal hobbits who are rescued from time to time by the genial white wizardy of Gandalf-like figures such as Henry Kissinger, Zbigniew Brzezinski, or Richard Allen.

This is an overstatement, for in fact most of the contributors to this issue say little about politics at all. A Manichean world view is assumed, and the rest is politically null. That is, perhaps, what a top-flight 'defence expert' is: a person with a hole in the head where politics and morality ought to be, who can then get along all the better with moving around the acronyms, in a vocabulary of throw-weight, delivery systems, megatons and the extrapolation of ever-more-tenuous worst-case scenarios.

'Controlling the escalation process by providing NATO with a wider menu of realistic nuclear options has become an important priority.' That is a sample of the use of English of one of these experts, Mr Richard Burt, whose extremist views on the abject decline of American military strength were presented extensively in the *New York Times* in the weeks before the late American elections. (He is now one of President Reagan's senior defence advisors.) And another notable expert, Professor Michael Nacht, comes forward proudly as the inventor of a new 'defensive' concept, that of 'pre-emptive deterrence'. Pre-emptive deterrence consists in pre-emptive *aggressive* actions around the world in pursuit of strategic advantage or scarce minerals, raw materials, oil and so forth, and he recommends this brave new concept to the attention of the new United States administration — but in a moderate kind of way, of course, and only when 'US security interests' or 'the intrinsic value of the assets' are important, and, even then, only in 'favourable circumstances'.

It turns out from Professor Nacht's tables that assets with 'intrinsic' or strategic value can be found in most parts of the Third World. That is a sobering reflection. But I have also been puzzling, as a European, to work out how this 'wider menu' of nuclear options might be consumed on this continent, and what 'pre-emptive deterrence' might lead on to here. The view of Europe of several of these distinguished contributors is somewhat hazy. Scholars so high in the world, whose advice is solicited by statesmen and editors, must take large and distant views. One expert notes that 'Western Europe (like South Korea) amounts geographically to a peninsula projecting out from the Eurasian land mass from which large contingents of military forces can emerge on relatively short notice to invade the peninsula.'

The vision informing such sentences merits our atttention. The juxtaposition of 'land mass' and 'peninsula' imposes the suggestion that the situation of Western Europe must perforce be precarious. (For the same geo-physical reasons the situation of Florida *vis-à-vis* the other United States must be precarious in the extreme.) This is the vision of the circumnavigating satellite: from its point of observation, Greenland or the Kola peninsula are more significant than Italy or the two Germanys. The vision excludes all historical or political dimensions: it would be futile to remind the author of two occasions in the past 200 years when large contingents of military force have 'emerged' from the peninsula and invaded the land mass. But the largest of political assumptions has been assumed in the vision itself: the ineluctable opposition of Eriador and Mordor, and the aggressive intent of the latter.

I have indicated matters of style and stance rather than particular arguments. For what we are confronted with — and I am now trying to identify the intellectual credentials of deterrence theory — is not a branch of scholarship but a scholasticism. Like all scholasticisms the practitioners are trapped within the enclosed circularity of their own self-validating logic. Every conclusion is entailed within the theory's premises, although a finely-wrought filigree of logic may be spun between one and the other. And the same premises may give rise to varied and contradictory conclusions, since so much of the exercise is a speculation in futurology which admits of no empirical validation: the matter of the argument deals with linkages, thresholds and ceilings, 'windows of opportunity', the 'balance' of unlike quantities and qualities, alternative perceptions, the 'credibility' of 'postures', the probable and possible outcome of weaponry decisions in ten or twenty or thirty years time.

I do not know whether the academic community realises what an extraordinary intellectual creature co-habits with the high scholarship of American universities. (I do not refer to Russian universities, since this is beyond my knowledge, but I suppose that a blunter, more militaristic, and more segregated, creature co-habits there also.) This creature is increasingly cutting every bridge which might link it with adjacent humanities: with political theory, with history (in all but its military branches), with sociology, with the analysis of culture. It operates on the basis of second-hand

and contaminated data, provided in large part by the intelligence services or by the public relations lobbies of the armed forces; and the official secrecy protecting much of its subject matter inhibits close empirical engagement with the data. The discipline, or pseudo-discipline, attracts indicative funding. It also attracts ambitious men and women who aspire to be advisors to Presidents and who know that if they do not maintain good relations with Defense Department officials and the military they will be starved of information and denied an audience for their work.

The more one examines this specialist literature, the more one is driven to ask the same question as Professor Michael Howard has already asked: *What is it about?* And what are its methods? The only proof which the theory can offer rests upon an exercise in counter-factual history. Its major procedures are predictive, yet its predictions are of a kind which can never be verified or falsified: they consist, rather, in speculative exercises in futurology, derived from worst-case analysis. These speculations commence (as we have seen) by excluding all variables not related directly to weaponry and strategy. This enables theorists to proceed by attributing a rationality to states which can rarely be found in history: that is, a rational calculation of advantage in the pursuit of self-interest, untroubled by those non-rational surges (of panic or of national self-assertion) which mark the historical record. The predictions also suppose, when they come to 'thresholds' or to menus of 'nuclear options', a fine tuning between 'posture' and 'perception' which strains any credibility. What if postures are misperceived by the adversary (as they commonly are), or if the alternative strategic premises of the adversaries do not mesh? What if the Russians are playing a different game from the Americans, and each ignores or misunderstands the others' rules? And, finally, this predictive theory can only operate by assuming an accuracy in the delivery of weapons, and a command and control of operations (with supporting communications) which is altogether improbable. This accuracy is neither evinced in history nor in today's world of the helicopter fiasco in Iran. The performance of new weapons, like the cruise missiles, is acclaimed

in the ecstatic terms of the manufacturers' advertising bro-
chures. I will not say that the first cruise missile deployed
at a target near Leningrad will in fact turn around and take
out Massachusetts. I will only say, as an old soldier, that
the claims of boffins and of staff officers for their perfect
weapons or their perfect battle plans only make me yawn.
Old soldiers know that the only general who commands
both sides on every battlefield is General Ballsup.

There are reasons why this very odd exercise in futurology has acquired some influence. The research and development of new weaponry requires a longer period of
forward planning than has ever been known before: ten,
fifteen, twenty, and now thirty years. Hence R & D, which
is a major *interest* in both blocs, requires a predictive
'science' to justify its inertia and expenditures. And the
SALT negotiations consolidated this 'science' and gave to
it credibility. Seven years were expended in the fruitless
pursuit of SALT II, and during this period many expert
minds were employed, on both sides, precisely in the work
of predicting consequences, searching for loopholes, and
imagining the new weapons and strategies of the adversary.
The humane experts of arms control first broke their teeth
upon a diet of SALT, and ultimately broke their hearts.
But, paradoxically, the SALT negotiations were also the
incubator of this inhumane scholasticism, as other minds
were tricked, by the continual elaboration of worst-case
hypotheses, into the ultrasophistication of contemporary
deterrence theory.

The methods of deterrence

Let us look more closely at two procedures: counter-factual
'proof' and worst-case analysis.

Counter-factual proof. Counter-factual history, as an exercise in historical logic, is not necessarily disreputable. But
the exercises in this case are trivial. The most commonly
found example, which is not part of everyday political
discourse, is that 'deterrence', in the past thirty years, has
'worked', in Europe if not in the rest of the world. The

proposition is made: there would have been a major European war, at some point between 1950 and 1980, if it had not been for 'the deterrent'.

Now this is not a stupid proposition. It might be true and it might not; it is a counter-factual proposition which does not admit of proof. And if we allow it some force (as I think we might) it establishes nothing about the future. There are episodes in those years — the Berlin air-lift, the Hungarian insurrection in 1956 — which might have occasioned war. This war (we should note) might equally well have been promoted from the West — to reunite Germany or to 'liberate' Eastern Europe — as (in the obligatory scenario of Russian tanks rolling upon the Channel ports) from the East. But this war did not happen. And there is some factual evidence which suggests that 'deterrence' was not the only reason for this. Thus Yugoslavia and Albania succeeded in detaching themselves from the Soviet Union, without recourse to the nuclear 'umbrella', and without war. Given the post-war settlement of Eastern Europe (and I am not apologising for this), there has been no further Soviet expansion upon adjacent non-NATO states: Finland, Austria, or Sweden. Moreover, as Alva Myrdal has argued, there are few territorial or national disputes in contemporary Europe so grave as to be evident occasions for war; and those which remain are found either between states *within* the same alliance (the Greco-Turkish disputes) or in grey areas removed from nuclear threat (the Yugoslav-Bulgarian dispute about Macedonia). And, finally, if we were to accept the argument that for thirty years the opposed alliances might have had recourse to war if they had not been 'deterred', this affords no proof that nuclear weapons were essential to this 'deterrence', and no proof whatsoever that nuclear weaponry on the present scale of overkill made 'deterrence' more efficient. For what might have deterred the opposing powers from war might have been war itself: that is, 'conventional' war, on a scale as great or greater than World War II — a war which had certain inconvenient and not wholly acceptable attributes. There was, as I recall, no particular appetite in Europe at the end of World War II to commence forthwith upon another. If the appetite at some time in the past thirty years revived, then I wish the counter-factual theorists would do a little serious historical work and show that this was so.

I am only making the obvious point that even counter-factual history must attend scrupulously to evidence, and must take the fullest view of this evidence (in its political, ideological, social and cultural as well as purely strategic aspects) in order to identify motivations and possibilities. That is, this is a problem requiring the full resources of the historical discipline. But the theorists of deterrence foreclose this examination by postulating as a premise exactly what research and analysis alone could find out. It is assumed that the armed forces of the rival blocs stand waiting to overwhelm each other at the first sign of weakness, and would have done so long ago had it not been for the fear of MAD.

Worst-case analysis. This assumption is premise *A* of deterrence theory, from which the rest of its alphabet follows. Our own weapons are for deterrence; but the weapons of the other side will, or may, be unloosed at the first sign of tactical or strategic advantage. It is not essential to say that they *will* be; to say that they *may* be is sufficient. Worst-case analysis then proceeds (and this is an extraordinary intellectual procedure) by excluding as inadmissable every other kind of evidence as to political, social and cultural reality. In monomanic fashion it applies its forecasting to this one thing: might there possibly be, now or at some future date, a point of tactical or strategic disadvantage, a weak link in the system of balance, or confusion of posture and perception, which would permit the adversary to strike? And it is assumed (for the purposes of this theory) that the adversary must at all times be malevolent, amoral, opportunist, and possessed by no motivations other than absolute hostility.

I can think of no reputable discipline which proceeds by such methods. Of course, any discipline — economics, demography or criminology — narrows its vision to certain phenomena only, and excludes the irrelevant. But it does not then — or it should not — smuggle back into its premises arbitrary assumptions as to the excluded phenomena. If criminology were to assume, as its first premise, that society is divided into two parties: the police and the law on one side, and all other citizens on the other; and, further, that all citizens will always seek opportunities to commit murder unless effectively deterred; then the theory would commence as apologetics for a police state, with a gibbet at every cross-roads. Criminology would then, by imagining murderers everywhere, actually provoke a state of conflict and induce more murders (judicial or other), just as deterrence theory is inducing nuclear war.

The elementary notion of deterrence — the cave men with their clubs, or a few ICBMs on each side — has a certain commonsense plausibility. It has even sometimes worked. But deterrence theory, in its scholastic or vulgar political expression, has long parted company with commonsense. By excluding all other phenomena, except the worst-case, from view, it offers, always, weaponry as a *substitute* for the diplomatic or political resolution of differences. It freezes all political process and, increasingly, on both sides, constricts even cultural and intellectual exchanges within the same ideological parameters.

More than this. Worst-case analysis (by excluding the possibility of any better cases, and by refusing to consider any measures which might bring the better about) actually *induces* the worst cases to arise. This is the entire record of weaponry, the pursuit of advantage, of the past two decades: the inducement of one worst case after another. Deterrence theory, by accelerating R & D and by summoning new weapons forward, is the ideological drive of addiction. In this, ideological, role it is indeed an operative force. Like an addictive drug, it induces euphoria, inhibits the perception of manifest consequences, and excuses the inexcusable.

A disreputable discipline

It is odd. The number of influential 'defence experts' in both blocs probably only amounts to a few hundred. All around these rocky islets there is a sea of authentic scholarship

— historical, political, sociological, and in military or peace studies. The scholars take little notice of the increasingly abstruse, acronymic and hermetic discourse which goes on on the islets; they think of these practitioners, perhaps, as rather well-funded freaks; those who have looked into the defence literature know that it is very weird.

Yet this intellectually-vacant pseudo-discipline carries greater influence upon the outcome of civilisation, and commands vaster human resources, than any intellectual exercise in history. Examine the history of the MX missile project. This originated in a classic exercise of deterrence theory, or worst-case alarmism. Eminent practitioners signalled that the increasing accuracy of Soviet ICBM delivery systems placed the United States land-based Minutemen silos at risk; the adversary was being offered a 'window of opportunity', and with a first strike could 'take out' every one of these silos. This afforded the theoretical rationale for the most expensive construction project in all history, the MX mobile 'shell-game', with its tracks and roadways which would have occupied half of the states of Utah and Nevada. The operative pressures behind this project were ideological and economic — in particular the vast pickings afforded to the arms lobby at a time of recession. But it was this paper-thin piece of worst-case analysis which provided the theoretical rationale.

Even as worst-case analysis it was badly flawed. United States nuclear menace stands on three legs: land, air and sea: and of these, only the first leg could possibly be imperilled by this fictional first strike. No Soviet command, however malevolent, could possibly unloose such a first strike in the expectation of remaining immune from an air- and sea-launched response. Moreover, as US interservice rivalries have built up — promoting alternative ventures — and as President Reagan's Republican friends in Utah and Nevada have become restive, it suddenly turns out that the original analysis was absurd also. The Soviet ICBMs are not as accurate as the worst case predicted; no first strike could possibly take out more than a proportion of the Minutemen silos. New learned articles are now being published, and the theory is undergoing revision.

How could it have come about that something above fifty billion dollars could be authorised to be spent upon a flawed argument based upon worst-case projections in a disreputable discipline? Or let us take another case. The ceaseless pursuit of advantage, rationalised by the worst-case analysis of both sides, has led to the present missile crisis in Europe: the build-up of SS-20s, the summoning on of cruise and Pershing II missiles. It is evident that neither weapon will contribute to European security: on the contrary, Europeans are feeling decidedly insecure.

Both sides justify their measures in terms of 'balance' within deterrence theory. The Soviet apologists argue that they are only modernising and replacing their S-4s and S-5s, and matching the (largely sea- and air-borne) forces of the West. What they disguise is that the modernised weapons are both more accurate, and are mobile and hence more difficult to target. The Western theorists are even less plausible. They designate as intermediate or theatre weapons missiles which can reach far behind Moscow and which can destroy the most densely-populated and densely-industrialised territory of their adversary: what may be intermediate to the Pentagon is as immediate as some five minutes flight to the Kremlin. In Russian perception these new missiles are not intermediate at all, but are forward-based United States strategic missiles which decisively tilt the 'balance' against them. If deterrence theory had been an objective discipline, one would have supposed that this self-evident difference in perception – what Sir Martin Ryle has called 'geographical asymmetry' – would have been registered impartially at the outset of the discussion. But, in my reading of the literature, this manifest point was universally overlooked; or was noted only by those distinguished advisors and arms controllers of an older generation who have been pushed out into the margins of protest.

Deterrence theory, then, has long parted company with science and has become the ideological lubricant of the arms race. Its theories can be turned to use by the arms manufacturers or by military lobbies; or they can be brought in afterwards to justify anything. To be anything more than that it would have to be fleshed out with some empirical substance;

it would have to engage with the full historical process; and, at the end of all its worst-case predictions, it would have to envisage some way forward to an ultimate better case — to proffer some little advice as to policies which might possibly advance the better and forestall the cumulative worst.

And how do deterrence theorists suppose that this race will ever end? Short of a final nuclear war, I suppose that there are these alternative scenarios. Soviet ideologists may suppose that, in the end, Western capitalism will collapse, with conjoint recession and inflation, shortage of energy resources, internal insurrection and revolt throughout the Third World. Western ideologists suppose that the Soviet economy will collapse under the burden of increasing arms allocations, with internal nationalist and dissident movements, and with insurrection or near-insurrection throughout Eastern Europe.

But these theorists need only cross the corridor and knock on the doors of their colleagues in History, Politics or Sociology, to learn that these scenarios might provide, precisely, the moment of the worst case of all. Each of these developments would bring the continent, and ultimately the world itself, into the greatest peril. Each would provide the conditions, not for the peaceful reunification of Europe, but the rise of panic-stricken, authoritarian regimes, tempted to maintain the discipline of their peoples by recourse to military adventures. The break-down of East or West, in a situation of massive military confrontation, would tend to precipitate war. And, indeed, already the military and political élites, both East and West, who are now sensing gathering difficulties within their own systems, are showing that they need the Cold War — they need to put not only their missiles but also their ideology and security systems into good repair — as a means of internal social control.

In doing this, these élites find deterrence theory to be of increasing service. We pass into a new, exalted stage where deterrence theory becomes the astrology of the nuclear age. It is a peculiar situation. In the case of internal ideological systems, the public normally have some experiential means of checking the ideology's veracity. Thus monetarism may appear as a superbly logical system, but we still know what prices are in the shops, which of our neighbours are unemployed, and who has gone bankrupt. But in the case of deterrence theory, the ideologists control both the intellectual system and the information input. None of us, in this hall, has ever seen an SS-20, nor can we count their numbers; none of us can check out the throw-weight or circular error probable of a Trident missile. We have no experiential means of critique whatsoever. The information itself is pre-processed within an ideological matrix (the intelligence services) and is presented with intent to prejudice.

This presents us with an extraordinary problem of epistemology. The sciences and social sciences alike have been subjected to epistemological criticism in past decades, and have sometimes been given a rough passage. But deterrence theory cannot bear any scrutiny of this kind at all. It is well established that President Kennedy was carried to power by an alarmed electorate who had been informed (by him) of a 'missile gap' in the Soviet Union's favour — a gap which was wholly fictional. President Reagan has now been swept to power upon a similar tide of prejudicial information and fictions. An academic discipline which has failed to challenge, frontally, these major exercises in public deception — which has covered up for them, or even provided the trumpeters and drummers for the whole mendacious exercise — a discipline which has left it to a handful of honourable dissenters, outsiders, and amateurs to contest, with small resources, the well-funded lies of State — such a discipline must stand self-condemned.

Ideology and symbolism

Militarisation in the advanced world today has these contradictory features. It is distinguished by the very low visibility of some of its activities and the high visibility of others. The actual military presence, in most parts of Western although not in all parts of Eastern Europe, is very low. This is not a time, as were the Jingo days before World War I or as was Hitler's Germany in the late 1930s, of ostentatious parades, rallies, tattoos, and the ubiquitous recruiting sergeant. The actual weapons are invisible, at Grand Forks, North Dakota, or on the Kola peninsula, or at sea. The attendant communications and security operations − although these may be our neighbours − are kept invisible behind a screen of Official Secrecy. The militarisation of nuclear weapons warfare is science- and capital-intensive; it does not require a huge uniformed labour force, nor does it necessitate conscription or the draft. The growing retinue of 'deterrence' is more likely to be in mufti: in manufacture, research and development; we may exchange smalltalk with them in the university commonroom − easy-going, civilian, decidedly unmilitary types.

But at the same time militarisation as ideology has an increasingly sensational visibility. It is presented to us, on television, in the speeches of politicians, as the threat of the Other: the Backfire bomber, the SS-20, the hordes of Soviet tanks. It is necessary − and on both sides − to make the public's flesh creep in order to justify the expense and the manifest risks of 'our deterrents'. With the break-up of the Cominform, and the weakness and disarray of Western Communist movements, nobody is much impressed today with the story line of the first Cold War: the threat from within. (This story line still works, to more effect, in the East.) What then must be imprinted upon the public mind is the escalating threat from without. Deterrence theory is elevated to the Chair of Propaganda. Professor Caspar Weinberger orders the neutron bomb; but at the same time he orders a sensational account of the build-up of Soviet weaponry to be sent on to Western Europe, to make plain the way of the bomb.

The other contradiction is this. None of these weapons − *none* of them − can ever be used, except for the final holocaust. As Mr Kennan has told us: 'The nuclear bomb is the most useless weapon ever invented . . . It is not even an effective defence against itself.' There is an existing state of threat: but to add and add to that threat is, in military terms, futile. Given the initial equilibrium of MAD, each additional weapon has been useless. They might as well not exist. The significance of these weapons is symbolic only.

I say 'symbolic only'; but as a social historian I have often offered the view that symbolism is a profoundly important constituent of historical process. Symbolic confrontations precede and accompany confrontations by force. They are often also a means of sublimating or displacing confrontations of force, with real and material consequences. A contest for 'face' may, in its outcome, confirm or call in question the authority of the rulers. The rituals of State, the public execution, the popular demonstration — all carry symbolic force; they may consolidate the assured hegemony of the rulers or they may bring it into disrepute with numbers and ridicule. Symbolism is not a mere colour added to the facts of power: it is an element of societal power in its own right.

New generations of nuclear missiles are counters in a contest for 'face'. But they are not less dangerous because they are only symbolic. They are carriers of the most barbarous symbolism in history. They spell out to our human neighbours that we are ready, at any instant, to annihilate them, and that we are perfecting the means. They spell out also the rejection of alternative means of resolving differences. That is why — as symbols — they must be rejected. As weapons they are useless, except for the final event; they exist, today, only as symbols of barbaric menace and of human self-defeat. And the consequence of the first rejections of these symbols will, in its turn, be of profound and hopeful symbolic significance. It will demystify the theory of deterrence, and symbolise the pursuit of alternative solutions.

A self-fulfilling prophecy

What should properly command our attention today is not the theory of deterrence — whether or not it may have 'worked' on this or that occasion — but the social and political *consequences* of its working over two decades. From one aspect these consequences are merely absurd. Anthropologists will be familiar with the potlach: the ritual and ceremonial destruction, by primitive peoples, of their surplus food and resources. From this aspect, the nuclear arms race is nothing but a gigantic potlach. From another aspect, matters are perilous. It is not only that these weapons do actually exist; their function may be as symbols, but they remain there, on their launch pads, instantly ready. The weapons themselves have been consumed in no potlach, only the human resources have been consumed. And there are now new and devilish strategies which propose that they might actually, in 'limited' ways, be used. Insane as it is, deterrence theory could, like other insanities, be self-fulfilling. By conditioning military and political élites, on both sides, to act in accord with the first premise of adversary posture — to seek ceaselessly for advantage and to expect annihilating attack upon the first sign of weakness — it could tempt one side (if a manifest advantage should arise) to behave as theory prescribes, and to seize the opportunity for a pre-emptive strike. And what would the war, then, have been *about*? It would have been about fulfilling a theorem in deterrence theory.

But the greater peril does not lie here. It lies in the consequences of a course of action which has frozen diplomatic and political process and has continually postponed the making of peace. Deterrence theory proceeded by excluding as irrelevant all that was extraneous to weaponry. But no theory can prohibit economic and political process from going on. Through these two decades, frustrated aggression has fed back into the opposed societies; the barbarous symbolism of weaponry has corrupted the opposed cultures; the real and material bases of the weapons systems — the military-industrial complexes of both sides — have enlarged and consolidated their political influence; militarism has increased its retinue of civilian retainers; the security services and security-minded ideologies have been strengthened; the Cold War has consolidated itself, not as between both parties, but as an indigenous *interest* within each one. This is a proper — and urgent — matter for scientific, economic, and political enquiry.

Deterrence theory proposed a stationary state: that of MAD. But history knows no stationary states. As deterrence presides, both parties change; they become addicted; they become uglier and more barbarous in their postures and gestures. They turn into societies whose production, ideology, and research is increasingly directed towards war. 'Deterrence' enters deeply into the structure, the economy, and the culture of both blocs. This is the reason — and not this or that advantage in weaponry, or political contingency — why nuclear war is probable within our lifetimes. It is not just that we are preparing for war; we are preparing ourselves to be *the kind of societies* which go to war.

I doubt if there is any way out, although increasing numbers are searching for it. Since the weapons are useless, and function only as symbols, we could commence to behave as if they do not exist. We could then resume every possible mode of discourse — inter-personal, scholarly, diplomatic — designed to break up the unnatural opposition of the blocs, whose adversary posture lies behind the entire operation. But the melding of the blocs can never take place upon terms of the victory of one side over the other; it must be done, not by the states, but in some part *against* the states of both sides. This means that we cannot leave the work to statesmen, nor to the functionaries of states, to do on their own. Political and military leaders, by the very nature of politics and military service, are the last to abandon adversary postures; and as soon as they do so, they are accused by their opponents of complicity with the adversary.

The work would have to be done, at least in the first stages, *beneath* the level of states. There would have to be an unprecedented investment of the voluntary resources of ordinary citizens in threading a new skein of peace. In this work scholars and intellectuals would find that they had particular duties, both because of their specialist skills and opportunities, and because of the universal humane claims of their sciences and arts. I am not inviting them to go into politics. I am saying that they must go *ahead* of politics, and attempt to put European culture back together: or all politics and all culture will cease.

References

1. G. Kennan, *New York Review of Books*, 16 July 1981.
2. 30 January, 1980.
3. Edited by Dan Smith and E. P. Thompson (Penguin books, 1980).
4. 'On Fighting a Nuclear War', *International Security*, Spring 1981.
5. I must apologize to American readers for inserting in this text (pp. 57–8) a passage which already appeared in 'A Letter to America', first published in *The Nation* (January 24, 1981) and in *Protest and Survive*, ed. E. P. Thompson and Dan Smith (Monthly Review Press, 1981).

5. THE SOVIET VIEW OF DETERRENCE: A GENERAL SURVEY

John Erickson

In the course of some recent exchanges on Soviet military science and Soviet military organisation, my perceptive colleague Professor Roger Beaumont from Texas A & M University enjoined me to read (or rather, to reread) an article on Russian military development by Edward L. Katzenbach, erstwhile consultant to the United States Air Force[1]. This proved to be a most revealing exercise, for while the article pointedly referred to 'a serious lag in Soviet strategic thinking' — lag which amounted to three years at least by this calculation — the markedly condescending judgement was supplemented by a platitude which deserved more attention, namely, that Russians do not necessarily think like Americans. Both these observations merit some closer inspection, for their relevance persists to the present day. The disdain shown towards the quality (or lack of quality) in Soviet strategic thinking was a marked feature of the 1960s, rooted in the supposed intellectual superiority of American sophistication in matters of 'deterrent theory' and encouraging the notion that during the SALT I process the Americans world perforce initiate the Russians into the mysteries of deterrent theory and the complexities of nuclear war. To general discomfiture, it soon became apparent that the Russians needed no tutoring in matters pertaining to war in general and nuclear war in particular, that there was a singular cogency to Soviet strategic thinking and that Russians did not necessarily think like Americans. While Western specialists in strategic theory refined their concepts of 'deterrence' into ever more complex (and arcane) theorems, a kind of nuclear metaphysics, the

Soviet command had worked much more closely within classically configured military concepts, inducing at once a much greater degree of military and political realism into what in American parlance is termed their 'mind-set'. Belated though this recognition of Soviet realism was, it had one unfortunate aspect, that Katzenbach's platitude went unremarked. Not only Western terminology but also Western preferences were frequently superimposed on the Soviet scene, even to the point of interpreting Soviet weapons programmes in terms of a *Western* rationale for such programmes, particularly the transposition of the notion of 'first stike'[2].

This process, long established though now subject to some limited change, has had damaging, not to say dangerous results; and paradoxically it could be said that this most abstract of items — let us call it 'doctrine' by way of intellectual shorthand — may well prove to be the most potent factor in the strategic equation. Indeed, it is becoming ever more apparent that improved mutual understanding of doctrine is a prerequisite of effective arms limitation and arms control as opposed to confining the matter to technicalities of weapons systems. True asymmetry may lie in doctrine (and perceptions) rather than in disparate numbers of weapons and characteristics of their presumed performance. By the same token, the dovish argument that there is actual convergence in doctrine (where no such convergence exists and where insufficient recognition is accorded to the factor of sheer military weight in Soviet priorities) can be misleading, while paradoxically the hawkish deprecation of American political will and the exaggeration of American vulnerabilities is yet another damaging distortion, leading in turn to crude over-simplifications of Soviet doctrine, all duly transmuted into a form of strategic demonology. While it would be mistaken to regard Soviet doctrine as an absolute master-plan prescribing all strategic objectives — including winning a nuclear war — it is equally feckless to be dismissive about (or ignorant of) doctrine as an indicator of *Soviet* perceptions of the deterrence process, of threat profiles, force structures and military precautions so involved (what I called 'deterring against what, with what') and, finally, of that military-operational provision relevant to the collapse of deterrence[3].

That latter point is the nub of the matter. If Soviet realism and adherence to military orthodoxy has inculcated a persistent scepticism towards the metaphysics of deterrence, if Soviet political attitudes preclude placing any reliance on the goodwill (or rationality) of an adversary and if Soviet practice precludes any mutuality which would imply dependence on an adversary for even a particle of Soviet security, this is still some distance from postulating the rejection of deterrence as it might be generally understood in favour of viewing nuclear war as a rational instrument of policy and, moreover, as a process which is winnable. I am not suggesting that doctrine *tout court* will elucidate all problems inherent in Soviet strategic policies, but there is a case for some inspection of the more recent Soviet pronouncements and analyses. And therein lies a small irony, for if two decades ago Edward Katzenbach was pointing to the 'serious' lag in Soviet strategic thinking, at this juncture Soviet specialists point to the 'serious lag' in Western appreciation of Soviet doctrine; appreciation and evaluation which rely on sources which if not actually outmoded have become inevitably passé — for example, the stylised recourse to Marshal Sokolovskii's *Voennaya strategiya* (*Military Strategy*)[4]. The convenient myth of Soviet nuclear troglodytes seemingly died hard, only to be replaced by the equally distorted simulacrum of Soviet nuclear supermen.

Peace and war, deterrence and defence

It is impossible to evaluate Soviet perceptions of 'deterrence' without some brief inspection of general Soviet theories of armed conflict, what might be called 'official doctrine' designed to suggest guidelines for weapons programmes in time of peace and rules for the use of such force in wartime. Such a sustained effort has produced a voluminous and complex literature (little of which is known in the West) and in which the *leitmotif* is the insistence that while nuclear weapons have clearly changed the character of any future war, they have in no way altered the essence (*sushchnost*) of war as a *political* phenomenon, to be understood as such. While it is frequently said that the Soviet view is 'Clausewitzian', in fact Lenin modified Clausewitz's dictum to read '*imperialist* wars are a violent extension of the politics of imperialism', where the essence of imperialism must generate chronic conflict. In this search for the 'laws of armed conflict' Soviet theory also departs from Clausewitz in refusing to regard wars as isolated phenomena: rather they have common features which inevitably involve 'the masses', as well as demonstrating various patterns in the relationship between war and politics[5].

Further to this search for laws and predictability, Soviet military doctrine (*voennaya doktrina*) is concerned specifically with disclosing 'the nature of contemporary wars which may be unleashed by the imperialists', as well as formulating the missions of the Soviet armed forces, specifying military-operational methods involved and estimating what is required in the way of defence preparations: Soviet military science (*voennaya nauka*) contributes analyses drawn from past wars and present weapons performance, while military art (*voennoe iskusstvo*) develops operational, battlefield methods. Thus, to the political awareness which is fundametal to the Soviet outlook must be added the infusion of military ideas which have a strongly orthodox cast about them. Both elements fuse in the notion that the essence of war has not been changed by nuclear weapons, that the nuclear weapon is not an absolute which has made war unthinkable — on the contrary, the situation must be thought through, into the situation where deterrence could well fail, or where it could be undermined by the malevolance of the imperialist camp. The nuclear weapon has not made conventional weapons superfluous; on the contrary, a flexible composition of military force is essential, exemplified in the Soviet 'combined-arms' concept. Whether any future war be long or short, large standing armies are indispensable: in what could well be a nuclear battle in the accepted sense of battle, the Soviet forces cannot remain inert, committed to absorbing an enemy strike and then lashing out in some indiscriminate punitive response — deterrence by punishment. And after the near catastrophe of

June 1941 when German armies were launched against the Soviet Union, it is inconceivable that any Soviet leadership will countenance absorbing any initial strike.

It follows, therefore, that this outlook places a premium on defence in the first instance, so that defence and deterrence must go hand in hand: the massive Soviet programme of defence (both active and passive) needs little or no advertising, though it has been the cause of misgiving and misunderstanding. Ironically, the Soviet interest in defence, including an extensive civil defence programme, fuelled American fears that here was indeed a major ingredient of a first-strike policy (with the Soviet Union taking major steps to protect itself), while Soviet opinion saw in the lack of a defence programme in the United States more than a hint that American policy was essentially one of first strike, surprise attack, an annihilating blow which would perforce eliminate any retaliation, with the prime emphasis on offensive forces in a high state of alert.

It is here that Soviet reference to the possibility of 'victory' in the context of general nuclear war makes what to many is a disquieting, even alarming appearance. This is an issue which requires some careful consideration, beyond the rather simplistic assertion that such statements confirm absolute Soviet belief in surviving and winning a nuclear war, indeed might even encourage any Soviet leadership actually to think of nuclear war as a rational instrument of policy. Are we talking about 'victory' and 'survival' being synonymous, or as separate elements? It would seem that stereotyped statements affirming that in the event of an American/imperialist attack on the Socialist camp the latter system would prove superior and axiomatically survive, are little more than expressions of ideological conviction, or ideological rectitude. However, once the discussion closes more immediately on the operational features of any nuclear war, the tone changes[6]. Soviet professional military writing (as opposed to that of the political officers) proclaims a much more cautious line, eschewing the notion that capitalist society will collapse like a pack of cards and demonstrating a ready appreciation of American second-strike capability to inflict a horrendous scale of damage on the USSR. By the same token, there is implicit recognition that rapid and total escalation is the most likely contingency arising from any so-called 'limited' war, speedily involving the full range of US strategic capabilities. This is the Soviet view.

Rhetoric and realism are obviously in conflict here. It is eminently understandable that political officers, responsible for moral and party-political education, should stress the superiority of the Socialist system and its potential for victory, but this is a far cry from asserting a military-operational reality. On the contrary, the military press stresses the unprecedented scale of damage following a nuclear attack, the huge volume of casualties and devastations of whole countries; observations supplemented very recently by the widespread publicity accorded to the exchanges between Soviet and American doctors on the effects of nuclear war, supplemented by the latest Ascot meeting[7]. While it is certainly impossible to specify just what 'unacceptable damage' would mean in the Soviet context (with one Western argument using the figure of Soviet losses in 1941–5 as evidence that the Soviet Union is somehow inured to a higher level of unacceptable damage), informed Soviet opinion seems inclined to the view that the scale of damage and loss would be unprecedented.

We should return, however, to the point of nuclear war as a means of politics, a rational instrument of policy. The possibility of nuclear war is recognised in terms of the Marxist–Leninist theory relating to the causes of war at large, namely, as a *political* product of a society composed of antagonistic classes pursuing competitive aims. Thus, the question of the essence of any future nuclear war must be kept separate from the other issue, the acceptability (or otherwise) of nuclear war as an *instrument* of policy[8]. On the whole, Soviet opinion seems to hold that nuclear war is not a rational instrument of policy, for means and ends lose any significance when the cost of destroying the enemy amounts to self-annihilation.

To take this logic a little further and returning to the fundamental tenet of the political essence of war, it is reasonable to infer that the sole contingency which could persuade any Soviet leadership of the 'rationality' of nuclear war in pursuit of policy would be the unassailable, incontrovertible, dire evidence that the United States was about to strike the Soviet Union: the political end would be the very survival of the Soviet Union through 'striking first in the last resort', to use Mr Malcolm Mackintosh's succinct phrase. Yet this form of 'rationality' is almost too fearsome to contemplate, hence the specific form of Soviet deterrence − to prevent the very emergence of that cataclysmic contingency[9].

In general, the role of military power is seen from the Soviet side as a major instrument in impressing on the 'imperialist camp' that military means cannot solve the historical struggle between the two opposing social systems, at the same time reducing (if not actually eliminating) the prospect of military gain at the expense of the Socialist camp. Putting this into the context of deterrent theory, while it might be said that the United States has embraced a concept of 'deterrence by punishment', the Soviet position is one of 'deterrence by denial'[10]. Obviously this is a somewhat simplified picture which must be developed in some detail, but it is worth noting that the terminology used in the Soviet Union to discuss deterrence tends to reflect this dichotomy. In the 1960s (and again in the 1980s) the Western deterrent concept has been defined as *ustrashenie* (which has a clear hint of threatening intimidation), while the Soviet stance is registered by the word *sderzhivanie* (conveying a sense of constraining and restraining an opponent, with even the word *oborona* − defence − used in a deterrence context)[11]. As we shall shortly see, this is more than mere semantic hair-splitting.

Some qualifications: While it is true that the Soviet leadership regards the capability to wage nuclear war − in terms of military preparation − as a major element of a visible deterrent, this does not indicate any preference for or inclination towards regarding nuclear war as a rational instrument of policy: even more, Soviet deterrent policies are designed to minimise the incentives for attacking the USSR and, above all, are aimed at preventing the outbreak of hostilities. This is 'denial' in an absolute sense. Certainly, this does imply reliance on Soviet capabilities rather than on enemy rationality or goodwill, the supreme importance of retaining the initiative and a certain scepticism about 'crisis management' when the crisis is (or could be) so apocalyptic. Thus, we have here not a commitment to 'war-avoidance' but to 'war-denial' (if that phrase can be admitted): at the same time, this does suggest some reduction in the notion of 'mutuality', where the Soviet Union is not willing to be dependent on an adversary for any element of its security, but, even more important, sees in the notion of mutuality in assured destruction nothing less than a disguise of what is essentially a US counter force (and first-strike) policy. Here we must return to the perception of the American notion of 'deterrence by punishment', which must be expanded to include 'compellence' which embraces 'escalation dominance' and connects military superiority with political, global dominance. Thus, the Soviet Union is to be 'deterred' into accepting this situation, where 'compellence' and 'extended deterrence' reflect an offensive military–political posture and commitment.

Mutuality is further diminished by the fact that while the Americans spoke of mutual assured destruction (MAD), in effect American policy was designed to increase counterforce capabilities: witness the MX missile programme, the Trident submarine-launched ballistic missile (SLBM) programme and the improvement in forward-based systems (FBS) which simply amounted to outflanking the SALT agreements. Even worse, Presidential Directive 59 (PD-59) allegedly reflected the real intent of US policy, reinforced and supported by the release of previously secret US documents such as the operational plan Dropshot[12]. US policy is designed to legitimise nuclear war by making the idea of limited nuclear war more feasible and thus more acceptable, resulting in a lowering of the nuclear threshold. A Eurostrategic nuclear war might then be pursued, leaving the USSR open to attack but giving sanctuary to the United States. Behind all this lies the intent of establishing (or re-establishing) escalation dominance and thus intimidating the USSR, or so the Soviet leadership reads the present situation.

While admitting the unremitting hostility of the adversary, Soviet military planners must take account in their deterrent calculations of the NATO theatre nuclear forces (TNF) modernization, which is seen as nothing less than a larger US design to regain military superiority. The idea is to tie NATO ever more closely into US strategic planning, to divert or to deflect Soviet counter-action towards Europe (rather than against the United States itself) and to adjust the overall strategic balance in American favour. More pertinently, the new weapons — above all, the Pershing II — can only be regarded as a first-strike counter force weapon, improving by a factor of ten the capabilities of Pershing I and capable of destroying not only inter-continental ballistic missile (ICBM) silos but also command and control centres[13]. What must impress Soviet military specialists is that the Pershing II has a flight time to target of only 4–6 minutes (as opposed to an ICBM which takes up to 30 minutes to reach its target): thus, with such a short flight time to target, the Pershing II nullifies any Soviet resort to launch under warning and even launch under attack[14]. Apparently the Soviet General Staff is prepared to regard the Pershing II range of 1500 miles (up to 2600 kms) as the truly effective range of the new missile, a figure which would mean much wider target coverage.

If we add the cruise missile, the Soviet sense of vulnerability can only deepen, leading to a denial concept without any measure of adequacy since it depends crucially on over-insurance — hence the preoccupation, not to say the obsession, with numbers and some numerical hedge of advantage. It is fair to comment here that this is not only a doctrinal requirement but one which also represents a number of bureaucratic and institutional interests (the Soviet equivalent of the military-industrial complex); yet by a fierce irony it is precisely this numerical fixation which will provide the coming crisis for Soviet deterrence policies. At the moment, the Soviet interpretation is that PD-59 plus NATO's TNF deployment plans amount to nothing less than an American push for superiority *tout court*, together with an attempt to implement a Eurostrategic variant for limited nuclear war.

The Soviet rejection of the idea of limited nuclear war is axiomatic, based as it is in the political notion that *political* objectives — not the performance of particular weapons —

decree the essence or scope of war: it follows, therefore, that if American objectives are unlimited in the sense of regaining military superiority and escalation dominance over the USSR, then any war operation cannot be limited, whatever the technicalities of the weaponry involved. At the same time Soviet attention is concentrated on the offensive nature of US 'deterrent forces', where counter force targeting was — and has remained — a prime US interest, bringing Soviet nuclear delivery systems into the tight focus of such a targeting philosophy. 'Punishment' was allegedly only part of the story: American lack of interest in defence (active and passive) pointed to a singular approach to deterrence, with important destabilising implications, while American emphasis on mutual assured destruction seemed to be in sharp contradiction to the development of a counter force capability[15]. The critical point for Soviet deterrence comes with the recognition that US counter force capability is not only expanding but will continue to expand in excess of a comparable Soviet capability.

Deterrence modes: We have already seen that the Soviet concept of deterrence is rooted in 'denial', designed to prevent the United States from the actual initiation of hostilities, to reduce the prospect of making military gains at the expense of the Socialist camp (a commitment which has steadily committed the Soviet Union to a global role), to assure the survival of the Soviet system (hence the priority accorded to strategic defence) and, through the development of actual military (war-fighting) capability, to minimise the incentives for attacking the USSR by guaranteeing counter-strike — hence the mix of pre-emptive and secondary retaliatory forces. What has certainly become increasingly prominent in Soviet military-political thinking is the idea of a more protracted war — should it come to war — with consequent emphasis on survivability and sustainability, including wartime force reconstitution. (One recent effect of Soviet command reorganization has been to blur the previous sharp distinction between strategic and tactical force elements, presumably in an effort to provide greater flexibility: a visible manifestation of this process is the greater autonomy now allowed to Soviet theatre commanders.)

On the other hand, for all the augmentation of military capability, Soviet military opinion cautions against any 'adventurist strategy' which might prematurely initiate a total struggle when the requisite 'correlation of forces' (*sootnoshenie sil*) cannot assure a favourable outcome (even 'victory') in such a struggle: as for the notion of a *blitzkrieg*, one Soviet general emphasized that 'blitz war can only lead to a blitz collapse'. *Blitzkrieg* for its own sake can only mean assuming unacceptable (and uncontrollable) risk: though the surprise factor has been enormously enhanced, the blitz solution does not seem to recommend itself to Soviet military planners, who have argued that the effect of modern weapons has been to extend the duration of war, as well as increasing its intensity, so that the interconnection of strategy, economics and the morale factor has assumed a correspondingly greater significance.

While eschewing any adventurist blitz strategy, Soviet military doctrine draws on its own established orthodoxy in linking military principles — speed, surprise, shock, fire-power the winning of the initiative — with what might be called the Soviet nuclear outlook. It is easy enough to label this after Western styles, such as 'pre-emption' or 'first strike', but I think this is better described as a preference for a strategic 'disruptive strike', not unlike Soviet artillery practice in World War II when the artillery *kontrpodgotovka* fired off its delicately-timed fire blow designed to disrupt enemy preparations for attack (it is worth noting that the Soviet missile forces were first developed by officers who had an artillery background). Equally, the Soviet principle of 'a succession of fires' (developed by military theorists in the 1930s) is also applied to the nuclear battle; hence we see Soviet strategic missile forces not only organized into 'missile armies' (with divisions, regiments, battalions and batteries) but also with first and second echelons, plus reserves. Yet the strategic disruptive strike may not succeed entirely, thus precipitating more protracted war and the utilisation of the 'combined-arms' forces; nuclear, conventional and chemical all interacting in land, sea and air operations with ICBM support.

Much confusion arises from over-simplification relating to the Soviet mode of simultaneously working to prevent nuclear war and also preparing to wage such a war, should it occur. The Soviet leadership with its military and political segments has no wish to embark on nuclear war, an outlook which seems to have wide popular support; and in this sense war-avoidance is fundamental to Soviet policies. But that immediate transposition of a Western term is somewhat misleading. The essence of Soviet deterrence is not the avoidance of war but the prevention of war — thus giving Soviet deterrence a positive, active cast. Here actual military capability has a prominent role — Soviet deterrence as restraint of the imperialists. There is mutuality of deterrence in recognizing that both sides have overwhelming capability to inflict unacceptable damage if nuclear war were to be initiated by any act of rational (or supposedly rational) calculation, but this cannot be construed as accepting the posture of hostage and thus denying any initiative to the Soviet Union, even to the point of forcing surrender upon it. A natural and inevitable scepticism pervaded the Soviet view of mutual assured destruction, not only because this ran counter to the principle of any dependence on a potential adversary for Soviet security, but more importantly because Soviet specialists perceived that the real issue was not MAD as such but rather that mutual deterrence in broad terms was being modified as the Americans moved away from deterrence via punishment and into greater emphasis on 'compellence', all with the aim of ensuring that 'US deterrence of the Soviet Union [will be] "more efficient" than Soviet deterrence of the United States'[16].

'Deterring against what, with what': threat profiles, force structures: In the United States and the 'imperialist camp' at large, the Soviet Union faces a formidable adversary, whose real purposes arguably are not disclosed by declaratory doctrinal positions (such as 'assured destruction' or even 'mutual assured destruction'). The reality in Soviet eyes lies in the American pursuit of war-waging counterforce capabilities with offensive strategic forces eminently capable of first strike: the 'punishment' concept has steadily given way

to coercion and constraint, with counterforce capability growing constantly. American programmes, according to Professor Trofimenko (and others) are aimed at regaining unilateral deterrence, to which end the United States works to realign the balance in its own favour and to outflank the SALT agreements. As for counterforce capabilities and options, the Soviet side insists that their own recourse to such capabilities was a reaction to American initiatives and weapons programmes. In particular, the Schlesinger doctrine and more recently PD-59 are viewed as the development of a 'strategy of victory in a nuclear way through build-up of counterforce potential'.

In this counterforce context it is also important to recognize significant Soviet–American differences over what exactly comprises 'the balance': while Western sources evaluate the 'net balance' (ICBMs, SLBMs and long-range bombers as strategic weapons systems) Soviet reckoning perforce includes the Pershing II medium-range ballistic missile and the ground-launched cruise missile — due for deployment in Europe — as strategic components (if only because of the Soviet definition that any weapon which can strike the USSR is 'strategic', irrespective of its geographical basing). The same criterion is applied to the whole nexus of forward based systems (FBS), including land- and carrier-based aircraft. More pertinently, Pershing II with its high accuracy and extended range, is perceived not as a counterpart to restoring imbalance in theatre nuclear forces[17] but expressly as a high-precision first-strike counterforce weapon: witness the 4–6 minute flight time of Pershing II to target, which effectively rules out launch on warning (assuming even rapid launch detection); and with strikes against Soviet missile silos and command and control centres, launch under attack will be hazardous if not actually impossible. In brief, the Soviet command sees itself facing the development of nothing less than a Eurostrategic nuclear capability associated with existing (and expanding) American offensive first-strike weaponry.

If such are Soviet preoccupations and perceptions (let me add the proviso here that these observations have been drawn almost exclusively from Soviet materials), it is worth examining briefly the present Soviet view of the 'correlation of forces', the strategic equation and Soviet effectiveness in terms of missions. In other words, what explains the Soviet military build-up? On the current count, Soviet strategic forces consist of 1398 ICBM launchers, 950 SLBM launchers and 156 inter-continental bombers (without Backfire), encompassing some 7000 nuclear warheads. The ICBM force is made up of 580 SS-11s, 60 SS-13s, 150 SS-17s, 308 SS-18s (the largest ICBM in the world) and 300 SS-19s, with the latter group (17s, 18s and 19s) carrying multiple warheads; while the submarine-launched missile, the SS-N-18, is the first Soviet SLBM to carry multiple warheads. The primary mission of the Soviet strategic missile forces is to destroy enemy means of nuclear attack (including command and control systems). Thus, while numbers are important, the progression of improvement in the Soviet ICBM force must be related to greater effectiveness against given target arrays. While concentrating on effectiveness against 'time-urgent hard targets', Soviet planners can now envisage attacking the entire hard and soft target array in the United States with a mix of Soviet systems. Also, the addition of heavy bombers and Soviet cruise missiles can at least provide some compensation for the growing vulnerability of land-based missiles, though the Soviet deterrent has not yet put to sea on anything like the American scale.

If there is any measure of sufficiency in Soviet force planning, then it must be reckoned against the requirement to cover the entire hard/soft target array with mixes of Soviet weapons, plus a survivable reserve — a position which is being steadily attained with the modernization of Soviet strategic forces. While launch on warning has been and remains part of the Soviet operational repertoire, the development of a survivable reserve force could have tempered this option. Refire and reload for Soviet ICBMs using the 'cold-launch' mode also provides a possible hedge for more protracted nuclear war, with a Soviet exercise in the autumn of 1980 rehearsing the reloading of 25–40 SS-18 silos over a period of 2–5 days (technically no breach of SALT, for this was not 'rapid reload' but tending to confirm the notion of the echeloning of missile armies).

The heart of the Soviet strategic system is the heavy bombardment force of 308 SS-18s (in two versions, MOD-1 with a single warhead, MOD-2 with 8–10 multiple warheads). While there is much talk about missile accuracy, the problem of reliability has recently come to the fore and must be introduced into projections of any attack mode. Discounting the reliability aspect, it can be made to seem that a relatively few Soviet ICBMs could wreak havoc on US silos, but this is to assume well nigh perfect performance: 125 SS-18s each with eight 1.5 megaton warheads could theoretically take out 1000 US silos, but Soviet prudence would dictate some insurance against equipment failure and assigning more war-heads (and more missiles) to wave attacks, each of diminished effectiveness[18]. 'High-confidence first-strike capability' (to use Dr Schlesinger's phrase) is demonstrably an elusive animal, a point not lost on the Soviet command.

The Soviet ICBM structure, both present and planned, could well be seen as the best approach to the real world of the nuclear battle, with a high numerical ceiling for the heavy bombardment force and a recognition that multiple (wave) attacks on ICBM silos could be less effective than one-on-one attacks with heavy megatonnage; with the multiple warhead (MIRV) arsenal available for dealing with soft targets and also for cross-targeting Minuteman silos; and with MOD-2 (single warhead SS-17s and SS-19s) also assigned to the hard target array including command and control centres. Thus, the Soviet command will continue to have at least two heavy ICBM systems committed against the hard-target array, while SLBM systems will be improved and developed as a survivable reserve force.

There are, however, some disturbing problems which face Soviet planners. While there is undoubted Soviet advantage in 'time-urgent hard target kill capability', this is matched — some would say outweighed — by US 'discretionary force potential' (the capacity to meet its overall targeting plan). Here we come to the US MX missile, which poses a major threat to Soviet land-based ICBMs (where a large segment of the Soviet deterrent is housed; much larger than US land-based systems). The net result of deploying the MX would be the massive degradation of Soviet counter force/counter-strike forces, in which contingency the Soviet command would be forced to redeploy its submarine missiles to cover soft targets and thus deplete its crucial survivable reserve. In sum, the advent of MX must impose more severe dilemmas on Soviet planners than present Soviet 'time-urgent hard-target potential' poses to the Americans. Equally, the development of the B-1 bomber, the 'stealth bomber' and the loadings of air-launched cruise missiles (ALCMS) means urgent and necessary refurbishing of air defence systems, indeed of the entire Soviet system of strategic defence. Add to this the programme involved in modernizing the Soviet SLBM force (in terms of missile performance), and the modernizing of Soviet theatre nuclear systems, and the outlook is dispiriting, to say the least.

Summary

To sum up, Soviet opinion from the outset was not inclined to accept what might be called the metaphysics of deterrence, or any arcane system of scholasticism which merely screened the American policy of containment: the Soviet Union was deterred and was intended to remain in that condition, all in the age of *ustrashenie* (the West's concept of deterrence). In the Soviet view, though American declaratory statements ostensibly committed US policy to concepts of nuclear sufficiency, in the real world − in the world of military procurement − the American build-up belied the notion of 'sufficiency' and American capabilities were being developed beyond those which could be identified with 'deterrence through punishment'. It was impossible, therefore, for the Soviet Union to subscribe to the mutuality of 'assured destruction' when military reality appeared to suggest further expansion of US counterforce capability: it was no part of Soviet policy to increase Soviet vulnerability nor to pinion the Soviet Union in a 'hostage' concept. As for mutual deterrence, it had to be a mutuality stripped of American attempts at coercion (compellance) and without resort to the reimposition of 'unilateral deterrence'. Yet another contradiction was that certain American attitudes professed war-avoidance and the 'unthinkability' of nuclear war, while the Soviet Union determined on war-prevention coupled with the acceptance of the possibility of nuclear war, an admixture which produced no small degree of confusion, acrimony and accusation in Western circles, certain of which insisted on the implacability of Soviet intentions in a quest for unchallenged military superiority — thus demolishing deterrence and undermining any mutuality.

It is too easy to dismiss deterrence as some kind of word-game or a form of nuclear mumbo-jumbo meant to obscure the significance of nuclear weaponry, a form of academic-intellectual conspiracy on the part of 'strategists' against humanity. But if there is a fault, it may well be not that we have paid too much attention to this phenomenon but too little, particularly in the matter of perceptions and, specifically, Soviet perceptions. These require at the very least close inspection, fair evaluation and due application of mutuality: as a very senior Soviet official put it in the course of our 'Edinburgh Conversations on Survival in the Nuclear Age' (a meeting held at Edinburgh in October 1981), what is sauce for the goose should be sauce for the gander. Whatever the dispute over Soviet intentions and capabilities, whatever the disparagement of deterrence as a moral or metaphysical hoax, it is nevertheless fair to state unequivocally that it is no part of rational Soviet design to see our collective goose cooked.

References

While the avowed purpose of this paper is to present (or represent) the *Soviet* view of deterrence, to which end I have drawn upon a variety of Soviet sources (not least Professor Trofimenko's recent paper), I have also tried to include materials which are either actual translations or identify translated materials. Finally, I have drawn on reputable non-Soviet items for certain purposes of clarification or, yet again, to attempt some balance of views and interpretations.

1. Edward L. Katzenbach Jr, 'Russian Military Development', *Current History*, November 1960, pp. 262–6.
2. Katzenbach did not fall into this trap: he argued, (*Current Hsitory*, loc. cit., p. 264) that the Russian theory and weapons developed round 'high explosives and megatons', to limited nuclear war 'they have never given a moment's thought', nor did they demonstrate

much interest in 'system redundancy'. A much more cogent and penetrating analysis of the misleading nature of simple transition of terms — particularly 'first-strike' — is presented in Benjamin Lambeth's paper, 'How to Think about Soviet Military Doctrine' in *Soviet Strategy*, edited by John Baylis and Gerald Segal (Croom Helm, 1981), pp. 112–14. An important work utilising much historical material (and original Soviet sources) is Peter Vigor's monograph, *The Soviet View of War, Peace and Neutrality*, RKP, London 1975.

3. See Benjamin Lambeth in *Soviet Strategy* (footnote 2), under 'Key Themes in Soviet Doctrine', pp. 108–9.

4. See interview with Lt Gen. M. Milshtein, 'Moscow Expert Says US is Mistaken on Soviet War Strategy', *International Herald Tribune*, August 28, 1980: the same point is made in Professor Henry Trofimenko's study *Changing Attitudes towards Deterrence*, University of California ACIS Working Paper No. 25 (July 1980), Note No. 32 (p. 54), which recommends works by Grechko, Gorshkov, Ustinov (Defence Minister) and Marshal Ogarkov (Chief of the Soviet General Staff).

   Professor Henry Trofimenko is a distinguished Soviet expert, a Professor of History and Diplomacy, Head of the Foreign Policy Department of the Institute of US and Canadian Studies of the Soviet Academy of Sciences, an observer of the American scene for more than thirty years and author or co-author of fifteen books, two of which are major studies of US strategy. His paper, 'Changing Attitudes towards Deterrence', was published in the United States of America.

   I have always maintained and still maintain that Marshal Sokolovskii's *Voennaya Strategiya* was reprinted in 1968 in the series *Biblioteka ofitsera* (*The Officer's Library*). This was not exactly demotion but it removed the book from the current operational code. Also, as I understood from my talks with Marshal Sokolovskii himself, his book was intended only as a first primer, not the final word.

5. It is possible to cite only a bare sample from a massive literature, e.g. *Marksizm-Leninizm o voine i armii* 5th edition (Moscow, Voenizdat, 1968), *Filosofskie nasledie V.I. Lenina i problemy sovremennoi voine* (Moscow, Voenizdat, 1972); M. V. Popov, *Sushchnost zakonov vooruzhennoi bor'by* (Moscow, Voenizdat, 1964) and an important recent study, K. V. Tarakanov, *Matematika i vooruzhennaya bor'ba* (Mathematics and the Laws of Armed Combat) (Moscow, Voenizdat, 1974). Meanwhile, I am much bemused to see that virtually no attention has been paid

to two important studies, *Metodologiya voenno-nauchnogo poznaniya* (Moscow, Voenizdat 1977) (a volume from the General Staff Academy) and I. A. Korotkov, *Istoraya sovetskoi vennoi mysli* (Moscow, Nauka, 1980). I fear that many of our 'Soviet experts' do not read Russian and must perforce wait on official translations, which may or may not materialise. They are not captives of 'Soviet disinformation' but rather of *our* information process and processing.

6. See Robert L. Arnett, 'Soviet Attitudes Towards Nuclear War: Do they really think they can win?', *Journal of Strategic Studies*, Vol. 2, No. 2, September 1979, pp. 172–91. This article, in addition to being eminently fair, contains many references to Soviet materials which are available in translation.

7. See *The Guardian* report, 'Brezhnev's Doctor is Anti-Bomb', 6 October, 1981: conference of Russian, American, and European doctors. The previous Washington congress was widely reported in the Soviet press.

8. For an elaboration, see Colonel T. Kondratkov, 'War as a Continuation of Policy' in *Soviet Military Review* (English version published in Moscow), No. 2, 1974, pp. 7–9.

9. I noted with much interest a statement in Donald M. Snow's excellent new study, *Nuclear Strategy in a Dynamic World*, (Univ. Alabama Press, 1981) to the effect that war *prevention* 'is arguably not only the first but the only true military objective'.

10. This distinction, which still retains its validity, was formulated by Glenn Snyder, *Deterrence and Defense*, (Princeton U. P., 1961).

11. See note 29 (pp. 53–4) in Professor Trofimenko, loc. cit., who also points out the confusion caused by the *Soviet* rendering of 'containment' and 'deterrence' by the single Russian term *zderzhivanie*.

12. For text see Anthony Cave Brown, *Dropshot: The United States Plan for War with the Soviet Union in 1957*, (New York, Dial Press, 1978). Inevitably this received fairly wide coverage in the USSR, with *Voenno-istoricheskii Zhurnal* subjecting Dropshot to more detailed examination. See also *Harmon Report* (12 May 1949–JCS 1953/1), 'Specific: the plan for the strategic air offensive in support of *Trojan*: a. An initial phase . . . attacks primarily with atomic bombs on 70 target areas. b. A second phase . . . continuation of the initial attacks with both atomic and conventional weapons.' The target area was the USSR: the initial phase was projected to last thirty days.

13. See Doug Richardson, 'Pershing II – NATO's Small Ballistic Missile', *Flight International*, 8 August 1981, pp. 431–4. Richardson cites

a range of 900 n.m. (1800 km) but, as I have noted, some Soviet sources increase this substantially. There is no official figure for Pershing II range, as far as I know.

14. With its 'Earth Penetrator', Pershing II is designed to attack command/control centres: this would inevitably force the Soviet command to 'launch on warning', but this requires high accuracy attack assessment and some estimates put this beyond the capability of Soviet computers — hence 'accidental launch' cannot be discounted with the danger of nuclear war by technological malfunction.

15. For a lengthy Soviet exposition, see A. G. Arbatov, 'Strategicheskii paritet i politika administratsii Karteva', *SShA: Ekonomika, politika, ideologiya* (Journal), 1980, No. 11, pp. 29–40. See also A. Arbatov, *Bezopasnost v yadernyi vek i politika Vashingtona* (Moscow, Politizdat, 1980), on American strategic policies. See also *SShA: Voenno-strategicheskie kontseptsii* edited by R. G. Bogdanov, M. A. Milshtein and L. S. Semeiko (Moscow Nauka, 1980). (On American strategic concepts, including limited nuclear war, also theatre nuclear warfare.)

16. Professor Trofimenko, loc. cit., note 30 (p. 54) defines four threats facing the USSR: (1) from NATO, including British and French nuclear forces, plus US forward based systems (FBS), (2) from US strategic potential, (3) from China with 'its huge reservoir of manpower', and (4) from large US naval units in forward deployment.

17. There is persistent Soviet denial that such imbalance does exist: see 'Russians deny the missile gap', *The Observer*, 11 October 1981, reporting observations by Lt Gen. Chervov.

18. On missile reliability, see under Missile Engineering, 'Panel reexamines ICBM Vulnerability', *Aviation Week and Space Technology*, July 13, 1981, pp. 141–8.

Bibliography

This bibliography extends the list of materials used and cited, and induces as much balance as possible in respect of interpretation.

Joseph D. Douglass Jr and Amoretta M. Hoeber, *Soviet Strategy for Nuclear War* (Hoover Institution Press, Calif. 1978). Analysis based on translated Soviet materials.

J. Erickson and E. Feuchtwanger (eds.), *Soviet Military Power and Performance* (Macmillan 1979). Collected papers on Soviet military organisation, strategic, land, sea, air forces.

Fondation pour les Etudes de Defense Nationale, *Les Fondements Doctrinaux de la Stratégie Soviétique*, Cahier No. 13, Paris 1979.

Raymond L. Garthoff, *The Soviet Image of Future War*, (Public Affairs Press, Washington, 1959) This book should be read and reread.

S. G. Gorshkov (C-in-C, Soviet Navy), *The Sea Power of the State*, (Pergamon Press 1979) Translation.

A. A. Grechko (Marshal Soviet Union), *The Armed Forces of the Soviet Union* (Moscow, Progress Pub., 1977).

Dennis Ross, *Rethinking Soviet Strategic Policy: Inputs and Implications* (Univ. California ACIS Working Paper No. 5, June 1977) A sophisticated analysis.

V. D. Sokolovskii (Marshal, Soviet Union), *Soviet Military Strategy* (translated by Harriet Fast Scott), (Crane Russak, New York 1975). Also *Soviet Military Strategy* (RAND Corporation, April 1963). Translation with analysis and annotation.

Strobe Talbott, *Endgame. The Inside Story of SALT II* (Harper & Row, 1979).

(US) Department of Defense, *Soviet Military Power*, (Washington, D.C., October 1981) 99 pp. See especially Pt. V, 'Soviet Strategic Forces', pp. 53–69.

Edward L. Warner, *The Military in Contemporary Soviet Politics*, Praeger Publishers, New York/London, 1977).

6. SCIENCE AND THE NUCLEAR ARMS RACE

Egbert Boeker

Introduction

Some 150 years ago, as the British Association adopted its name, people believed that the 'Advancement of Science' would heighten the level of rationality in human thinking and that the application of the scientific method would increase human standards of living. Few of the founders of the BA would have suspected that the Advancement of Science would lead to the point where the military application of science and technology threatens the very survival of the human race. This ambivalence of the scientific enterprise, working between human welfare and uttermost destruction, is the main theme of this paper.

As a working physicist, I would like to start with some examples from laser physics that show that this fascinating new field gives us new knowledge of nature and leads to techniques and instruments that are dangerous from the point of view of arms control. Next, I discuss how the scientific community deals with the ambivalence between welfare and destruction. I give a few examples of scientists' hesitancy and unwillingness to discuss these problems in public, and I try to understand the roots of this reluctance.

As a third and last point I indicate how one could try to lead the 'Advancement of Science' in a more positive direction. This would not necessarily amount to pacifism. I hope to show that science may contribute to the development of a non-nuclear defence that would serve the interests of the European countries.

Lasers, a mixed blessing

A laser is an optical instrument that produces coherent, virtually monochromatic light. A laser beam has very little divergence and will, in a vacuum, propagate as a straight line up to a distance of many kilometres. Recent developments are taking us in the direction of very intense, powerful laser beams with as little divergence as possible.

One of the first widely known applications of the laser was its use in holography, invented by the British scientist Dennis Gabor. This technique for recording and reconstructing light waves makes use of the monochromatic character of the laser beam. It produces three-dimensional pictures of objects and is used extensively. An application that most people would regard as a real advance is the non-destructive testing of materials. Two holograms are made on the same photographic emulsion, one with stress applied and one without. The holographic reconstruction then shows interference fringes from which the quality of the material can be gauged. Defective solder joints in gold dental bridges can be found in a similar way[1].

A second application of lasers makes use of the fact that lasers can be constructed with a very high energy density. In Rochester, lasers with a peak energy of 4 kJ, or 12×10^{12} W for some 50 pica-seconds, are used[2]. With such high power lasers we have gone a long way towards *laser fusion*. In this process glass micro balloons of 100 μm diameter are filled with a mixture of deuterium and tritium and irradiated by lasers. When the incoming energy is high enough and entering from all directions the balloon will implode and a d + T fusion reaction takes place. It is hoped that in the long run the energy balance might become positive, and the fusion process might contribute towards fulfilling our energy requirements.

Between now and this possible future there will be a time when the fusion reaction works, but does not result in net energy production. The major application of the process would then be military. By means of laser fusion the conditions of the nuclear battlefield could be imitated and its weapons systems tested under war conditions[3]. This example shows that the success of laser fusion may contribute to nuclear war. For it may encourage political and military leaders to believe that such a war is thinkable or even winable.

A third application of lasers leads still further into the military field. I am thinking of laser beam weapons. In these weapons the high energy of the laser beam is used in the kilowatt range cut or weld a variety of materials[4]. At higher powers, lasers can cut and weld at larger distances. They could then, for example, destroy satellites or missiles in powers, lasers can cut and weld at larger distances. They could then, for example, destory satellites or missiles in space. For this reason the United States spends some $200 million annually on these kinds of projects. These weapons are not deployed yet, and they will most probably encounter many technical problems[5].

Physical research on laser beam weapons puts pressure on the Anti Ballistic Missile (ABM) Treaty of 1972 between the US and the Soviet Union. The research itself is not forbidden by the Treaty. But if it leads to results, the pressure to cancel the Treaty will increase. And if that happens, any one of the superpowers might establish its ABM system. Subsequently, any of these powers might feel safe against a nuclear attack and give way to the temptation to start a 'limited' nuclear war. Whether or not they would succeed in keeping the war limited is a matter of concern, but it would still be a disaster for very many people.

It should be mentioned that research on laser beam weapons for use in space is against the spirit of the Outer Space Treaty of 1967 that forbids weapons of mass destruction in space. In spirit it promotes the peaceful use of space, but its formulation leaves the ABM application open. Most importantly, however, this scientific research hardly contributes to the advancement of science, but rather the destruc- of part or even the whole of civilization.

The silence of the scientific community

These three examples from laser physics demonstrate that this field produces applications that increase human well-being (the dental one or the industrial one of cutting and welding), other applications that leave us with mixed feelings, and still others that most people would regret, or even abhor. Of course, the scientific community, more than any other group of people, should be aware of the problem that faces us: is it possible to prevent the destructive potentialities of the advancement of science?

It must be said that, certainly since the two atomic bombs on Japan in 1945, many scientists have become concerned and quite a few spend part of their professional lives opposing the arms race — often in association with the national branches of the Federation of Scientific Workers, the Pugwash movement and the connected periodical *Bulletin of the Atomic Scientists*. The *Bulletin* publishes articles on the arms control implications of technology. It gives often outstanding political analyses and it puts forward alternatives to the development of weapons.

However, I guess that no more than a few per cent of scientists really do any reading on the subject. The worldwide circulation of the *Bulletin* is some 20 000: it reaches a few per cent of the world's scientists. In the Netherlands the membership of the League of Scientific Workers, the national branch of the Federation of Scientific Workers, comprises only a few per cent of the total scientific population. Although the number of scientists concerned about the arms race is bigger than these numbers suggest, in most countries it presumably does not amount to a working majority. This may be the superficial explanation for the fact that official scientific institutions — as far as I know — never speak out against the race to oblivion that we face today. I would like to illustrate this with the following examples.

The first one refers back to the laser applications I mentioned earlier. In a widely distributed weekly, a Dutch scientist reviewed laser development in essentially the same way that I have done here. The editors asked two Dutch laser physicists to respond[6]. One dismissed the possibility of military applications and played down the significance of the big military spending on the subject. The other one granted the military applications, admitted that he had no expert knowledge on arms control implications but presumed that the benefits of the civil applications would outweigh the social costs of the military ones. The publicity of this discussion was highly atypical: most scientific leaders choose to remain silent on the subject.

This brings me to the second and perhaps more telling example. In the same building where the British Association celebrates its 150th birthday, the European Physical Society (EPS) organized its fourth general conference in September 1978. Virtually all European professional organisations, including those in Eastern Europe, are EPS members. The Society boasts thousands of individual members as well. At the York meeting, attention was focused on the arms race on two occasions. In a plenary session, Dr Frank Barnaby presented a lecture on 'Physics and the Arms Race', which made quite some impression on the public. The chairman of the EPS subsequently emphasized that the unity of European culture should be one of peace and not of war. The general feeling was that all European scientists should be aware of the facts Barnaby referred to.

At the same meeting of the EPS there was a discussion group, organized by the Advisory Committee on Physics and Society. At the request of the audience, and following Barnaby's talk, the arms race was scheduled there. Proposals were formulated along the following lines[7]:

That the EPS ask its member societies to discuss at their national (annual) meetings the following propositions:
1. The EPS condemns the arms race in concordance with similar United Nations resolutions. Physics and physicists should not be used for the development of even more advanced weapons, but for peace and development.
2. The EPS advises its members not to participate in military research and development (R & D). It obviously cannot and should not put sanctions on physicists who do not follow this advice. However, such advice makes military R & D improper. This is a first step towards a consensus abandoning military R & D (or part of it).
3. The EPS advises its members to make public any scientific developments that may lead to new weapons systems. The

Society's own newsletter could print these details. This could make it possible to control these developments from a disarmament point of view.

4. The EPS and the American Physical Society should work out a scheme in which, in the course of 10 years, more and more laboratories would be open to inspection to see whether military R & D is taking place in them. This proposal is in the spirit of the first report of the UN Atomic Energy Commission (31 December 1946) in which, with regard to nuclear weapons and nuclear energy, a foolproof inspection system, with the right to travel without restraint for inspectors, is required. It is also in the spirit of the Baruch Plan (1946) that required the opening of (nuclear) research laboratories to all scientists in order to prevent a nation taking secret advantage of a scientific breakthrough.

5. Concurrently with the decision-making in the Advisory Committee on Physics and Society, Dr Frank Barnaby from the Stockholm International Peace Research Institute (SIPRI) and possibly other experts could be asked for their comments on the recommendations put forward here.

It should be understood that the only request was to discuss the propositions in the national societies. Subsequently the results were to be compared. It should also be noticed that the first proposition was not much more than a polite statement, to set the stage. In itself it had no practical consequences.

It is not hard to guess what happened. In the first place these discussions were not reported in the 'Conference impressions' article in the EPS bulletin[8]. The five propositions mentioned above were indeed discussed in a meeting of the Advisory Committee on Physics and Society at Rome, in March 1979. But even the first proposition was not approved. The discussion resulted in an agreement on a proposal to ask the developed countries to transfer one per cent of their military budget to development aid. This was subsequently rejected by the EPS Council. Neither this discussion nor the Council decision were referred to

in the Council Report to EPS members[9]. This *petite histoire* shows how difficult it is to get scientific institutions to cooperate in finding ways out of the arms race, despite the frequent statements by many individuals that this race is leading us to total destruction.

The difficulty of escaping

Where does the general reluctance to discuss the arms race originate? For there is no reason to single out the EPS for particular blame. Many more examples may be cited. I would like to try to understand this reluctance, as understanding is needed if we are to persuade the scientists to cooperate. I use the proposals to the EPS as a model for an escape from the arms race and, in the next section, try to adapt the model to the findings.

The first and second proposals point to the heart of the matter. According to many authors[10], military R & D is one of the driving forces behind the arms race. On the one hand, the weapons laboratories produce new ideas for weapons and it is then often very difficult for political leaders to reject funding for development and production: one of the reasons being the fear that an opponent might develop and produce the weapon. On the other hand, these new ideas may circumvent the few existing arms-control treaties or threaten the feasibility of new ones. The most drastic solution then, is to try to stop military R & D by urging people not to participate. This would apply both to scientists and technologists working in the laboratories as well as to the academic scientists who give advice to the military.

The problem here is that some 40 per cent of the world's scientists have a full-time job connected with military R & D. These people, members of scientific institutions, would object to prosposals 1 and 2. Besides, academic scientists do not like to close off so many careers for their pupils. The answer here should be the conversion of military R & D to civil R & D, e.g. to the needs of developing countries. It is not obvious, however, that these countries need the very advanced expertise of the weapons experts. Even if the conversion were possible, therefore, it would take many years.

The first two proposals assume a distinction between military science and technology and the rest of science. The third proposal recognizes that many industrial inventions or academic discoveries may have military applications. This fact is usually ignored by academic people. Around Christmas 1979 for example, a questionnaire was sent to all physics laboratories in the Netherlands with precisely this question: 'Could your work possibly have military significance?' Most leaders of the laboratories just answered with 'no'; a few wrote that they did not know, but no one tried to give even the beginnings of an analysis.

The need for such an analysis is clear. Scientists could assess the arms control implications of potentially dangerous developments. Politicians would then be able to anticipate their effects instead of running behind the facts, as is now often the case. But the scientific community does not cooperate. The discussion on laser physics referred to above indicates the possible reasons for this. The second Dutch laser physicist quoted stipulated that he had no expert knowledge of the arms control implications of lasers. But instead of asking expert advice, he wrote that he gives the benefit of the doubt to the advancement of knowledge.

There are, presumably, a few connected reasons for this reluctance to think. First, the wide-ranging public discussion on the possible dangers of DNA research has caused a trauma within the scientific community. As soon as the public and politicians start to interfere, research is restricted and the free development of science threatened. Publication of the weapons aspects of science, which is bound to decrease the scientists' freedom, will not be popular. A related point is that public discussion of the negative aspects of the advancement of science is expected to tarnish the public image of science. In a time in which many universities and institutes have set up science information services to improve that image, negative information is bound to be suppressed. Both of these reasons are connected to the fact that research is supported by public finds. Public funding may involve restrictions; and a bad public image will decrease the total science budget.

It thus seems as if accepting proposals 1 to 3 is against the best interests of science. Proposals 1 and 2 diminish the job prospects and so the influx of science students, and no. 3 threatens the funding and the flexibility of research. My reaction to this is that it is also in the interest of the scientific community to survive by avoiding a nuclear holocaust. And with regard to the public image, I would say that the public is certainly aware of the negative aspects of the scientific endeavour. In the long run science will benefit from an open discussion in which scientists show their willingness to phase out the dangers and show their genius in finding useful applications.

This does not mean 'business as usual'. As already mentioned, the needs of society may be better met by having fewer highly specialised scientists and more scientists with a broader training. More and better-trained science teachers may be more useful than more research scientists. If these presumptions are right, the science system has to adapt. But even so, a *contrat social* between science and society would serve the survival of both.

The phrase 'science and society' points to the last and perhaps deepest objection to implementing proposals of the kind discussed here. 'Science and society' has connotations of left wing activism. And there is indeed some link with the middle left of the political spectrum. For people who are content with the status quo or even want to return to the privileged position that science had some 10 years ago, have not much to expect from public discussions and arms limitations proposals. One does not need to be an activist, however, to realize that the uncontrolled advancement of science has brought us the arms race and the threat of global destruction. Changes are needed, but they must be supported by a workable majority.

The need for security

Let us recall the origin of most military R & D. It began around World War I, when science and technology were used to counteract the weapons of the aggressor. Also, and as significantly, science was used to find substitutes for overseas products that were no longer easily available. The same happened in World War II and it is well known that scientists cooperated in the development of the atomic bomb in order to put an end to that war.

In these political contexts I certainly do not want to blame those that participated in military R & D. On the contrary, I appreciate it. However, it appears to me that the public esteem of the endeavour depends on its political context. And that has changed in two ways. Firstly, it is apparent from other chapters in this book that military technology has not brought us a safer world. Secondly, people's perception of the international situation has changed. Let me try to pursue this a little further.

A first observation is that the military threat from the East has to be reassessed. Developments in Poland teach us that the Warsaw Pact is no monolith and that it is difficult to think of a situation in which all the Eastern European armies would march to the West as comrades and with a will to fight. Also, the movement within Poland shows that the Soviet Union is very reluctant to use military force, even when it knows that it could do so without fear of military retaliation from the West. Granted, there would be economic countermeasures. But if these deter, it just shows that military arguments and military power are not always very useful.

A second observation is that the Soviets have some reason to fear an invasion from the West — there have already been two this century. We understand their trauma, and that they never want it to happen again. That must be the explanation for Soviet military doctrine on how to attack the West: if the worst comes to the worst, try to get the battlefield out of the country.

A third observation is that within NATO the interests of Europe and the United States are not always parallel. A trivial recent economical example is the high US interest rates that have made many European countries suffer. In the military sphere it is clear that a superpower like the United States feels obligations around the world and is prepared for military actions anywhere. For European countries, this is past. They do not like to become involved in military adventures elsewhere.

A fourth observation is the increasing talk about limited nuclear war. One obvious battlefield is Europe rather than the US. This means that the geographic situation of Europe between both superpowers makes this continent (including Britain) extra vulnerable.

A last observation is that the military effort originates in people's need for security. In the present economic situation, there are many more direct threats than the one from the East. Unemployment, even for the traditionally secure jobs in the civil service, is one example; another is social conflicts and riots that cannot be ascribed to foreign influences.

Economic and social policies should obviously take precedence over military policies in meeting people's need for security. Let us, however, return to military R & D. If the first four observations are correct, military R & D in Europe should no longer contribute to the nuclear arms race. It should serve a modest, but effective defence of Europe.

The principle of non-aggressive defence

An effective European defence could be based on the following principle: *The build-up, logistics and doctrine of the armed forces should be such that they could not be used for attack, but serve the demands of a militarily credible defence without nuclear weapons.* The advantage of this basic principle is clear: if it were put into effect an opponent would have no reason to fear the arms of the other party. To put it mildly, one of the excuses for the continuing arms race would be gone. The peace-keeping forces within the other party would hopefully be strengthened. If Europe were to follow this principle, the Soviet Union, even in times of severe international tension with the US or China, would not need to contemplate a pre-emptive strike against Europe, as it would have nothing to fear from that side. This shows that the proposed principle takes into account not only the security needs of one side, but also those of a possible opponent. In this way, a stable system might be created.

It is clear that the deployment of long- and middle-range

nuclear missiles would not be consistent with the principle, as they could easily be felt to be a provocation. It could also be argued that the use of short-range tactical nuclear weapons favours the attack more than the defence. For the attack is interested in movement where destruction does not matter; the defence is interested in keeping its strongholds and keeping its system manageable. Tactical nuclear weapons do not help much in that. Also, defence positions are easier to identify than a moving, attacking army, and are therefore more vulnerable to nuclear attack. Nuclear weapons should, therefore, be ruled out. As this is in line with the feelings of an increasing number of people, it makes sense politically.

It is easy to see that the principle is consistent with the observations made earlier. It could first of all be applied in Europe, thus diminishing the threat of a limited nuclear war on this continent. It would reduce the need for the Soviet Union to have a barrier of satellites on its western flank, thereby making change more possible in Eastern Europe. It is consistent with the position of e.g. Rumania, and it would stimulate other countries to take similar positions.

Earlier I argued that military R & D should be evaluated within a political context. I admit that no Western European government adheres in public to the ideas put forward here. However, campaigns for nuclear disarmament are gaining strength; churches and political parties are discussing the subject of defence; and similar changes are taking place in many countries[11]. The scientific community must therefore choose either to join forces with these new movements or to remain neutral. To remain neutral favours the status quo and must be interpreted as a choice against them.

I believe it serves the advancement of science when the scientific community and the scientific institutions take a stand. If propositions such as those to the EPS, taken as a model, go too far, they could be modified. It would be unwise to change the first one, the condemnation of the arms race, as it is perfectly in concordance with many UN resolutions. The second one, the advice not to participate in military R & D, could be changed to

(a) a task for the scientific institution to find ways of converting military R & D to civil R & D and slowly diminishing the military R & D.

(b) advice to participate in military R & D only if it is consistent with the principle of non-aggressive defence, explained above.

(c) a task for the scientific institution to discuss the social aspects of science in general and military R & D in particular.

Proposition (c) could help the people in military R & D to make their decisions. It would also result in discussions on the other propositions.

The organization of non-aggressive defence

When in mathematics one encounters a complicated differential equation, it is sometimes possible to give a 'proof of existence', although the solution itself has not yet been found. It would be most convincing if this sort of proof could be given for the defence principle explained above. We should realize, however, that no such proof has been given for the present NATO strategy either: no one can prove that without nuclear deterrence the Soviet Union would have occupied Western Europe. Suffice it, therefore, to give a brief indication of how defensive, non-nuclear deterrence could look. The reader may judge whether that would satisfy his or her need for security.

First a remark on the current NATO war scenarios. It is generally assumed that a conventional attack by the Warsaw Pact (WP) would be made over the plains of northern Germany, the easiest entrance to Western Europe. This conventional attack would at first be countered by conventional forces and, when the enemy was about to break through, the President of the United States would allow the use of nuclear weapons, either tactical or long-range. The latter could cut off his supply lines (although this would not be felt for several days), so tactical weapons would be most immediately useful.

This scenario on the firing of nuclear weapons is under

attack in military circles. It invites the use of the same weapons by the WP who, according to this scenario, do not care too much about the destruction of enemy territory. This destruction of the country to be defended is not a pleasant prospect for the defender. Moreover it is very difficult to plan such a war in advance: managing it may easily get out of hand. Planners in the armed forces therefore, discuss non-nuclear defence extensively. They think of a region some 40 km wide at the borderline between NATO and the Warsaw Pact, where the use of Precision-Guided Missiles and advanced intelligence systems should be able to stop virtually any attack.

To understand this, one should realize that an attack — if it comes at all — would use tanks and armoured cars, protected by aircraft. It is known that these are quite vulnerable to cheap anti-tank or anti-aircraft missiles. If NATO defence were to be organized this way, its numbers of tanks could be reduced to the minimum required for defence, and the money saved spent on strengthening the defensive system. This reduction of tanks would make a NATO counter-attack impossible, but that would not matter if the system worked. For NATO does not seek to occupy Eastern Europe, but simply to protect its own territory.

A revision of NATO strategy along these lines is technically feasible and within the realm of political reality as long as it did not overrun the current defence budgets. It might also be set up in such a way that it would be consistent with the principle of non-aggressive defence. I envisage one major drawback: i.e. that it would maintain within Europe the separation between NATO and the Warsaw Pact. Bipolarity, and the focus on the Soviet Union as the potential enemy, would remain. This would give Europe less freedom to act in world politics and make the process of liberalisation in Eastern Europe more difficult. It would also block development towards a European system of security in which e.g. the superpowers would accept a neutral Europe as a 'big Austria'.

For these reasons it is worthwhile working out a more decentralized system of defence as a second step after the de-nuclearization of Europe.[12] This could entail the division of Western Europe in units of the order of magnitude of the

German *Länder* or Benelux (Belgium, Netherlands, Luxemburg). Each unit would be protected by the most advanced technology, similar to the system described previously Of course the defence of each unit would be weaker than it would be if all the forces were deployed along the East–West dividing line. This weakness should be compensated for by a stronger territorial defence by local reserve groups as well as by a stronger reliance on civil resistance, once the country were occupied. An occupant should pay a high price for his attack. Admittedly, this system would not be cheap to set up.

There are three current objections to this decentralized system. The first is that an attacker, say the Soviet Union, could occupy just one unit and then make political claims. A counter argument is that this worst-case analysis is not consistent with political reality: the Soviet Union has difficulties enough with its present WP states. Also, there is no strong group in West Germany that is willing to take control on behalf of the Soviet Union. And finally, in an intermediary situation, emphasis could at first be placed on a common conventional 'forward defence', and a decision taken later at an appropriate time to move towards more decentralization.

A second objection is that a conventional defence is vulnerable to nuclear blackmail. But this blackmail has up to now had no effect in regions outside NATO or the WP. The Soviet Union has repeatedly offered to negotiate a 'no first use' agreement on nuclear weapons.

A final objection is that non-aggressive defence could easily lead to an arms race in electronic warfare, draining yet again the funds that are so needed for development in the poorer parts of the world. However, the R & D needed for non-aggressive defence would focus on the defensive side only, instead of both offence and defence as is the case at present. This would save money to begin with. And as the purely defensive posture reduced international tension, the rationale for military R & D would weaken and more money would flow into the civil sector. This could happen on a significant scale only when the Soviet Union and the US established a détente again. A non-aggressive Europe could help to bring about détente. A non-aggressive defence strategy is, therefore, urgently needed.

References

1. Charles M. Vest, *Holographis Interferometry*. (New York: John Wiley, 1979).
2. The 12TW Omega Laser of Rochester. Cf. Jack Wilson, 'Non-fusion applications for TeraWatt Lasers', *Laser Focus* (July 1981), pp. 47–50.
3. Actually, the funding of laser fusion by the US Congress has been supported in virtue of these military arguments. Cf. Wim Smit *et al. Laserfusie: verwevenheid van civiel en militair onderzoek* (transl.: *Laser fusion, link between civil and military research*) (De Boerderij, Technische Hogeschool Twente 1978) nr. 7801. As a typical example see Hearings on US House of Representatives 6566, fiscal year 1978.
4. I. J. Spalding, 'Industrial Applications', *Europhysics News 12*, 7 (1981) p. 10.
5. *Science 211* (1981) p. 148.
6. W. A. Smit, 'Militaire toepassingen van hoog-vermogen lasers' (transl.: 'Military applications of high-power lasers') *Intermediair 17*, 5 (1981) pp. 17–21.
7. This formulation is taken from a letter to the Chairman of the EPS Advisory Committee on Physics and Society, at his request (by E. Boeker on behalf of ten Dutch EPS members, 24 October 1978). It is a more precise formulation of the text presented at the York meeting. In the letter these statements are coupled to the resolution of the special UN session on disarmament, 23 May–1 July 1978.
8. *Europhysics News 9*, 10 (1978) contains only a reference to Barnaby's talk.
9. *Europhysics News 10*, 5 (1979). The information is a private communication from Dr W. Turkenburg.
10. Frank Barnaby, 'Military Scientists', *Bull. Atomic Scientists 37* 6, (1981) p. 11 and SIPRI yearbooks (London: Taylor & Francis Ltd).
11. Examples are the positions of the British Labour Party, the reluctance of the Dutch to place cruise missiles on their territory, the Hearing of the World Council of Christian Churches (November 1981, Amsterdam).
12. Frank Barnaby and the present author are working out such a system for the Netherlands. They have defined the principle of non-provocative defence.

7. THE PHYSICAL AND MEDICAL EFFECTS OF NUCLEAR WEAPONS

Joseph Rotblat

It is important, at the start, to delineate the scope of this article, namely, the distinction between the effects of nuclear weapons and those of a nuclear war. A nuclear war is one in which nuclear weapons are used, but a discussion of the effects of nuclear weapons differs greatly from a discussion of the effects of a nuclear war. The difference is not simply a quantitative one, e.g., that in a nuclear war a large number, 1000 or 10 000, individual nuclear weapons might be used. There is a basic conceptual difference, in that a nuclear war covers an almost infinite variety of parameters and assumptions that have to be made in any estimate of the consequences of a nuclear war. Most of these parameters interact with each other, and some of them are of such a nature that very little can be said about them with any degree of confidence, simply because there is no knowledge about them. For this reason any estimate of the effects of a nuclear war is bound to be highly speculative. On the other hand, a description of the effects following the detonation of a nuclear bomb as an isolated event, would not only be a purely academic exercise but could also be grossly misleading, because the effects can be properly evaluated only in the context of a nuclear war. For this reason, this chapter, while being primarily concerned with the effects of individual weapons, will also refer to their relevance in a nuclear war.

But even within the limits of a discussion of the effects of single nuclear weapons, there is a very wide range of uncertainty, sometimes amounting to more than an order of magnitude. The reason is that nuclear weapons differ from conventional weapons both quantitatively and qualitatively; while extrapolation sometimes helps to evaluate the quantitative differences, there is no experience to guide us in respect to the qualitative differences.

The quantitative differences arise from the fact that the destructive power per unit weight is millions of times greater in nuclear than in conventional weapons. For example, in World War II Tokyo was to a large extent destroyed and many people were killed in air raids which involved several hundred bombers carrying explosives whose total weight was nearly 2000 tonnes. Approximately the same number of people perished in Hiroshima after *one* aircraft delivered *one* bomb weighing 4 tonnes, with the actual weight of the nuclear explosive being only about 60 kilogrammes. But the Hiroshima bomb was a first and very inefficient weapon; a modern nuclear warhead, with a nuclear explosive weighing only 100 kg, can produce the same destruction as 350 000 tonnes of TNT. A single bomber can carry an explosive yield equivalent to some 10 000 Tokyo raids; if the same explosive yield were to be produced by a conventional explosive, such as dynamite, its weight would be greater than one of the largest man-made structures, the Cheops Pyramid. Or to put it in a different way, one nuclear bomb can have an explosive power greater than that of the total of all the explosives ever used in wars since gunpowder was invented.

The qualitative difference, which makes nuclear weapons unique, is that in addition to causing loss of life by mechanical blast, or by the heat from the fireball, nuclear weapons have a third killer: radiation. Unlike the other two agents of death, the lethal action of radiation can stretch well beyond the war theatre, and continue long after the war has ended, into future generations.

The extent of damage produced by a nuclear weapon depends primarily on the explosive yield of the weapon, and here we immediately enter into the realm of arbitrary assumptions. Nuclear weapons exist with a huge range of explosive yields: at one end, in the so-called mininukes, they bridge the gap with conventional weapons; at the other end we find yields in tens of megatons (one megaton is the equivalent of a million tons of TNT). In the strategic forces alone, there are warheads with yields ranging from 40 kilotons (0.04 Mt), as in the Poseidon SLBMs (submarine-launched ballistic missiles), to 20 megatons, carried by Russia's Bear bombers — a range covering a factor of 500. Thus, by choosing bombs of different yields one can arrive at widely divergent conclusions about the effects produced by these weapons.

The following example will illustrate this. The official pamphlet *Protect and Survive*, issued by the Home Office, starts with the following sentence about heat and blast: 'The heat and blast are so severe that they can kill, and destroy buildings, for up to five miles from the explosion.' This is a definite statement; the lethal limit is 5 miles; if you happen to be at a distance greater than 5 miles from the explosion, you will not be killed. This statement is of course true for some nuclear bombs, but not for others. Available information (included in another Home Office publication, *Nuclear Weapons*) enables us to calculate the lethal area for blast injuries from bombs of different explosive yields. The lethal area is defined as the circular region within which the number of survivors is equal to the number of people killed outside that region; in other words, deaths will occur even beyond the radius of the circle. Now, a 5-mile radius for the lethal area for blast is obtained for a bomb of 5 megatons. But, as already mentioned, the Russian strategic force includes bombs of 20 Mt, and for these the lethal distance for blast is 8 miles. So people may be killed by blast at distances considerably greater than the limit in *Protect and Survive*. The divergence is much larger when the heat effect is considered. One can calculate — although with somewhat less accuracy — the distance at which a person in the path of the heat flash from the bomb might suffer third-degree burns, which in wartime conditions are very likely to be fatal. The calculations show that such burns may occur at a distance of 5 miles for bombs of 0.4 Mt. For a 20 megaton bomb, the lethal distance is about 17 miles. The Home Office cannot assure us that bombs with an explosive power more than 0.4 Mt will not be used, and therefore the above statement is misleading.

Another parameter of importance in discussing the effects of a nuclear weapon is the height above ground at which the weapon is detonated. This affects the lethal areas for blast and heat effects, for a bomb of given yield, but above all it affects the fall-out. Although all nuclear detonations (except those underground) produce fall-out, local fall-out occurs only if the bomb is exploded sufficiently close to the ground. Ignoring this fact may give rise to a falsely optimistic assessment of the radiation hazard. Statements have been published that the worry about radiation is exaggerated, quoting as evidence that in Hiroshima and Nagasaki there were not many deaths from radiation. This is not true in any case, however the main point is that the bombs were exploded over these cities at such heights that no local fall-out would have occurred. But, by present day standards, these were very small bombs; if bombs with an explosive power, say, 0.4 Mt or more, were exploded at the same height, there would have been intense local fall-out.

The bombs on Hiroshima and Nagasaki were the only ones to have been used in warfare so far, but although their consequences were the subject of extremely thorough investigations, very large uncertainties remain. Indeed, it appears that the more the effects of these bombs are studied, the greater the confusion. We are not even sure now what the actual explosive yields were. The largest uncertainty concerns the number of people who died as a result of the bombings. In Hiroshima the estimates vary from 68 000 to over 200 000, a factor of three. The main speculation is about the number of deaths in the months after the bombing, up to 1950 when the first population census was taken. Some estimates indicate that perhaps three times as many people died during those few years than on the first day. If this were true, it would suggest that the acute effects of radiation were far greater and took a much longer time to manifest themselves, than is generally assumed.

In addition to this the long-term effects of radiation, such as the estimates of the risk of cancer induction, which are based mainly on the experience of Hiroshima and Nagasaki, have now been thrown into doubt. Recent analyses have shown that the whole dosimetry system (the determination of the doses received by the survivors), arrived at after a fantastically huge effort, was in considerable error. Some believe that it led to a significant underestimate of the radiation hazard. We have no real basis for calculating the long-term effects of nuclear weapons.

Having thus illustrated the flimsiness of the bases on which the estimates of the effects of nuclear weapons rest, these effects will now be reviewed in the light of current knowledge. They will be described in terms of the agents which contribute to the casualty toll of nuclear weapons. Table 1 lists seven such agents, each contributing in a different way, quantitatively and qualitatively, with the uncertainties and unknowns increasing as we go down the list.

Table 1   Contributors to the casualty toll of nuclear bombs

1. Blast
2. Heat
3. Initial radiation (neutrons and gamma-rays)
4. Fall-out: (a) local; (b) global
5. Electromagnetic pulse
6. Depletion of ozone layer
7. Synergism

1. The blast effect

Of all the effects this is the best known. It produces the same type of damage as ordinary high explosives but immensely magnified. About half of the total energy released in the explosion of a typical nuclear weapon is contained in the blast wave, which produces very high pressures in the air through which it passes. Death can result from either direct or indirect injuries caused by that wave. The human body can withstand quite high overpressures, and most deaths occur from indirect effects, from the collapse of buildings, from being blown into objects, or from falling debris. Experience accumulated in past wars enables us to calculate, with a considerable degree of accuracy (about 30 per cent), the effect of the blast wave on human beings from a bomb of a given explosive yield, detonated at a given height, over a given type of terrain. Bombs do not always explode at the specified height, or have the designed yield; nevertheless, there can be no doubt that a large bomb detonated over a centre of population would contribute the largest number of immediate casualties.

To be more specific, we shall consider the effects of bombs of two specified yields: 1 Mt and 10 Mt, exploded at a height about 300 metres (1000 ft). The lethal areas for the blast effect (as defined previously) would then be 70 and 300 km^2 respectively. The number of fatal casualties could be calculated if the population density were known. On the assumption that bombs may be dropped anywhere in the UK, the average density for the country can be taken i.e. 230 per km^2. This would lead to about 16 000 and 70 000 deaths respectively. But if the bomb were detonated over a large city, with a population density of 4600 per km^2, as in London, the casualties could of course be very much higher, namely 320 000 and 1.4 million. The actual toll might be either higher or lower than these figures. If the explosion occurred in day time, when many suburban residents come to town for work, there would be many more casualties than if the bombing were at night, or if people did not go to work. The toll could be considerably lower if — contrary to official policy — people left the cities before the bombing, or if well-designed shelters were available for the majority of citizens.

In addition to deaths there would be many injuries, abrasions, fractures, ruptured internal organs and loss of blood. Many of the wounds would be of such a nature as to give a high probability of recovery in normal circumstances with medical care. But in conjunction with the other effects of nuclear weapons, burns and radiation exposure, and particularly if a number of bombs were exploded in the country, the chances of recovery would be greatly diminished, largely because medical help would be hampered by fall-out.

2. The heat effect

The hazard due to the heat wave is less predictable than from the blast wave. Man has experienced incendiary bombs and massive fires; but in the case of nuclear weapons, the heat hazard is caused by a temperature several orders of magnitude higher than anything reached on the earth before, and this introduces uncertainties in casualty estimates.

About one-third of the total energy released in the explosion appears in the form of heat emitted from the fireball. This emission consists of two pulses: a short pulse, of a few millisecond duration, followed by a longer pulse, of the order of seconds; its duration is the longer the greater the explosive yield of the bomb. The bulk of the thermal energy is carried by the second pulse. It can cause fatal or severe burns, and start fires, over a large area. The distance at which a given heat effect (measured as the thermal energy per unit surface area) is produced, depends primarily on the explosive yield of the bomb, but it also depends on atmospheric conditions. With fairly good visibility, the heat wave can cause fatal casualties at distances much greater than from the blast wave. Thus, with a visibility of about 20 km, persons caught in the path of the heat flash would have a 50 per cent probability of suffering third degree burns, over an area of 400 km^2, for a 1 Mt bomb, and over an area of 1600 km^2, in the case of a 10 megaton bomb. People with third degree burns can survive if they receive medical treatment, but under war conditions this would be very unlikely, and most of these people would probably die. The areas where such burns may occur are about five times larger than from the blast effect, but it is impossible to say how many people will be affected, because this depends on how many happen to be in the open.

But even those indoors may become casualties of the heat effect, because it can cause death and injury through fires started by the ignition of flammable and combustible materials. These fires are quite separate from the fires started indirectly by the blast wave from damaged furnaces and stoves, overturned electric radiators, broken gas pipes, and petrol in cars, Under certain circumstances, the individual fires may consolidate into one huge fire, covering a large area. Two types of such events are distinguished: a firestorm and a conflagration. In the firestorm the merging of many small fires causes a single convective column which blows inwards from an outside perimeter, and creates temperatures over 1000 °C. Within the area of the firestorm people, even in shelters strong enough to withstand the blast effect, may die through asphyxiation due to the lack of oxygen, or be cremated in the high temperature. It has been stated that such firestorms are unlikely to occur in our cities, but this is disputed by others; there is no direct experience to go by. In a conflagration, the fire front moves outwards and spreads as long as there is material to fuel it. The area and extent of damage due to these fires may far exceed those caused directly by the heat flash.

3. Initial radiation

The two effects described so far, blast and heat, are qualitatively similar to those from conventional weapons, but the next two items in Table 1, initial radiation and fall-out, are unique to nuclear weapons, because they result from nuclear interactions with matter.

The initial radiation consists of neutrons and gamma-rays, most of which are emitted simultaneously with the explosion, but by convention this category includes all ionizing radiation emitted within one minute after the detonation. For the type of bomb discussed here, about 5 per cent of the total energy released appears in the form of initial radiation.

The processes which govern the interactions of neutrons and gamma-rays with matter, and their attenuation as they pass through the air are known with a high degree of accuracy from nuclear physics. But the actual number of neutrons, or gamma-photons, emitted after the explosion depends markedly on the amount and type of material used in the assembly of the bomb. An example of this is the neutron bomb in which, in theory, 80 per cent of the total energy released could be carried by the neutrons. Thus, even for bombs of the same explosive yield, the intensity of the initial radiation may vary over very wide limits. The intensity of the radiation at a given distance, and thus the radiation dose received by people, depends on other factors as well, such as the density and humidity of the air. But more importantly, there is considerable uncertainty about the acute effects of radiation; i.e. the magnitude of the dose which may cause death, as well as about the time of death. By making some plausible assumptions one can arrive at an estimate of the hazard, but it should be kept in mind that the estimate may be greatly in error.

The main characteristic of the initial radiation is that both neutrons and gamma-rays are absorbed in air exponentially. The consequence of this is that the explosive yield of the bomb does not influence to a large extent the range of the lethal action of the radiation. This means that with large bombs the lethal effect of the radiation occurs in an area already devastated by blast and heat. Table 2 shows the lethal areas (in km^2) for the three effects described so far, for bombs of different explosive yields. As is seen, with big bombs the heat effect produces the largest lethal area, and radiation the smallest. The proportions change for small weapons; with a 1 kiloton bomb radiation would cause the largest number of casualties. The lethal areas for blast and radiation are about equal for a 10 kt bomb.

Table 2   Areas of lethal damage from various effects (km^2)

Type of damage	Explosive Yield				
	1 kt	10 kt	100 kt	1 Mt	10 Mt
Blast	1.5	4.9	17.7	71	313
Heat	1.3	11.2	74.2	391	1583
Radiation	2.9	5.7	11.5	22	54

The effects of nuclear weapons were described mainly with the examples of 1 and 10 megaton bombs, but many of the warheads in strategic MIRVed weapons have a much lower yield, although now there appears to be a reverse trend, towards increased yield. (For example, the warheads in Minuteman III have a yield of 170 kt, while in the new MX system the missiles are planned to have 10 warheads with 500 kt each.) However, the use of lower-yield weapons does not diminish the destructive effect; on the contrary, the effect per unit explosive yield is increased. For example, the total lethal area from the blast effect produced by five bombs of 200 kt each is nearly twice as great as that from a single 1 Mt bomb.

The main effect of dividing a given megatonnage into a number of smaller bombs would be to increase the number of people killed and injured. If this were done, a much larger number of injuries would need to be catered for. Since — due to fall-out — medical help would be unlikely to be available at the time most needed, the majority of the injured would die; and the net result would be much more pain and agony. Therefore, by presenting the data for single large bombs, a more optimistic, or rather more merciful picture is painted.

4. Fall-Out

The fourth agent of destruction in Table 1, fall-out, is probably the most insidious of all, as well as being the least predictable. The action of the three agents described so far is of short duration; the all-clear could have been sounded after a few minutes and those who have survived could have come out into the open and begin the process of rehabilitation. But the fall-out makes this impossible; the danger is extended in time as well as in space. Since the presence or absence of radiation cannot be conceived with our senses, and since the population is unlikely to be equipped with radiation monitors, the terror of the unknown will compound the visible and audible terrors.

Fall-out consists of the radioactive fission products created at the instant of the explosion (plus some other radioactive materials). If the bomb is detonated at such a great height that the fireball does not touch the ground, then the fission products — which are in a gaseous form — rise with the fireball to high altitudes into the stratosphere. There the particles are carried by the stratospheric winds round the globe, and eventually, after some months, come down all over the earth, but mostly in the hemisphere in which the detonation occurred. By the time the particles have descended, the intensity of the radioactivity has greatly diminished and no acute radiation effects would be expected. Nevertheless, the exposure of people to this *delayed*, or *global*, fall-out may cause long-term effects, such as cancer and genetic damage.

If the bomb is detonated on the surface, or at such a height that the fireball does touch the ground, then huge quantities of earth and debris are sucked up with the fireball. As the fireball cools, the radioactivity condenses on the particles of earth or debris, and since many of these are large particles, they come down by the force of gravity within a day or so, at distances to which they were carried by the wind, some hundreds of kilometres. This is called *early*, or *local fall-out*. It may contain about 60 per cent of the radioactive content of the explosion. The actual location, the time of occurrence, and the extent of this early fall-out depend primarily on the speed and direction of the wind prevailing at the time.

There is no real experience of handling local fall-out. As already mentioned, in the Japanese cities there was no early fall-out (except for a 'rain-out' in a few locations). The atmospheric tests of nuclear weapons were generally carried out in uninhabited areas. The only documented event of exposure of people to local fall-out was the Bravo test of 1 March 1954, when a thermonuclear device of about 15 megatons was exploded near the ground on the coral reef of the Bikini Atoll. Due to an unexpected change of wind, the radioactive cloud came down in a long plume in an easterly direction (Figure 1), covering the Marshall Islands, several of which were inhabited. An area of about 20 000 km² was intensely contaminated with radioactivity. Two days after the test the inhabitants were evacuated but many exhibited symptions of radiation sickness, nausea and vomiting. Almost all the children of the Rongelap Atoll — nearly 200 km away — later had to undergo surgery for the removal of thyroid nodules. There were also several cases of cancer of the thyroid. Three years after the test the population of the Rongelap Atoll were allowed to return, but even after 25 years, in 1979, the northern islands of the Atoll were still declared too radioactive to visit. The islands of the Bikini Atoll, where testing continued until 1958, remained

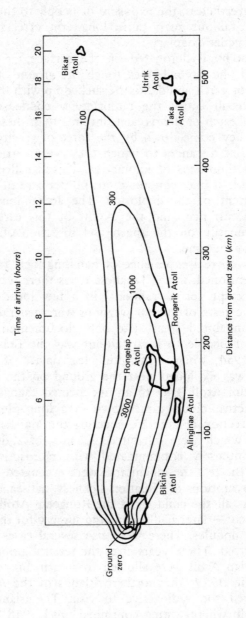

Source: *The Effects of Nuclear Weapons*, edited by Samuel Glasstone and Philip J. Dolan (US Departments of Defense and Energy, 1977).

Figure 1 Dose contours (rads) after the Bravo test explosion

uninhabited for many years. Vigorous decontamination measures were taken, including the removal of two inches of topsoil, but this still did not help. In 1967 the Atoll was declared habitable, but later it was evacuated again; it was not until the end of 1980 that the population was allowed to return, but even then with certain restrictions. This gives some idea of the persistence of fall-out.

In addition to the exposure of the inhabitants, a Japanese fishing boat was showered with fall-out particules. Although, after landing, the crew underwent rigorous decontamination procedures, nearly all of them developed liver damage from which one died soon afterwards, and it is alleged that another died later.

The radioactivity in the fall-out can expose populations to radiation in several ways, in different time sequences: (a) external irradiation by the radioactive cloud, as it passes overhead; (b) internal irradiation through the inhalation of radioactive particles in the air; (c) external irradiation, mainly from the gamma-rays from the radioactive particles deposited on the ground; (d) internal irradiation by drinking contaminated water, or through eating meat or by drinking milk from animals which had ingested radioactive substances, or by eating vegetables or other plants which had incorporated such substances; (e) internal irradiation by inhaling radioactive particles resuspended in the air. Routes (a) and (b) are relevant for a short time after the explosion; route (c) acts mainly during the first few weeks; routes (d) and (e) are of longer duration.

In the case of local fall-out, route (c), that is the gamma-ray exposure from material deposited on the ground, represents the most important hazard. It gives rise to total-body exposure. The rate at which the radiation dose is delivered is proportional to the explosive yield of the bomb. Unlike the other three agents described before, the amount of fall-out is in direct proportion to the explosive power, and it does not make a significant difference whether it came from a single or a number of bombs. However, the actual dose-rate is modified by two factors: the decay of the radioactivity with time, and the diminishing of its intensity with distance due to spreading out of the fall-out.

The decay of the radioactivity is initially very rapid. Thus, it is ten times less after two days than it was after seven hours. But later the decay is slower; a further reduction by a factor of 10 will occur after fourteen days, and then after 100 days. Therefore, if the activity· was very high at the beginning, the exposure levels could remain dangerously high for a long time.

The second factor is the gradual spreading of the radio-activity over larger areas, so that the further the distance from the explosion the lower the dose-rate, and the total dose that could be accumulated. Under ideal conditions,

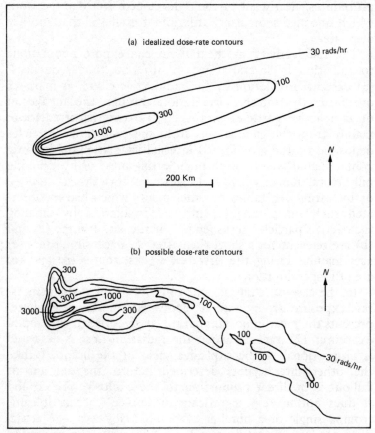

Source: as for Figure 1.

Figure 2 Idealized (a) and possible (b) dose rate contours for a 10-Mt surface burst and a wind velocity of 50 km per hour

when the wind has a constant speed and direction, the lines which join the points with the same dose-rate are cigar-shaped, or elongated ellipses (Figure 2a). In practice the contours may be greatly distorted; Figure 2b shows a pattern that might actually result from variations in local metero-logical and surface conditions.

Nevertheless, an idealized picture is still useful in providing an approximate estimate of the possible radiation hazard from early fall-out. Table 3 shows the calculated time of arrival, the dose rate and the total accumulated dose at various distances for a 1 and 10 megaton bomb. As is seen, even as far away as 800 km (500 miles) the dose which a person in the open might accumulate from one 10 Mt bomb is 100 rads. To provide a yardstick, it should be mentioned that the dose from natural sources is about 0.1 rad per year.

Table 4 shows the areas within which doses up to given limits could be received. The detonation of one 10 Mt bomb could result in a dose of at least 25 rads over an area greater than the whole area of Great Britain (227 000 km^2). In order to compare the effect of fall-out with the effects described before (Table 2), one has to take the area within which a lethal dose might be accumulated. Assuming a value of 600 rads for the lethal dose, the area comes out to be about 20 000 km^2 for a 10 Mt bomb; this is over 50 times greater than the lethal area from the blast effect.

The actual situation could be far worse. In a nuclear war, electricity-generating power stations are likely to be primary targets. Should a nuclear power station be hit by a nuclear bomb, the radioactive content of the reactor would be sucked up with the fireball, carried by the wind and deposited as local fall-out together with the fission pro-ducts of the bomb. However, the decay of the radio-activity from a reactor is much slower than that from a bomb, and therefore a given area would be contaminated for a much longer time. As an illustration, Figure 3 shows the contours of fall-out areas in which a dose of 100 rads would be accumulated in one year, starting two weeks after the explosion of (a) a 1 Mt bomb dose, and (b) the same bomb plus the radioactivity from a reactor whose capacity was 1 gigawatt of electricity. In this latter case,

Table 3   Dose rates and accumulated doses in an idealized pattern of fall-out

Downwind distance (km)	1-Mt bomb				10-Mt bomb			
	Time of arrival (hrs)	Reference dose rate (rads/hr)	Accumulated dose (rads)		Time of arrival (hrs)	Reference dose rate (rads/hr)	Accumulated dose (rads)	
100	3.3	270	850		2.8	1410	4570	
150	5.4	160	440		4.9	670	1870	
200	7.5	110	280		6.9	450	1160	
250	9.6	76	180		9.0	330	800	
300	11.7	54	120		11.1	260	600	
350	13.7	42	92		13.2	220	480	
400	15.8	32	67		15.3	180	380	
450	17.9	25	51		17.3	160	320	
500	20.0	20	39		19.4	130	260	
550	22.1	16	30		21.5	110	220	
600	24.2	13	24		23.6	98	180	
650	26.2	12	21		25.7	87	160	
700	28.3	9.0	16		27.8	74	130	
750	30.4	7.4	13		29.8	66	110	
800	32.5	6.3	10		31.9	61	100	

Table 4   Areas covered by given accumulated doses in fall-out

Upper limit of accumulated dose (*rad*)	Area (km²)	
	1-Mt bomb	10-Mt bomb
1000	1000	12 000
800	1300	16 000
600	1700	21 000
400	2600	29 000
200	5500	52 000
100	10 000	89 000
50	18 600	148 000
25	32 700	234 000
10	56 000	414 000

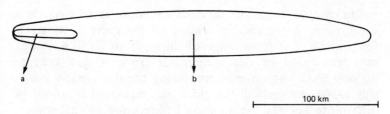

a   b

100 km

Figure 3   Contours for cumulative dose of 100 rads in one year, starting 2 weeks after the explosion of (a) 1 Mt bomb; (b) 1 Mt bomb + radioactivity from 1 GWe reactor.

the area is thirty times larger than for the bomb alone. Many reactors already exist in this country, and a number of new ones are to be built; therefore, the prospects of post-war recovery may be far gloomier than hitherto believed.

In order to assess the number of deaths from fall-out (or from the initial radiation) one needs to know the dose of radiation which would kill a person. This brings in another uncertainty, since there is little human experience on which to draw. Figure 4 shows a supposed relationship between

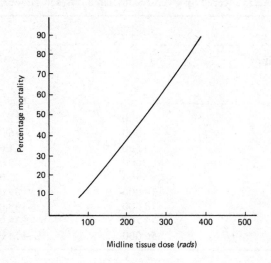

Figure 4 Probability of death from acute effects

mortality and radiation dose, if the dose is received in a short time. A remarkable feature of the curve is its steepness; within a narrow range of doses, from 90 to 400 rads. the probability of death increases from 10 per cent to 90 per cent. The error in measuring the dose nearly covers this range, so even if the dose was measured it would be difficult to say whether a person had received a lethal dose.

In this connection another important factor must be mentioned. The dose on the horizontal axis of Figure 4 differs from the doses mentioned before (e.g. Tables 3 and 4) in that the former is the dose delivered inside the body (mainly to the bone marrow) while the latter present dose levels on the surface of the body. The two are different because radiation is attenuated as it passes through the body; a surface dose of 450 rads may result in a bone marrow dose of 250 rads. However, the degree of attenuation depends on the size of the body; infants, for example, attenuate much less than adults. Consequently, with the same fall-out exposure, an infant will receive a larger dose to the bone marrow than an adult. When this is combined with the greater intrinsic sensitivity of children to radiation, it can literally mean a difference between life and death. A level of external exposure which gives an adult a reasonable chance of survival is likely to kill a child. It is the babies and infants who will be the main victims of exposure to radiation from nuclear weapons.

For a given radiation level, people staying indoors — or better still, in shelters — will receive much smaller doses. But with high intensity bombing the indoor doses may still be high enough to kill, or at least to produce radiation sickness. The symptoms of radiation sickness are anorexia, nausea, vomiting and diarrhoea; some of them start at quite low doses (Table 5). These symptoms are very much like

Table 5 Radiation doses to midline tissue (in *rads*) which produce radiation sickness symptoms

Symptom	Percentage of exposed population		
	10%	50%	90%
Anorexia	40	100	240
Nausea	50	170	320
Vomiting	60	215	380
Diarrhoea	90	240	390

symptoms resulting from nervous tension and crowding in shelters. The witnessing of genuine symptoms of radiation exposure in others may evoke similar symptoms, with epidemic results, particularly in young children. This would make it very difficult for the doctor to decide who should receive treatment. In the case of a nuclear war this is likely to be an academic question because with high fall-out levels, doctors and nurses will not be able to move about; by the time it is safe for them to reach the afflicted, nature will have made the selection.

As Table 3 shows, local fall-out stretches over long distances. In a nuclear war in Europe it would not respect neutral countries; the civilian populations of combatant and non-combatant countries would be affected. The long duration of the fall-out, which makes post-war recovery so much more difficult, has another sinister aspect: it may reach into yet unborn generations, through the genetic effect of radiation.

The ubiquitous and iniquitous nature of radiation exposure, its extension both in time and in space, has made the use of radiation in warfare obnoxious to society. Indeed, the United States and the Soviet Union jointly proposed in 1979 a treaty to prohibit the development, production, stockpiling and use of radiological weapons. The hypocrisy of the superpowers in proposing the treaty lies in the specific exclusion from it of radiation from nuclear weapons. In other words, they consider the use of radiation as unacceptable on civilized standards, but they sanction it in nuclear warfare.

5. The electromagnetic pulse (EMP)

The EMP is associated with the intense ionization of the atmosphere by the radiations from the bomb. It results in a short but very powerful pulse of electromagnetic radiation; it is like a radiowave but millions of times stronger than from a radio transmitter. The range of the EMP depends on the altitude of the explosion; if the bomb is detonated high up in the air, it can cover an enormous area (Figure 5). The EMP is not directly hazardous to man, but the electric surge produced may damage electric and electronic equipment, and disrupt electricity supplies as well as telephone and radio communications. Modern solid state devices (transistors, etc.), which have almost completely replaced thermionic valves in radios and TV sets, are particularly sensitive to the EMP. It has been estimated that the cost of anti-surge devices would be so high as to make this preventive measure impractical. *Protect and Survive* advises the public to listen for instructions on the radio, as this would be the only link with the outside world, but if the enemy deliberately produces a powerful EMP in order to disrupt communications, the whole edifice of the civil defence policy may be undermined.

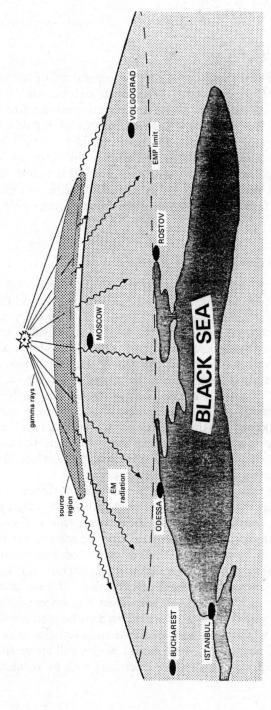

Source: *Comprehensive Study on Nuclear Weapons*, (UN Report, 1980).

Figure 5 Electromagnetic pulse

6. Depletion of the ozone layer

It is believed that the very high temperature of the explosion favours the formation of nitrogen oxides, and that these compounds act as catalysts in converting ozone into ordinary oxygen. We know very little about the effect which such a depletion of the ozone in the atmosphere would have, but it could result in a large increase in the intensity of ultra-violet radiation. The consequence of this would be an increase in the incidence of cancer of the skin and melanoma. This is quite apart from possible but not assessable climatic changes.

7. Synergism

Synergistic action (potentiation of the effects of separate traumas) is not usually included among the contributors to the effects of the bomb, but it may be responsible for a significant proportion of the total casualty toll. The various agents of injury and death are usually considered as if each of them acted alone, but the synergistic interaction between them is bound to aggravate the situation. A person who has suffered a burn from which he would normally recover, would stand much less chance if his immune mechanism was weakened by the action of a sub-lethal dose of radiation. Similarly, damage to the skin and soft tissue by mechanical injury could lead to a fatal infection if the white blood cells and platelets were depleted by radiation.

Synergism assumes a much greater importance in the case of multiple detonations in a nuclear war. In addition to the physical, biological and medical interactions, there will be the psychological, sociological and economic factors. This chapter is concerned with the effects of individual nuclear weapons, but it is of the utmost importance not to be misled by considering them in isolation. If one thinks only in terms of a single weapon, then the impression may be created that those fortunate enough to be outside the lethal circles for blast and heat, or the acutely lethal area of the fall-out, will be all right; doctors and nurses will arrive from other cities to tend the injured, electricity will be reconnected to the grid, food will be supplied from the rest of the country, and soon life will return to normal. Nothing can be further from the truth. Should a nuclear war start, it will not mean one or a few bombs. At the least it would mean an attack on all military targets, but there is a high probability that it would escalate into an all-out nuclear war. The Home Office, when considering the scale of a nuclear war, assumes that a total of 200 megatons is likely to be exploded over Great Britain, but the Secretary of State for Defence said recently that more than 1000 Mt would be needed to destroy the cruise missiles in this country. With an attack on such a scale, it would make little difference whether or not cities were direct targets.

The Home Office estimates of the effects of a nuclear attack are presented in the form of the percentage of survivors as a function of the total megatonnage of the weapons employed (see chapter by S. F. J. Butler). By quoting single figures for a given level of attack the impression is created that it is possible to estimate the casualty toll with some degree of accuracy. This is wholly unwarranted. Moreover making calculations on the basis of 'the most likely case' is an irresponsible approach. The whole range of the possible casualty toll should be stated; if a single figure is to be given, it is more appropriate that it is based on the worst case analysis.

Quite apart from the incredibility of presenting the outcome of a nuclear war in figures, it is psychologically impossible to comprehend the scale of destruction in an all-out nuclear war. When the magnitude of a disaster is very large our senses become dulled; we start to register events on a contracted, something like a logarithmic scale; a hundred million deaths appear only as a small difference from ten million, and ten million deaths impress us only a bit more than one million. To grasp the consequences of a nuclear war, we need to bring them down to the personal level; we have to think how each of us would be affected by witnessing the suffering or death of our child, our spouse, or our parents. This type of approach was used in the book *Children of Horoshima*,[2] which contains essays written six years after the bombing by children who were 4 to 16 years at the time. Reading even a few of those individual accounts is enough to make one comprehend the personal tragedy amidst all the horrors of a nuclear war; enough to force one to the solemn resolution: a nuclear war must never happen.

References

1. J. Rotblat (SIPRI), *Nuclear Radiation in Warfare* (Taylor and Francis, 1981).
2. *Children of Hiroshima* (Publishing Committee for *Children of Hiroshima*, 1980).

8. SCIENTIFIC ADVICE IN HOME DEFENCE†

Sidney Butler

British defence policy development

Before discussing my main topic, the part scientific advice can play in home defence matters, I need to spend some time considering national policy aspects. In major matters affecting the security and well being of the British people, our national policy invariably combines preventive and remedial elements. National policies in the fire and law and order fields, for instance, prominently feature fire and crime prevention, but there are complementary provisions for remedial action to control and limit outbreaks of fire, crime and disorder. Although prevention is always preferable, remedial measures must be available and are regularly used. The price when prevention fails in these cases is not prohibitively high and total prevention of course is not feasible.

When we consider the limited scope for the protection of the nation against modern war, the potentially disastrous consequences are such that prevention must take absolute priority. Nevertheless, prevention of war cannot be guaranteed by a single nation or a group of nations. The national policy of Great Britain therefore must include measures to provide some protection for the nation should prevention fail. *The Hiroshima Diary* of Dr Hachiya[1] should persuade all readers that it is absolutely vital to prevent modern war and especially nuclear war. But it also shows what was achieved by a small, resolute team of doctors, nurses and administrators in the midst of absolute devastation with little outside help, without preparation or warning, at first without knowledge of the weapon which had been used, and throughout without adequate knowledge of nuclear weapon effects on man.

The importance the British Government attaches to effective measures for the prevention of war is demonstrated by the following excerpts from the 1981 Statement on the Defence Estimates:

> . . . the terrible experience of Hiroshima and Nagasaki must be always in our minds . . . Our task now is to devise a system for living in peace and freedom while ensuring that nuclear weapons are never used, either to destroy or to blackmail . . . Nuclear weapons are the dominant aspect of modern war potential. But they are not the only aspect we should fear . . . Non-nuclear war between East and West is by far the likeliest road to nuclear war . . . We must therefore seek to prevent any war, not just nuclear war, between East and West.[2]

Accepting that prevention of war must take top priority, modest civil defence precautions to mitigate the effects of war should prevention fail are nevertheless essential. The lead in UK Home Defence policy and planning is taken by the Home Office, within the wider context of NATO home defence planning. Policy developments take place within Cabinet Office because most government departments are involved and national survival is ultimately at stake. Major policy decisions are, of course, taken by Ministers.

European warfare using modern weapons would involve widespread damage and large-scale civilian casualties from which the UK could not expect to remain immune. Chemical weapons are far more lethal than when they were last used widely some 60 years ago, and their use could offer important military advantages in temporary denial without causing physical damage. Escalation from conventional warfare to continental or global nuclear warfare would increase the scale of damage and casualty levels, possibly by a factor of 100 or more, quite beyond human experience and, indeed, our full comprehension. However, should we fail to prevent war, and in particular nuclear war, the studies I will be discussing indicate that there would always be large numbers of survivors in Great Britain needing help and succour. Moreover, there would always be limited prospects for ultimate national revival, albeit to an impoverished economic state in the more extreme situations one can envisage. Everyone would *not* die in the nuclear holocaust. There is, then, a clear governmental humanitarian responsibility for the development of realistic and effective home defence contingency plans capable of quick activation, firstly to increase the number of survivors and improve their prospect of survival, and secondly to promote national revival and regeneration in a constitutional democratic form. It is, of course, arguable that a home defence posture, convincing to potential adversaries, is an essential component of the defence strategy of any country, especially a country relying on the prevention of war by a policy ultimately involving the nuclear deterrent. However, home defence measures are necessary whilst the prevailing conditions in Europe continue, irrespective of the defence strategy of the UK and the nature of its treaty obligations to other countries.

Scientific advice in the Home Office

As in other areas of responsibility, the Home Office retains professional assistance and advice for the administrative division responsible for home defence policy formulation and implementation. For half a century or more, a major continuing contribution has been made to home defence matters by the small group of Home Office scientists specialising in home defence science. However, as their spokesman today, I should make it clear that these scientists are only responsible for the home defence policy selected by successive governments to the extent that they provide some of the inputs to policies under consideration.

Home Office scientists, although not responsible for policy formulation and approval, currently are encouraged to take (and do take) initiatives affecting policy development within official circles. We also participate closely in activities directly connected to policy. As an example, a senior scientist leads the Working Party on Domestic Shelters which produced the technical publication[3] made available earlier this year. I myself serve on a Cabinet Office Committee which is involved in a continuing review of home defence policy. Occasional opportunities arise to discuss scientific aspects of home defence matters directly with the Minister responsible. We also contribute to studies on selected aspects of home defence policy and planning (in which invited representatives from local government and other appropriate organisations participate) which are convened by government departments on an *ad hoc* basis.

The need for scientific advice in home defence

The contributions scientists can make fall naturally into two parts:

   (a) Scientific inputs to home defence policy development, planning and training (including the training of scientific advisers);

   (b) Membership of home defence scientific advisory teams at all administrative levels during and after a war situation affecting the British mainland.

Wartime government (Figure 1) would be dispersed in a crisis, on a basis of 10 regional groups for England and Wales, with comparable arrangements for Scotland and Northern Ireland. Each regional team would be headed by a regional commissioner who would be a peacetime government minister, carrying full powers for internal government. The regional team would include a cross-section of selected central government staff, strengthened by regional representatives from utilities, broadcasting, emergency services (fire, police etc.), military etc., and supported by a group of regional scientific advisers. In a crisis, each regional team would be dispersed in the region in several groups to improve survival prospects. Some time after a nuclear attack, the surviving groups would join together to set up a regional headquarters at a location selected by the regional commissioner. Buildings for sub-regional headquarters exist and would be manned in a crisis period, but would not become operational unless and until a widespread nuclear attack took place. Sub-regional commissioners would also

Central Government

Assumed cease to function in event of nuclear attack
Selected ministers and officials dispersed in crisis to form regional and
    sub-regional teams
Reconstructed by amalgamation of surviving regional teams

Regional government groups

Government ministers as regional and sub-regional commissioners
Split up in several locations prior to attack
Cross-section of central government staff
Regional representatives (utilities, emergency services etc.)
Regional scientific advisory team

County

County chief executive as county controller
Local government staff
County scientific advisory team

District

District chief executive as district controller
Local government staff
County scientific advisory team
Appropriate local organisation within each district

Figure 1 Wartime government organization

be government ministers, and their staffs would be similar
to those of regional commissioners. They also would have
scientific advisers attached to their staffs.

At county level, chief executives would become county
controllers responsible to the regional commissioner and
would assume delegated powers after a nuclear attack.
District chief executives would likewise become district
controllers, responsible to the county controller. The teams
under the county controllers would include personnel re-
presenting emergency services (fire, police etc.), public
health, local food distribution etc. Similar, less wide-ranging
forms of organisation are specified for district control.
Volunteer home defence scientific advisers are recruited and
trained to provide scientific advice to country and district

controllers. Appropriate forms of local organisation at community level are required within each district.

It is recognised that, although diversified communications and limited physical protection for the control teams have been provided, some teams might cease to exist and loss of communications might interrupt the chains of command temporarily. Survival operations necessarily would be centred mainly at community, district and county levels in the early days after a nuclear attack, with responsibility gradually reassumed by the higher levels. Each sub-region would concentrate, at first, on assessing the overall impact on its area, identifying surviving resources, determining the needs of the population, and monitoring the overall fallout radiation situation. Later on, sub-region teams would rationalise the use of surviving resources and direct overall policy, having particular regard to longer-term considerations. Sub-regions would pave the way for the regional commissioner to take over some time after the attack. Regional commissioners would develop regional policies for survival and regeneration, and reconcile inter-regional problems. Regional commissioners would also prepare for the restoration of democratic national government. At regional, sub-regional, county, and district levels, the principal source of advice on the effects of modern weapons would be the groups of voluntary home defence scientific advisers. Their role would be particularly onerous and vital in the immediate aftermath of a nuclear attack; they would have a continuing long-term role to provide scientific advice during the national survival and national regeneration phases, as discussed later.

By definition, home defence scientific advisers should be practising scientists who have made a special study of the contribution scientific advice could make to the understanding and treatment of selected problems likely to arise in wartime. The full-time home defence scientists in Home Office are small in number. In peacetime, all other home defence scientific advisers (Figure 2) are part-time and most are volunteers. In each regional team, however, there would be a Principal RSA (regional scientific adviser) who is a nominated senior civil service scientist (either serving or recently retired). All the other regional scientific advisers,

Home Office	Small team of full-time specialist home defence scientists	
Region and sub-region	Principal regional scientific adviser }	nominated senior government scientists
	Chief regional scientific adviser }	
	Regional scientific adviser }	volunteers
County/District	County scientific adviser }	volunteers

Home defence scientific advisory committee

    Chairman (from Chief RSAs)
    Chief RSAs
    Representatives of PRSAs

Senior Home Office home defence scientists
Senior Home Office home defence policy makers

Figure 2 Home defence scientific advisory organisation

including the Chief RSA, are volunteers selected and appointed by the Home Office. There are also a number of regional scientific lecturers who assist with the teaching of Home Defence science. At county levels, all scientific advisers are volunteers (although, of course, many are in full-time employment as local government and central government scientists).

The Chief RSAs, and the RSAs in general, are regarded as the UK peer group for home defence science. The collective views on home defence scientific matters of the Chief RSAs, within the Home Defence Scientific Advisory Committee, have a strong influence on Home Office scientists and policymakers. The persisting efforts of the RSA organisation and of Home Office scientists over many years, including the 'care-and-maintenance' period, have served to reinforce acceptance of the necessity for the provision of up-to-date realistic scientific information on all aspects of home defence. I would like to stress the major personal contribution to home defence thinking made over the past

decade by John Clayton, soon to retire as Director of Home
Office Scientific Advisory Branch, to whom I am indebted
for much of the material now presented. I also wish to place
on record the value placed by the Home Office on the vital
part being played by the dedicated regional and county scientific advisers in home defence. It is perhaps appropriate to
note at this point that some of these volunteers have been
subjected to criticism and pressure from disarmament campaigners. Civil defence does not exist to encourage war, any
more than ambulances exist to promote accidents: it may in
fact contribute to the *prevention* of war as part of the pre-
ventative UK defence policy. Volunteer home defence scientific advisers are making a vital contribution of an honourable
and humanitarian nature to the national home defence
insurance policy, essential whether or not the UK possesses
nuclear weapons and relies on a policy of war prevention —
based ultimately on the nuclear deterrent.

The Home Office home defence scientific work programme must support the need for scientific inputs to
policy, planning and implementation, for general home
defence training, and for thorough training and preparation
of volunteer home defence scientific advisers (Figure 3).
We keep under review weapons effects on living things
and on structures, having to rely mainly on data from defence science sources at home and overseas. Close liaison
in particular is maintained with our NATO counterparts.
The most reliable open publications on the basic damage
and casualty effects of nuclear weapons remain Glasstone[4]
and the HMSO publication on *Nuclear Weapons.*[5] Possible
protective measures mainly centre on blast and fallout
shelters. The casualty and damage models essentially support
studies of policy options. A wide range of policy options
are studied in the UK context. Substantial continuing effort
has to be applied to training and operations. The limited
Home Office effort is augmented significantly by voluntary
help from RSAs, and some topics are the subject of external
research contracts. However, it will be obvious that we must
concentrate research effort on a few selected areas at any
one time, gradually strengthening the overall position over a
period of years.

Objectives: To provide reliable scientific information and professional
　　　　　　support to:

(a) Policy development, policy implementation, and training of
　　emergency management teams;
(b) Training of volunteer regional and county scientific advisers.

Main activities:

(a) Effects of nuclear and other weapons, and possible counter measures	(1) Effects on man, agriculture, industry, housing etc (2) Shelter designs and surveys (3) Radiac instrumentation
(b) Operational research studies and assessments	(1) Casualty and damage models (2) Policy option assessments (3) Post-attack recovery measures
(c) Training and operations	(1) Regional and county procedures (2) Assistance to UK Warning and Monitoring Organisation (3) Training scientific advisers and home defence science lecturers (4) Management training game development (5) Exercise support

Figure 3 Home defence scientific work programme

Damage and casualty effects of nuclear weapons

The principal immediate effects of a nuclear detonation are
the electromagnetic pulse (EMP), heat/light flash, initial
radiation, blast/shock wave, and thermal radiation from the
fireball.[6,7] I do not propose to discuss the important specialised subject of EMP damage[8] to electrical and electronic
apparatus, although it is important in home defence planning
to recognise the potential effects on attack and fall-out
warning procedures of interruptions to communications. The
remaining immediate effects can be considered (Figure 4)
in terms of a set of damage rings centred on the ground
zero and defined in terms of the peak over-pressures created
by the blast shockwave at the edge of each ring (11,6, $1\frac{1}{2}$
and $\frac{3}{4}$ psi). The damage rings for a ground burst would be

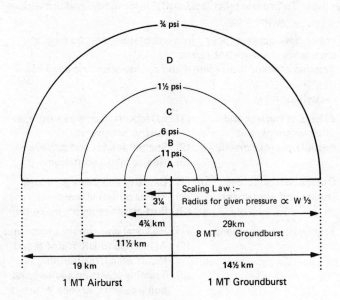

A Ring   Crater + lip for groundburst covers 6% of A ring area
         Total house destruction
         Fatality level could exceed 85% without blast shelter protection

B Ring   Irreparable house damage. Streets impassable.
         Severe blast dynamic effects on an exposed man.
         Fatality level could exceed 40% without blast shelter protection

C Ring   Severe to moderate house damage. Streets obstructed.
         Blast could cause lethal flying missiles.
         Main fire zone would reach outside limit of C ring in average
         visibility.

D Ring   Light house damage. Streets open.
         Isolated fires would occur in average visibility.

Figure 4 Nuclear weapon damage and casualty model

significantly smaller than for an air burst at a given weapon
power, because considerable energy is expended in crater
formation. The crater, in fact, would only cover a small
part of the A damage ring. Similarity laws can be derived[9]
based on weapon power as far as blast effects are concerned.

The damage ring radii are proportional to the cube root of weapon power, so that the radius would be doubled and the damage area quadrupled when the weapon power is increased eightfold. The spreading blast wave creates pressure patterns on the outsides and insides of building structures, varying rapidly in a complicated fashion. Approximate damage levels are indicated (Figure 4) which would apply to stoutly constructed brick houses. In addition, the blast wave induces violent winds which could carry objects and people, and would create potentially lethal flying debris.

The heat and light flash, together with the subsequent thermal radiation from the ascending fireball, causes fires and charring at large distances in good visibility. Typically, the main fire zone would extend to the outer edge of the C damage ring and isolated fires would be caused in the D ring. General firestorms would not be expected[9] to develop in UK cities after a nuclear attack; however, the possibility of widespread fires could be greatly reduced by suitable precautions and by the control of incipient fires by survivors of the attack.[10]

Approximate rules can be derived concerning the average casualty rates to be expected in each damage ring. Such factors as warning, advance preparations, availability of blast protection, and the behaviour and posture of the people during and after the attack can affect the casualty rates significantly. In the absence of general blast shelter protection, most fatalities from immediate effects are likely to occur in the A and B rings, directly or indirectly from blast. However, further fatalities from blast and thermal effects would arise in the C ring, especially among those caught in the open. Because of the limited range of initial radiation (usually defined as that radiation emitted in the first minute after bomb burst) this would only cause additional fatalities among any people close to ground zero with protection adequate against blast but not initial radiation. Therefore, the principal factors determining the level of fatalities from immediate effects are the number of people located in the A and B rings, and the level of protection they achieve against blast. In the absence of adequate blast protection, fatality levels in A-ring areas would be expected to exceed

85 per cent (included those trapped, which the casualty rules assume, on a worst case basis, will die), and to exceed 40 per cent in the B-ring areas.

The remaining cause of death directly attributable to nuclear weapons in the short term would be the radioactive fall-out from groundbursts (or near groundbursts). Fall-out, consisting of irradiated earth, rock, etc., is drawn upwards in the fireball and the larger radioactive particles fall quickly back to the ground. Typically, two-thirds could return in the first day or two; close to ground zero, the fall-out process could be complete in the first hour or so. Fall-out would lie in approximately elliptic-shaped zones with the maximum density and highest radiation level in the innermost contour (Figure 5). The radiation rate from fall-out dust would normally decay very rapidly following approximately a $t^{-1.2}$ law.[11] (Should radioactive wastes be scattered by an explosion, these would exhibit much higher persistence of radiation and so could constitute a more persistent local hazard to living things.) Thus, the radiation rate would fall by a factor 10 as the time from detonation increased sevenfold. Providing fall-out was complete at 1 hour the dose rate 7 hours after detonation (DR7) would be only 1/10 that applying 1 hour after detonation (DR1). By 2 days and 2 weeks, the radiation levels would have decreased to 1/100 and 1/1000 of those prevailing at 1 hour.

Since the probability of death from radiation sickness depends essentially on the total dose received, it would be particularly important that those surviving the immediate explosion achieve adequate protection against fall-out radiation before fall-out reaches significant levels. They should remain so protected in fall-out areas until the radiation levels decayed to intensities at which controllers would operate progressive public release procedures locally. Such release procedures may begin within one or two days after attack, but in areas of high dose rate radiation may still be restrictive after a fortnight. In practice, of course, the fall-out contours would be much more complicated than the idealised contours. The advice provided by scientific advisers would be based on detailed local radiation measurements, analysed by standardised methods carefully taught and practised.

Fall-out casualty level predictions involve assessment of the distribution of fall-out protection achieved by the people in their refuges. For any refuge, the fall-out protective factor (PF) is defined as the ratio between the dose which would be received in the open and the dose which would be experienced in the refuge (Figure 6). This factor depends partly on the distance between the people in the refuge

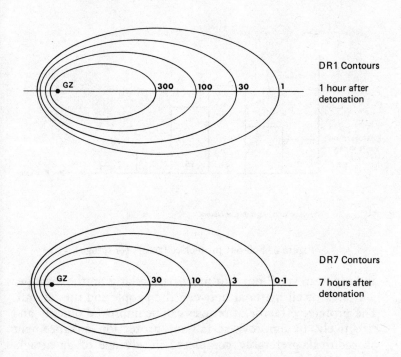

In steady wind conditions fall-out deposited in elliptic-shaped contours

Normally radiation rate follows $t^{-1 \cdot 2}$ law

Thus radiation rate is reduced by factor 10 as time after detonation is increased by factor 7

DR1 Contours

1 hour after detonation

DR7 Contours

7 hours after detonation

Figure 5 Idealised fall-out radiation contours

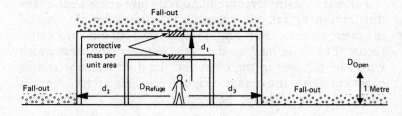

$$\text{Protective factor (PF)} = \frac{\text{Dose rate in open}}{\text{Dose rate in refuge}} = \frac{D_{Open}}{D_{Refuge}}$$

PF increases with distances from fall-out (d_1, d_2, d_3)
and increases with increased protective mass/unit area

(a) *Protective factor for a refuge*

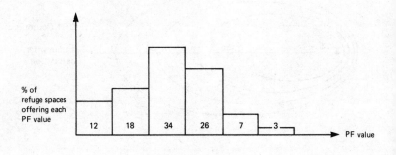

(b) *Spectrum of protective factors*

Figure 6 Fall-out protective factors for refuges

and the nearest fall-out, but more particularly on the mass per unit area of all material between the people and the fall-out. The protective factor of refuges can be improved quickly and effectively by improvised fall-out protection enhancement procedures[12] preferably completed in advance of an attack. For casualty estimation, a spectrum of protective factors must be assumed, with due allowance for such enhancement.

The fall-out casualty model for radiation casualties is based on the advice of a Medical Research Council working party (Figure 7). Because the human capacity to resist radiation sickness varies, it is necessary to use a probability approach. $LD_{50/60}$ is the estimated immediate radiation dose at which 50 per cent death rates would be expected within 60 days. The probability curve is comparatively steep so that limits can be set in practice, outside which probabilities of 100 per cent and 0 per cent effectively apply as far as death from radiation sickness is concerned. A comparatively small change in protective factors of a refuge therefore could make the difference between inevitable and neglible risk of death in marginal situations. The basic fatality curve relates to an acute (immediate) dose. If the radiation is received over several days or longer, an allowance needs to be made for body recovery effects. Assuming a constant protective factor and a $t^{-1.2}$ decay law, the effective radiation dose reaches a maximum 5 to 8 days after detonation for possibly-fatal dose levels. This reinforces the need for close adherence to fall-out protection and public release procedures, based on reliable fall-out analyses provided by scientific advisers.

Blast and fire damage would affect the fall-out protection available to survivors in A, B and C damage rings. Post-attack improvement or repair of fall-out protection and refuge occupation activities would tend to conflict with the need for initial fire fighting and rescue operations in the immediate aftermath of a nuclear attack. Further complications can be envisaged with nuclear attacks spaced out over a period.

Further casualties, including fatalities, will arise from disease deprivation and other causes, depending on the effectiveness of the help and succour which is available, partly governed by the extent to which effective precautionary measures are devised and implemented prior to any nuclear attack on the UK. Communal shelter confinement of large numbers of people, for instance, would encourage the occurrence and spread of epidemic infective diseases, which would be likely to be exacerbated by water usage restrictions. The general strain on extremely limited surviving medical and hospital resources and limitations on medicines would

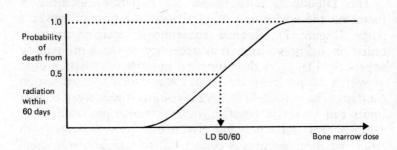

LD 50/60   Acute (immediate) bone marrow dose
for 50% chance of radiation death
within 60 days.

(a) *Probability of death from acute bone marrow dose*

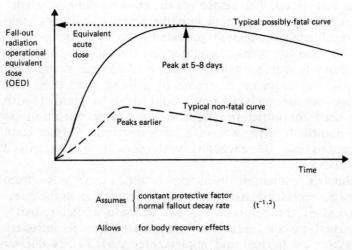

Assumes | constant protective factor
         | normal fallout decay rate $(t^{-1.2})$

Allows   for body recovery effects

(b) *Fatality curves from radiation received over time.*

Source: Medical Research Council advice to the Home office from the Protection against Ionising Radiation Committee (PIRC).

Figure 7 Radiation injury model

force recourse to more basic techniques and reduced standards of treatment of a selective nature.

The general elevation in background radiation would be expected to cause a small but noticeable rise in long-term effects and illness, notably an increase in cancer induction, hereditary damage and damage to the developing embryo. Such effects must be viewed according to the time of appearance post attack and their probable severity, when considering survival and regeneration strategies. Cancer is a generic term covering all types of malignant disease including leukaemia. Apart from skin cancer, cancers have a mortality rate of 10 to 98 per cent, according to type and stage at time of diagnosis and treatment. It seems probable that cancer treatment would command a low priority in view of the other problems which would beset the country in the survival and regeneration phases. Currently, the lifetime risk of naturally-occurring cancer (excepting skin cancer) is 20 to 25 per cent. Additional cancer fatalities would be induced in survivors exposed to fallout radiation at the rate of about 1 per cent at an exposure level of 100 rads. Leukaemia mortalities might be expected to peak at 10 years after irradiation, whereas lung cancer mortalities would peak after 20 to 30 years.

About 5 per cent of all normally-conceived children are affected by severe congenital abnormality; the frequency of embryonic damage from an exposure of 100 rads spread over 1 to 2 weeks is likely to be much smaller. Hereditary damage could present itself in the children and later descendants of irradiated survivors; about half the cases would occur in the first two generations. It is estimated that about 2 cases per 100 people (of reproductive age) might occur at an exposure level of 100 rads of gamma radiation. Summarizing, although the long-term consequences of exposure to fall-out radiation should not be dismissed, their significance to survival and regeneration planning suggests they should command a comparatively low priority.

Fall-out radiation would certainly impose severe limitations on agricultural systems. Livestock reared for meat production would suffer radiation casualties in a similar manner as humans. Food production in general would be disrupted for a number of reasons. The vulnerability of growing crops to radiation and their subsequent yield would depend on the time of year of an attack. Even at the stage of growth where radiation resistance is at a maximum, dose rate levels could inhibit harvesting, the delay of which could lead to spoilage and waste. The specialized nature of modern strains, together with present reliance on chemical fertilisers, pest control measures and energy-intensive methods using specialist equipment, thus placing a heavy burden on limited resources (probably irreplaceable in the first few years after a nuclear attack), present further problems of major significance. The Ministry of Agriculture, Fisheries and Food takes the lead on such matters. However, home defence scientific advisers would make a significant contribution at local level in helping to weigh priorities and the selection of practical policies balancing immediate, short-term survival, and longer-term regeneration considerations.

Prediction of the damage and casualty effects of a multiple nuclear attack

It is necessary to combine our knowledge, necessarily imperfect, in a model which allows us to provide predictions and understanding to aid policy-makers and Ministers. In order to make systematic estimates for different national attack scenarios, population distributions, and assumptions of protective levels against immediate and fall-out effects, it is convenient to use computerised models[13]. The country is divided into a fine grid and the population distribution stipulated on a one kilometre square basis (Figure 8). (A similar systematic approach (manual or automated) would also be used by scientific advisers to provide early post-attack casualty and damage estimates for controllers and commissioners, using the best available local information on bomb falls and fall-out.) As a standard population distribution, we use the 1972 census, which represents the night-time residential situation and is also equivalent to the distribution on which the current *Stay-put* policy is based. Other distributions can be represented readily, including day-time at work and partial or complete evacuation

Stipulate population of square at attack

Specify shelter posture at attack
Estimate peak over-pressure for square
Specify casualty/damage rules

Estimate damage

Estimate immediate effect casualties

Specify shelter posture post attack
Specify wind conditions at attack
Estimate effective fall-out dose for square
Specify casualty rules

Estimate fall-out casualties

Figure 8 Casualty and damage — general estimation procedure

distributions. For a particular attack scenario, the peak over-pressure in each square is calculated. The casualties from immediate effects are then estimated square by square, using rules which take into account the availability or other-wise of blast protection and the posture assumed to be adopted by the people. Damage estimates are also made for each grid square. For the attack scenario specified, and assumed wind conditions, the total fall-out from ground-bursts is similarly estimated for each square. Assuming post-attack shelter postures and the distributions of fall-out protection available, casualties from fall-out can be estimated. The results can be presented in detail, for example on a county district basis, as well as in aggregate. I should stress that precise casualty and damage estimates are not possible. Rather, it is a question of determining the most likely levels for a particular case and assessing confidence limits.

As an example, I have summarised the main results for a multiple nuclear attack on Britain with nearly 200 MT (179 weapons) including 109 MT of ground bursts generating fall-out (Figure 9). The principal assumptions include the night-time residential population distribution (equivalent to *Stay-put* policy), no specific blast shelter provision, and general adherence to *Protect and Survive* advice especially as regards fall-out protection procedures[14]. The attack includes a number of airbursts over city targets, as well as

| 129 airbursts | Power 84 MT |
| 50 groundbursts | Power 109 MT |

| 179 weapons | Total power 193 MT |

Key assumptions The attack includes city targets
There is no blast shelter provision
There is full adherence to *Protect & Survive* advice
Stay-put or night-time residential population

A Ring area	(11 psi +)	$2\frac{3}{4}$%	24% Population
A & B Ring area	(6 psi +)	5%	38% Population
A, B & C Ring area	($1\frac{1}{2}$ psi +)	15%	60% Population

Severe fall-out area   9%

(Dose rate DR 7 — 100 *rph* or more 7 hours after attack — accumulated dose in open 4000 *r* or more in first 14 days)

Initial population	56	Millions	
Killed or trapped	16	Millions	30%
Fall-out sickness deaths	under 1	Million	
Serious injured	$3\frac{1}{2}$	Millions	32%
Other homeless	up to 14	Millions	
Immediately available housing		40%	
Housing reparable in wartime		10%	

Figure 9 Casualty and damage summary for a multiple nuclear attack

attacks on military targets. About 5 per cent of the land area would lie in the A and B damage rings, with a further 10 per cent in the C damage rings. However, because so many of the targets selected in this attack lie in or near to densely populated areas, nearly 40 per cent of the population (over 21 million) would normally be located in the A and B rings and a further 20 per cent in the C rings. In the absence of general blast shelter provision, for this attack some 16 million fatalities (those trapped in buildings again being assumed, on a worst case basis, to die) are estimated from immediate effects. The most severe fall-out zones (dose rate greater than 100 rph at 7 hrs) would be reasonably compact, covering about 9 per cent of the land area.

Assuming full adherence to *Protect and Survive* fall-out protection procedures, fall-out radiation sickeness deaths might be limited to under a million. In this case, perhaps 70 per cent of the population would survive the first 60 days. However, nearly half of the survivors would need to be moved and rehoused, including several million seriously injured; and only about 40 per cent of the housing stock would remain immediately usable.

Casualty estimates obviously must depend directly on the rules governing casualties. For the attack under consideration, the effects of varying the casualty rules over the limits considered applicable to UK circumstances are shown in Figure 10 for both immediate and total fatalities. The fatality estimates from immediate effects would almost double if the more severe blast criterion were used, and the estimated survival level would drop to about 50 per cent. In this example, the fatality levels are not affected greatly by variation of the radiation injury model, as we have assumed general adherence to good fall-out protection procedures. The casualty levels at a given weight of attack would be affected significantly by the targetting strategy adopted by the attacker (Figure 11), especially with the normal night-time population distribution associated with current *Stay-put* policy. With the population more uniformly distributed as a result of dispersal, the survival level naturally would be expected to become less dependent on the attack strategy. It is, of course, possible to postulate levels of attack on the UK higher than 200 MT. The approximate results shown in Figure 12 indicate that the casualty levels would not be expected to increase linearly with weight of attack. Perhaps the most important point to note is that even with an attack an order of magnitude greater designed to produce A-ring damage to virtually all population centres in Great Britain (and clearly not defensible on military grounds), millions of survivors would be expected to need assistance and there would still be limited prospects for national revival, though in a very impoverished state.

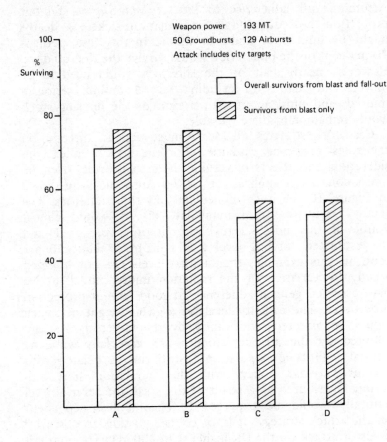

A   Standard current casualty model
B   With less severe fall-out radiation criterion
C   With more severe blast criterion
D   With both criteria changed

Figure 10   Some effects of changing casualty criteria

Measures to mitigate the effect of nuclear attack

Of the three main measures (warning, shelter, and evacuation) available to reduce casualty levels, warning is regarded as vital and potentially very effective at comparatively low cost. The UK Warning and Monitoring Organisation, which can be

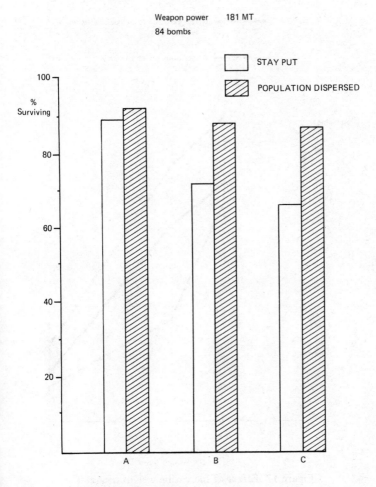

Weapon power   181 MT
84 bombs

A   Attack primarily on military targets
B   Attack extended to include population centre targets
C   Attack primarily on civilian targets

Figure 11   Some effects of changing population distribution and enemy targetting assumptions

fully activated at very short notice, would broadcast a nationwide attack warning, monitor bomb fall and radio-activity, and distribute details of bomb falls and warnings

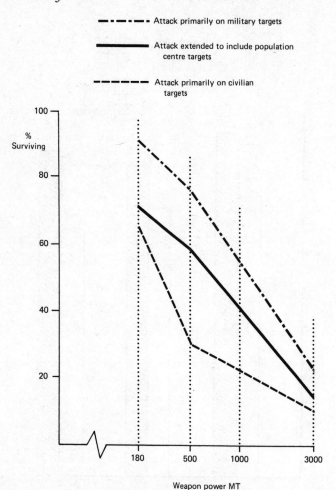

Figure 12 Effect of increasing weight of attack

of imminent fall-out to county controls. One vital function of the county scientific advisers would be to obtain supplementary bomb fall and fall-out data locally (the only data if communications failed). This information would be used by county scientific advisers to provide the county and district controllers with early damage and casualty estimates, and fall-out contours on which to base public release procedures. Reliably interpreted fall-out information would also be essential to allow controllers to organise movements of essential workers and to start rescue operations. The county scientific advisers would have a particularly vital task to play initially: the Home Office therefore places great importance on the provision of competent, well trained county scientific advisers in large numbers and devotes considerable effort to their training and exercising.

I have already mentioned that Home Office scientists are involved in continuing consideration of policy options. The provision of improvised shelters against fall-out on the lines suggested in *Protect and Survive* is a low cost measure which could reduce fall-out fatality levels possibly by several millions. The general provision of blast shelters however would be expensive, even if it were possible to identify accurately the most likely targets and concentrate on providing blast shelters close to such targets. For example, it might cost £8000 million to provide over a decade or more deep shelters for the 10 per cent deemed most at risk, basement-type communal shelters for a further 15 per cent with the remaining 75 per cent relying on home refuge rooms, approaching a year's total spending on defence. Certainly, such a policy would significantly reduce casualties, providing we judged correctly on targets. However, is the insurance premium justified to meet the very low perceived level of risk of nuclear war? It is true that Scandinavian countries and Switzerland have decided to pay this premium. Most countries appear to consider the cost too high, including both the USA and USSR, neither of which is providing general blast shelter protection for its population.

Instead, both the USA[15] and USSR[16,17], with the advantage of large land masses, appear prepared to rely extensively on population dispersal during a major crisis, as a lower cost means of limiting possible casualties by reducing the numbers of people close to probable target areas, including major conurbations. Undoubtedly, spontaneous evacuation would occur in Great Britain from areas perceived as target zones to areas perceived as safer from attack. Problems which would be associated with a directed dispersal policy for a compact densely populated country like Great Britain include:

(a) Reliable assignment of risk area grades;
(b) Timing of dispersal initiation;
(c) Transportation during the crisis, probably in conventional war conditions;
(d) Maintenance of essential wartime activities;
(e) Economic dislocation costs of prolonged dispersal;
(f) Provision of sufficient host area accommodation, life support, and fall-out protection in a small, densely-populated country with limited low risk areas.

Very little can be done to limit damage to transport, industry, and physical structures of all kinds. Particularly careful consideration is required regarding the measures a government should take to stockpile supplies and conserve scarce resources before and after the attack. Generally speaking, it is costly to stockpile vital resources for long periods and difficult to store them in safe and accessible places. Moreover, the concentration of production and distribution for economic reasons and the use of lightweight industrial building structures causes industry generally to be vulnerable to nuclear attack. Plans exist to disperse medical and emergency services staff and equipment in a crisis, but such plans may prove difficult to implement if conventional war were to precede a nuclear strike. Home Office scientists become involved in the selection of cost-effective strategies on these types of problems.

Although it is not possible to anticipate in detail all the major problems which would be likely to arise in the early years following a major nuclear strike against Great Britain, nevertheless many can be identified, structured and examined in advance with consideration of alternative forms of treatment. Home Office scientists and the regional scientific advisers participate in the analysis of selected problems and the assessment of the merits of possible strategies. Many aspects of science are relevant (including psychology and human factors) and other professions have potentially important contributions to make.

Regional and sub-regional commissioners and their staffs would have to consider in the survival phase such matters as:

(a) The need to establish themselves as the recognised, legitimate and effective government;
(b) The provision of emergency services and the restoration of normal services as far as possible;
(c) The assessment of the viability of the different areas in their region;
(d) The contrast between the complexity and fragility of pre-attack society and the post-attack impoverished community struggling for survival;
(e) The conflicting priorities of using scarce resources for short-term problems, and conserving them for the future;
(f) The need to cope with attitudes and reactions of communities which have suffered severe loss and face continuing deprivation.

However, commissioners would also need to look forward to the problems of national regeneration, aiming at creating a stable democratic society, inevitably reduced substantially in economic and social terms. Vital aspects would include:

(a) The choice on a regional and a national basis of long-term objectives which are realistic;
(b) The establishment of sustainable living standards bearing in mind the availability or otherwise of international assistance;
(c) The selection and development of appropriate technologies;
(d) The formation of a national government and the restoration of democratic procedures and freedoms;
(e) Generally, the adoption of policies appropriate to the conditions actually prevailing.

In the aftermath of nuclear war, scientists and other professionals at regional, county and district level would need to play a part both in decision-making and in vital actions. Improvization would frequently be required, with the reversion to simpler, manpower-intensive techniques requiring less sophisticated materials and processes. The immense accumulation of human knowledge and experience, however, should remain available and would need to be utilised. The creative professionals available to commissioners and controllers would need to provide sound advice and leadership in innovation and improvisation. The volunteer regional and county scientific advisers, versed in home defence matters and made aware in advance of possible revival measures, would make essential contributions.

Concluding remarks

Reverting to my initial themes, I would reiterate that the prevention and deterrence of war between East and West is the essential and permanent objective[18], but sensible home defence precautions are necessary on humanitarian grounds and worthwhile for Great Britain in prevailing circumstances. The UK Government will continue to strive to prevent all war, not just nuclear war; no home defence protective measures could ever make the consequences of nuclear attacks on the UK acceptable to the UK Government. However, in the conditions which have prevailed in Europe for the past 35 years, the UK Government has a duty to make arrangements to help survivors singly and collectively if we were ever attacked, irrespective of the UK defence policy, or its treaty commitments. I hope to have convinced you that scientists can and must make an important contribution to home defence contingency planning, and that trained volunteer scientific advisers would have an honourable and vital humanitarian role to play were prevention to fail. I look forward to hearing Professor Humphrey discuss what scientists collectively and individually might do to persuade the statesmen and nations of the world to achieve a stable situation where war between nations can be excluded effectively and the ultimate threat of modern continental or global war removed permanently. But nuclear and other horrific weapons have been invented and cannot be ignored by home defence planners. The following extract from the *Statement on the Defence Estimates 1981* is relevant and, I think, thought-provoking:

We have to seek unremittingly, through arms control and otherwise, for better ways to order the world. But the search may be a very long one. No safer system than deterrence is yet in view, and impatience would be a catastrophic guide in the search. To tear down the present structure, imperfect but effective, before a better one is firmly in our grasp would be an immensely dangerous and irresponsible act.[19]

References

1. M. Hachiya, MD, *Hiroshima Diary* (Victor Gollancz, London, 1955).
2. *Statement on the Defence Estimates* (HMSO, April 1981), Part 1, pp. 13, 14.
3. *Domestic Nuclear Shelters — Technical Guidance* (HMSO, January 1981).
4. *The Effects of Nuclear Weapons*, edited by S. Glasstone and P. J. Dolan (US Departments of Energy and Defence, 1977).
5. *Nuclear Weapons* (HMSO, 1974).
6. Glasstone and Dolan, op. cit.
7. *Nuclear Weapons*, see reference 5.
8. Glasstone and Dolan, op. cit.
9. *Nuclear Weapons*, see reference 5.
10. *Protect and Survive* (HMSO, reprinted 1980).
11. *Nuclear Weapons*, see reference 5.
12. *Protect and Survive*, see reference 10.
13. P. Bentley, *Blast Overpressure and Fall-out Radiation Dose Models for Casualty Assessment and other Purposes* (Home Office report, to be published).
14. *Protect and Survive*, see reference 10.
15. *Guide for Crisis Relocation Contingency Planning — Overview* (DCPA CPG 2–8–A, January 1979).
16. Yegorev *et al.*, *Civil Defence*, Executive Summary in English, (USAF, 1970).
17. Leon Gouré, *Recent Developments in Soviet Home Defence (1969–70)* (Centre for Advanced International Studies, University of Miami, May 1971).
18. M. E. Quinlan, *Deterrence and Nuclear Weapons*, 1981 Annual Study of the Association of Civil Defence and Emergency Planning Officers (July 1981).
19. *Statement on the Defence Estimates 1981*, see reference 2.

9. THE CONSEQUENCES OF NUCLEAR WAR

George Rathjens

My charge when I was asked to speak here was to talk about the possibilities of survival in nuclear war. What they might be will depend very much on the nature of the war, and I have chosen to partition the problem according to three possibilities: a virtually unlimited exchange, involving the full-scale use of nuclear forces — and in dealing with this, I shall, with your indulgence, talk mainly about the consequences of the United States and the Soviet Union using their so-called strategic forces against each other; second, the use of those forces in a disarming attack against adversary strategic forces, a possiblity I take up not because I think it serious but because the very lively issue of US strategic arms modernization is so tightly coupled with it; and then the use of nuclear weapons in other limited ways, particularly in Europe: the case, I presume, of greatest concern to this audience.

Of the three necessary steps in trying to estimate the consequences of a nuclear war the simplest, or at least the one in which one can have the most confidence, is calculating the response of individuals and structures to the effects of the explosion of invididual weapons, a task that can be carried out without difficulty, albeit with considerable uncertainty, using standard reference materials.[1] In addition, one has to develop a scenario for events after the first weapon is used — how those in authority will react, and how command and control capacity will degrade; and then, one must envisage how societies might respond to the synergistic effects of many weapons having been used, probably in a very short period of time.

With very little experience that is relevant to the second and third tasks, nothing definitive can be done. But still, we must do what we can, especially as we hear increasingly these days about the possibility of nuclear weapons being used in highly controlled and limited ways, and because it is of the greatest importance that political and military leaders not be misled into believing that this is possible if it is not.

Those who believe they can be so used could be right — a nuclear war may be winnable, as the Vice President of the United States has said; a limited Soviet attack against the US Minuteman ICBM force should perhaps be considered a serious possibility; and it may be that a nuclear war in Europe could be so limited that having ground-launched cruise missiles, Pershing IIs, and neutron bombs at NATO's disposal would be to its advantage — but we have no basis now for believing these things; and acting on such beliefs could be at least costly and at worst, most perilous. Colin Gray has written, 'One of the essential tasks of the American defense community is to help ensure that in moments of acute crisis the Soviet general staff cannot brief the Politburo with a plausible theory of military victory'.[2] It may be at least as important that that community and others in the West concerned about these matters try to ensure that in moments of crisis the *military staffs of the Western nuclear powers* not brief *their* political masters with a theory of military victory, at least if the use of nuclear weapons is in any way at issue.

I might note here that in the case of many military men there is little danger. I quote from the last public paper of the late Lord Mountbatten,

> In all sincerity, as a military man I can see no use for any nuclear weapons which would not end in escalation, with consequences that no one can conceive. In warfare the unexpected is the rule and no one can anticipate what an opponent's reaction will be to the unexpected.[3]

In the United States at least, it is the civilian advisors of which Mr Gray is a prolific example[4] who seem to be more persuaded that limited nuclear war is a realistic option and one for which we should be better prepared, and even that damage might be limited to something within the range of historical experience — a few million fatalities — in the event of expenditure of the full nuclear stockpiles of the superpowers.

Doctrines and realities

As a point of departure in dealing with damage in the event of a full nuclear exchange, let me go back twenty-five years in American experience. In a scarcely remembered but seminal speech, entitled 'How Much is Enough?'[5], Donald Quarles, then US Secretary of the Air Force, spelled out the doctrine of sufficiency: the idea that in the structuring of strategic nuclear capabilities, what was needed was enough to destroy the Soviet Union, and that whatever the level of adversary forces, capabilities in excess of this would be superfluous. This foreshadowed Robert McNamara's 'assured destruction' capability as a criterion for strategic force planning. Some of you are old enough to remember that he suggested that a capability to destroy 20 to 25 per cent of the population of the Soviet Union and 50 per cent of its industry would suffice to deter the Soviet Union from actions that could lead to a nuclear exchange, amounts achievable with the delivery of 200 or 300 one-megaton weapons or their equivalent.[6]

There has been a great deal of confusion about whether these percentage figures were best estimates of what would be required for deterrence and of the damage level that might be expected with the delivery of the stated number of weapons. Actually, the estimates of damage sufficient to deter were upper bounds — surely those levels would suffice; perhaps much less would do — and the estimates that these levels would result, given the delivery of 200 or 300 megaton-equivalents, were lower bounds; amounts calculated on most conservative grounds. Almost certainly, the damage would be much larger were account taken of the unpredictable effects of fall-out and fire, and particularly of the secondary consequences of societal distruption; for example, breakdown of food and energy distribution systems and medical services. The figures and the 'assured destrustion' idea were adduced and, during the McNamara years, used, not to define levels of strategic force capability which the US should attain, but rather more to argue against expansion to much higher levels.

Their use has contributed greatly to confusion about US targetting policy: to a belief that destruction of Soviet population and industry was the primary criterion for allocation of US strategic weapons. In fact, the weapons were allocated against targets believed to be of military importance — air fields, nuclear storage sites, etc., including some industrial facilities, e.g. oil refineries and tank factories, but generally not against what we would call light industry and certainly not against population *per se*. It is true that many Americans in positions of responsibility felt that it was primarily the threat of unacceptable damage, of 'assured destruction' of the Soviet Union as a going society, that would serve as a deterrent to a Soviet attack or other events that might lead to the use of strategic arms, and if hard choices between being able to inflict heavy damage on military targets or simply destroying Soviet cities on a massive scale had had to be made there would have been serious differences of opinion between advocates of the two alternatives. But such choices did not arise, at least during the sixties and seventies, because those interested in the former, e.g. the military planners who wrote the SIOP (the Single Integrated Operations Plan) for US strategic forces, could allocate the weapons to targets of military importance, and others — for the most part, civilian authorities — could be confident that 'assured destruction' objectives would be met. This was a consequence of many of the targets being located in or near cities and of the characteristics of strategic weapons: of the fact that the yields were very large, at least during the sixties, and accuracies of delivery of the order of a mile, at least for missiles. The situation may be different in the future, and I will discuss that possibility.

Before doing so, I should like, however, to clear up some other confusion relating to ideas about 'assured destruction'. As strategic capabilities of the Soviet Union grew, it became increasingly clear that assurance of destruction in the event of large-scale use of nuclear weapons would be mutual, and the late Donald Brennan coined the acronym MAD to describe 'mutual assured destruction'. In recent years it has been commonly suggested, by, incidentally, Henry Kissinger among others, that many in the American arms control and defence community thought mutual vulnerability a desirable state of affairs[7]; and much has been said and written about a doctrine of 'mutual assured destruction' (which, in the views of Gray and Brennan respectively should be abandoned in favour of doctrines of 'victory' and 'defence'). In fact, 'mutual assured destruction' is not a matter of doctrine at all: it is rather a short-hand way of describing the physical reality of the circumstances in which the United States and the Soviet Union have found themselves. Whatever the doctrines or policies for using nuclear weapons in limited ways, and there have been flirtations with both trying to avoid destroying adversary population and industry and with trying to defend one's own, mutual assured destruction *capabilities* have been an unfortunate reality of at least the last twenty years: certainly not something that is desirable but a reality inherent in the superpowers' having large nuclear forces, and from which, in my view, there can be no escape short of radical disarmament.

This becomes apparent when one considers the size of current nuclear stockpiles: about 4000 megaton-equivalents for the United States, ten to twenty times McNamara's assured destruction force level, and even larger for the Soviet Union.

Since McNamara produced his figures there have been a number of more refined studies of the consequences of the employment of nuclear weapons. Among the more recent and best known in the United States is one by the Office of Technology Assessment of the US Congress.[8] It explores the consequences of the use of nuclear weapons against Detroit and Leningrad, both of which metropolitan areas have populations of somewhat over four million, and finds that a single 1 MT weapon airburst over Detroit would be likely to produce about 470 000 direct fatalities and 630 000 injuries. Both fatalities and injuries would be about twice as large in the case of Leningrad, a consequence of its higher population density, and other Russian cities. A very large fraction of the injuries would surely prove fatal

because of the gross disproportion between medical needs
and capabilities — a point brought home forcefully by the
Japanese experience, by a study done by Arthur Katz for
a US Congressional committee[9], and by work by members
of Physicians for Social Responsibility, a group of American
doctors who have become convinced that there is no way
to deal with the medical problems of nuclear war except
through avoidance. The problem is made so difficult because
medical facilities — physicians, nurses and hospitals — are
concentrated disproportionately in central cities, the areas
where destruction would be most complete; because, in the
event that many cities are attacked, of the near total destruction of the pharmaceutical industry; and because of the
likely high incidence of serious burns among the injured
and the fact that burns pose an especially serious burden
for medical resources.[10] In summary, a 1-MT weapon or its
equivalent can be expected to kill of the order of a million
people in a very large city; the number varying a great deal,
however, depending on the construction of the city, living
patterns, meterological conditions, and the height of the
burst of the weapon. But, in fact, cities are likely to be
more heavily struck, and damage is likely to be much greater.
This was driven home to me by an experience in 1960.
I was sent to the headquarters of our Strategic Air Command to inquire into the structure of the SIOP. As I looked
through the atlas I picked a city in the Soviet Union about
the size of Hiroshima, but which otherwise had nothing
I was aware of to distinguish it, and asked about the weapons
allocated to targets in that city. There were four weapons
as I recollect, one of about 4 MT and three of over 1 MT
each, yields equal respectively to about 300 and 80 times
that of the Hiroshima weapon.

When consideration is given to the aggregate effects of
attacks in which large numbers of weapons are used against
the United States, direct and relatively immediate fatalities
are likely to be around 100 million and industrial damage
around 70 per cent.[11] Levels of damage for the Soviet Union
would probably be similar. In addition, in the weeks following there would be many additional fatalities as a result of star-
vation and disease, consequences mainly of the unavailability

of fuels and the breakdown of transportation and medical services.

In recent years there have been a number of suggestions that the seriousness of such attacks could be greatly mitigated by civil defence measures: by protecting machinery and by evacuating populations from cities and through the use of shelters. The more optimistic studies, notably those of T. K. Jones[12], have suggested that Soviet fatalities from a heavy American attack might be reduced to a few million and that full recovery would be possible in two to four years following such an attack. Jones' works appear though to have been based on erroneous assumptions about Soviet population distribution[13], and his studies and some others appear to be based on other assumptions that are also dubious. These studies have been largely refuted, particularly by the US Arms Control and Disarmament Agency[14], the CIA[15], and the Office of Technology Assessment[16], as well as by one of my former students, Fred Kaplan[17]. While there can be little doubt that removal of people from cities *could* lead to substantial reduction in near-term fatalities, it is doubtful that evacuation could be implemented on anything like the scale proposed or that it would be effective on a longer time scale in either saving lives or in facilitating recovery, given the massive destruction of industry, services and living space from a heavy attack.

There is even less hope in active defence.

Soviet ballistic missile defences could intercept tens of American (or British, French or Chinese) re-entry vehicles at best, and would more probably be totally ineffective; its air defences would do somewhat better but the majority of US air-delivered warheads would almost certainly get through; and it has virtually no anti-submarine warfare (ASW) capability against US missile-launching submarines. The US has better ASW capabilities, but no ballistic missile defence at all, and virtually no air defence capability.

There have been interesting developments in optical discrimination techniques that could have relevance to ABM (anti-ballistic missile) defence but when account is taken of possible countermeasures neither these nor the more exotic possibilities of laser and particle-beam technologies offer much hope of making ABM defence of cities (as distinct from defence of a limited number of hardened military facilities, e.g. missile sites) an option that merits serious consideration. Also, air defence of cities and ASW are likely to become more difficult rather than easier with the development of cruise missiles, low radar cross-section aircraft and longer-range sea-launched ballistic missiles.

While one can understand the wish to improve defences, it has to be recognized that the situation has not changed for the better in the more than thirty years since Louis Ridenour argued persuasively that, in a world of nuclear weapons, 'There is No Defense'[18]. Cities are so fragile and the weapons so powerful that for defence to be meaningful it must be nearly perfect, and that is not feasible now nor likely in the future. I would rank the prospects somewhere between those of finding the Grail and the Fountain of Youth.

Some of those who have damned 'assured destruction' as a doctrine, rather than recognizing it as a capability inherent in large nuclear forces, have suggested escape from its threat through mutual forbearance in the way weapons are targetted. Even McNamara, who surely laboured under no such confusion about the meaning of 'assured destruction', flirted with this possibility in 1962 with what became known as a 'spare-the-cities' doctrine. The approach made little sense at the time for the reason I have given earlier: the co-location of targets of military significance with cities and the unfeasibility of destroying the one while sparing the other, given the technology then available. The technology has, however, improved and will continue to do so. Missile delivery accuracies of hundreds of metres are now feasible and accuracies of tens of metres will be before the end of the decade. With that, and with weapons of low yield, it would be possible, at least conceptually, to execute so-called surgical attacks, perhaps destroying the Kremlin while sparing the Intourist Hotel, a few hundred metres away. I shall turn to the special case of limited attacks against ICBM (inter-continental ballistic missile) sites in a moment, but before doing so, let me generalize and say why I think spare-the-cities options are distant possibilities, at best, notwithstanding changing technology.

Firstly, if damage is to be limited to actual targets, there will have to be not only dramatic improvements in accuracy, but further great reductions in weapons yields. Reductions have been occurring. The average yield of weapons in the American strategic stockpile is now only about a tenth of that in the early sixties, and those in the Soviet stockpile are also much smaller, on the average, than they were then. Even the *aggregate* yield of the strategic force warheads of each superpower had diminished in the last decade and, with that, the potential for covering large areas with thermal or blast effects or fall-out. But this does not mean that the damage-producing potential of the two stockpiles has been reduced. Quite the contrary. Much of the effect of large weapons would be 'wasted' because of the discrete size of targets. With more weapons, damage *potential* is probably increasing, even though yields are much lower. If we are to get away from a mutual assured destruction capability, the damage-inflicting potential of each superpower would require reduction by a factor of at least ten.

Secondly, because of the area they cover, many targets of military significance, e.g. military bases, air fields, shipyards, and manufacturing facilities, are most efficiently destroyed with moderately large-yield weapons. For this reason, both sides will continue to keep weapons in at least the high-kiloton yield range — and as long as they have many of these, they will have assured destruction *capabilities*, however the weapons are targetted.

Thirdly, this aside, those who believe that an assured destruction capability is needed as a deterrent are likely always to have the last word, however weapons may be targetted and whatever the rationale for their development and procurement. Thus, each of the superpowers is likely to retain an assured destruction capability just as a matter of last-resort insurance. While the United States has not, for many years, had to make choices between targetting installations of military importance and posing an assured destruction threat, I wonder about the United Kingdom, France and China. My guess is that 'assured destruction', or something very like it gets priority, at least in the case of the last two.

Fourthly, the trend to smaller warheads is unlikely to go much further, at least for the United States. The MX, if it is deployed, will have warheads of larger yield than we put on the Minutemann III, and the Trident, larger warheads than the Poseidon.

Although we may turn to a greater commitment to 'nuclear war-fighting', it is a complement, not an alternative, to living under the spectre of mutual assured destruction. I repeat, we, and I have in mind both the East and the West, can escape the latter only through *radical* reductions in strategic arms.

The Nitze scenario

That is not likely to happen soon. On the contrary, Soviet strategic forces continue to grow and the impetus in the United States for expansion of capabilities is greater than at any time since the 'missile gap' of more than twenty years ago.

A major rationale for this expansion is the possibility that, with improving missile accuracies and deployment of multiple independently-targettable re-entry vehicles (MIRVs) on its missiles, the Soviet Union could, with but a fraction of its large ICBM force, destroy the great bulk of the US ICBM force in a disarming attack. This would not in itself deprive the United States of an assured destruction capability. Some US ICBMs would surely survive, but even if the numbers were very small, the other two components of the US strategic triad, the bombers and the missile-launching submarines, could together or, for that matter, each individually, deliver a devastating retaliatory blow against the Soviet Union. But it is alleged by many thoughtful Americans, of whom Paul Nitze is the most prominent and influential, that it might be foolish for any president to give them the order to do so, given the great likelihood that such an American retaliatory strike would be followed by the Soviets' countering with the destruction of American cities. Mr Nitze goes further and suggests that the Soviets would very probably never even feel the need to execute a disarming strike: their simply having the capability to which the US could have no reasonable response could permit the effective exercise by them of coercive pressure on the United States.

At issue in considering if the Nitze scenario should be taken seriously is the question of whether the Soviet Union could, in fact, make such an attack with confidence that the outcome would be satisfactory of whether they would be deterred by the prospect of escalation involving a devastating US response.

The decision was made by President Carter and then reaffirmed by President Reagan that there would be unacceptable risks in improving Soviet capabilities and that something had to be done about what is referred to as the Minuteman vulnerability problem. Mr Carter's answer was a programme to develop and deploy a new and larger ICBM, the MX, with its yet-to-be-decided basing scheme. For better or worse, there appear to be no deployment options which would provide the desired degree of invulnerability that could be implemented very quickly. There will, therefore, be what President Reagan refers to as a 'window of vulnerability', no matter what basing option is selected. Also, there have been serious objections to each of the proposed schemes and there have been concerns about the cost of the programme, lately, even within the Administration. These last factors will be important and possibly decisive in decisions about the MX programme, but whether or not there continues to be a belief in the 'window of vulnerability', the Nitze scenario will be important too.

In the view of many of those engaged in debate on the issue, the credibility of a Soviet disarming attack is, and will be, critically dependent on the 'collateral damage' that might result from it and on whether escalation might follow. It is argued that if many Americans were to be killed as a collateral consequence of an effort to destroy US strategic forces, the likelihood of an American retaliatory response would be high. In that case, or even if there were an expectation that fatalities might be high, the Soviets would probably be deterred from such an attack. On the other hand, if they could be confident that a disarming strike could be executed with little risk of much collateral damage, and hence with a lowered risk of escalation, they would be more likely to attack, or at least the threat would be more credible and the US would be, therefore, more vulnerable to coercion.

It becomes, then, a matter of some moment to try to estimate the magnitude of damage to US population from such attacks, whether and how the US might respond, and how events might develop thereafter.

There have been a number of attempts to deal with at least the first step, i.e. to estimate collateral damage from Soviet disarming attacks, some of them involving not only Soviet targetting of US ICBMs but of missile-launching submarine bases and Strategic Air Command bomber bases as well. The range of fatality estimates is astonishingly great: from under one million to over 50 million.[19] Much of this dispersion is due to variations in the scenarios: to factors which would presumably be under the control of the Soviets. For example, whether they chose to attack or spare those facilities near population centres – the submarine bases, most of the bomber bases and one of the six Minuteman sites – would probably make a large difference in fatalities produced; so too, would other details of the attack: the number and yield of warheads used, and whether they were burst in the air or on the surface. But for each particular scenario there would still be great uncertainties about collateral effects, a consequence of such uncontrollable factors as local meterological conditions (particularly important in determining fall-out patterns and the propagation of thermal radiation and fires), where 'wild' missiles might impact, and what individuals in the impact area might be doing at the time. The range of uncertainty is reflected in substantially different estimates of effects that have been made by different US government agencies for similar hypothesized attacks.

Should such an attack occur, reporting and assessment of damage to both the US missile force and US population would surely be subject to distortion, whatever had actually happened.

With the compounding of uncertainties, US political leaders, who would be confronted with the question of how to respond to the Soviet attack, would almost certainly be acting on the basis of a very different picture than the Soviets might have had in mind in planning it. And, were a response ordered, there might well be at least some confusion in its implementation.

Lord Mountbatten's observation about the difficulty of predicting events in war is surely germane. For any given Soviet attack, estimates might be made for lower and upper bounds on damage: at the one extreme it might reasonably be estimated that some fraction of US missiles would be destroyed and that there would be a few million, or even only a few hundred thousand, fatalities, but a reasonable upper bound would probably be that virtually all of both societies would be destroyed. There would be no real basis for estimating a probability distribution for outcomes over this range.

I would suggest that whatever the Soviet objective, whether to improve its military posture relative to that of the US, to demonstrate to third parties the impotency of the US, or to demonstrate Soviet resolve in a crisis, a Nitze-type disarming scenario is simply not something that a rational Soviet leadership would contemplate — nor would an American leadership contemplate the inverse. The uncertainties as to effectiveness, given the use of missiles that have never been used under operational conditions and the uncertainty as to adversary response, including the possibility of its launch of missiles on warning of their imminent destruction, would be simply unacceptable. Yet, a disarming 'first-strike' against the US Minuteman forces has been shaping US strategic arms development policy and its approach to arms control negotiations more than any other single factor.

Nuclear war in Europe

I turn now to the potential use of nuclear weapons in other limited scenarios, particularly the European case. The issues will be clear to virtually all of you for they have not changed qualitatively in many years.

There is a presumption of a threat from Warsaw Pact forces, perhaps having its origins in conflict elsewhere. On the assumption that the threat in Europe will be from conventional forces, at least initially, NATO has conceptually three not-mutually-exclusive options for coping with it: meeting it with adequate conventional forces; through a policy of 'escalation dominance', i.e. by developing and maintaining superior 'nuclear war-fighting' capabilities that would permit a successful defence across a range of levels of conflict; or relying for deterrence on the possibility of mutually unacceptable escalation somehow occurring.

Now, I have long thought that Warsaw Pact capabilities and potential at the conventional level have been much overestimated, but it is not within my charge to discuss that matter here. So, let me turn to the nuclear options.

Judgements about the relevance of the two alternatives will depend on assumptions about command and control relationships and on personal experience and views about how organizations and individuals are likely to function in crises with imperfect information. My own views have been foreshadowed by my quotation of Lord Mountbatten on the unpredictability of adversary behaviour in war and by my comments on what I have called the Nitze scenario for a disarming attack against the US ICBM force. It is the uncertainty of outcome far more than the relative balance of forces that is likely to be decisive in decisions that might lead to the use of nuclear weapons.

I would not go so far as to argue that nuclear weapons could not be used at all, based on having superior capabilities. They have been, after all, against Japan. They might be again against powers that have no significant capability to retaliate; and, although I have my doubts about the wisdom of it, I can conceive of rational, presumably prudent men ordering their use even against another nuclear power in certain special circumstances where there might be a basis for unusual confidence in the predictability of both the physical effects and adversary reactions. Sinking a ship at sea or destroying isolated radar stations or satellites might be examples.

But talk of using nuclear weapons in Europe raises in my mind just the opposite spectre, a situation fraught with even more uncertainty than the disarming attack against US missile silos: greater, mainly because of the complications of command and control. In the case of the disarming attempt, the attack would be pre-planned against immovable targets, the orders would be given to a single military unit — the Soviet Rocket Forces — over an intact command and control system, and execution would presumably require a few minutes. Even then, I would have doubts about all orders being executed properly. At least I would in the inverse case of a US counterforce attack. In the case of nuclear war in Europe, even the initial use of weapons would be likely to be ragged, given the many different units involved, different perceptions of the seriousness of the situation, and the evanescent nature of many of the targets. And within hours of the first use of nuclear weapons, if it had not happened before, there would probably be catastrophic degradation in command, control and communication capabilities.

I do not propose to go further into the command and control problem here — I have said a little more about it elsewhere[20] — except to remark that I know of no one who has looked at the problem who believes that the United States, much less NATO, now has capabilities that would permit effective centralized control of nuclear weapons for more than hours, if they were used in moderately large numbers. Certainly, we do not have capabilities that are in any way consistent with implementation of the much-discussed Presidential Directive 59 on the flexible use of nuclear forces, and there is near-consensus in the American defence community on the high priority that should be accorded to greatly improving what we call C^3I (command, control and communications intelligence) capabilities. I might just interject here that one of my great fears is that with a great deal of such effort, political leaders might become misguidedly convinced that they could prudently use nuclear weapons in a war-fighting role, when they could not; convinced, if you like, of a theory of victory, to use Colin Gray's phrase.

In summary, I cannot tell you any more about the prospects for surviving the use of nuclear weapons in Europe than had Lord Mountbatten in his statement that there would probably be 'escalation, with consequences that no one can conceive'.

But I would not want to drop the subject quite so quickly, especially since Europe is now so torn over the question of the deployment of new kinds of nuclear weapons, which are alleged by some to be a menace but by others to be essential.

If I am right that all of the talk about flexible response, escalation dominance, countervailing strategy and nuclear war-fighting is illusory, there can be no military rationale for .these new weapons. Having them will certainly not give their possessors an exploitable military advantage. Nor will their use make much difference in the levels of damage to Europe in the event of nuclear war, considering all of the other nuclear weapons that might be used. A judgement about whether or not they should be acquired must, then, be based on other considerations: their cost, their political effect, and on whether their presence might affect the likelihood of escalation in a crisis. I shall say nothing about the first two matters, and only a bit about the last.

Whether nuclear weapons will be used at all in the event of conflict in Europe and whether their use is likely to be limited would, it would seem to me, depend only remotely on the characteristics of individual weapons. Other factors to which I have referred — C^3I capabilities, and I mean that to take in a lot, including the individual idiosyncracies of many people — will be far more important. But if the characteristics and numbers of weapons have any effect at all, I should think the new ones will make escalation a little more likely. Someone is likely to want to use them, and others to destroy them.

Now, whether NATO needs greater potential for escalation is arguable. If so, there may be better — certainly, there are cheaper — ways of getting it. My own view is that the potential is more than sufficient, and that we may not survive indefinitely without reducing it.

References

1. The best I know of is *The Effects of Nuclear Weapons*, edited by Samuel Glasstone and Philip J. Dolan (US Departments of Defense and Energy, 1977).
2. Colin S. Gray, 'Nuclear Strategy: the Case for a Theory of Victory', *International Security*, 4, 1, Summer 1979, p. 56.
3. Louis Mountbatten, 'A Military Commander Surveys the Nuclear Arms Race', *International Security*, 4, 3, Winter 1979, p. 4.

4. In addition to the above, see Colin S. Gray and Keith Payne, 'Victory Is Possible', *Foreign Policy*, No. 39, Summer 1980, and for a critique, Michael E. Howard, 'On Fighting a Nuclear War', *International Security*, 5, 4, Spring 1981.

5. *Air Force Magazine*, September 1956, p. 51.

6. Alain C. Enthoven and K. Wayne Smith, *How Much Is Enough?* (New York: Harper & Row, 1971), p. 207.

7. Speech in Brussels, 1 September 1979. For text see 'NATO: The Next Thirty Years', *Survival*, 21, 6, November/December 1979, p. 265.

8. *The Effects of Nuclear War* (Office of Technology Assessment, Congress of the United States, May 1979).

9. *Economic and Social Consequences of Nuclear Attacks on the United States* (Joint Committee on Defense Production, Congress of the United States, March 1979).

10. Although it would be very dependent on time of day and year and on meteorological conditions, the ratio of burn injuries to others could well be substantially higher in the case of weapons in the megaton range than in the Japanese experience because thermal effects become increasingly important relative to blast and radiation as weapons yields increase.

11. The OTA (reference 8) cites the following estimates (pp. 94–5) for Soviet attacks against US military and economic targets: Department of Defense (1977), 1955-65 million; Defense Civil Defense Preparedness Agency (1978), 122 million; Arms Control and Disarmament Agency, 105–31 million — all without civil defence measures.

12. T. K. Jones, 'Industrial Survival and Recovery after Nuclear Attack', A Report to the Joint Committee on Defense Production, (US Congress, 18 November 1976), and T. K. Jones and W. Scott Thompson, 'Central War and Civil Defense', *Orbis*, Fall 1978.

13. See Alfred Lieberman, 'Critique of T. K. Jones' Computation of Soviet Fatalities' (United States Arms Control and Disarmament Agency, 3 May 1979).

14. *An Analysis of Civil Defense in Nuclear War*, (United States Arms Control and Disarmament Agency, December 1978).

15. *Soviet Civil Defense*, (Direction of Central Intelligence, July 1978).

16. Op. cit.

17. 'The Soviet Civil Defense Myth', 2 parts, *The Bulletin of the Atomic Scientists*, March 1978, p. 14, April 1978, p. 41 (and Leon Goure for a rebuttal, April 1978, p. 48).

18. Louis N. Ridenour, 'There is No Defense', in *One World or None*, edited by Dexter Masters and Katharine Way, (McGraw-Hill Book Co., Inc., 1948).

19. *Briefing on Counterforce Attacks*. Hearing before the sub-committee on Arms Control, International Law and Organization, Committee on Foreign Relations, United States Senate, September 11, 1974. See also reference 8, pp. 81–90.

20. *How the Use of Nuclear Weapons in Europe Might Arise*, a talk given in Groningen, the Netherlands, April 1981. To be published.

10. PROSPECTS FOR NUCLEAR DISARMAMENT: DIPLOMATIC TENSIONS AND PERSPECTIVES

Nicholas Sims

A paper on *Prospects for Nuclear Disarmament* must begin by recognising that the range of answers to the question implied by such a title is confined, in present circumstances, to the alternatives of 'dim' and 'non-existent'. In the context of *The Way Ahead*, the theme chosen for today's session, it behoves us to make the relatively optimistic assumption that the prospects are no worse than dim, and, having asked why, to consider how they might be improved.

Unfortunately the fact that nuclear weapons are now widely regarded with revulsion is in itself no guarantee of nuclear disarmament. To go further, and recognise that we need to rid ourselves of them, is not at all the same as finding a way to do it. Even if it were universally accepted (which is by no means the case) that nuclear disarmament could make a surer contribution than nuclear deterrence to the peace of the world, the problems of reaching agreement on how to move from where we are now to where we would like to be would remain. They cannot be wished away or denounced as invented obstacles. There are no short cuts to disarmament, though wishful thinking often suggests that there are.

I tried to tackle some of the most prevalent illusions in my book *Approaches to Disarmament* when I revised and expanded it after the first UN Special Session on Disarmament in 1978; I called the relevant chapter 'No Easy Answers',[1] and I still believe just that. There are no short cuts, no easy answers, but a long haul encompassed with uncertainties, and it does the cause of disarmament no service to pretend otherwise.

Some of the problems which accompany the pursuit of nuclear disarmament arise at the level of diplomacy, and it is with them that this paper will be concerned.

The significance of diplomacy

Diplomacy is, of course, not the only level at which problems arise. There are others: the deficiencies of international organisation; the economic pressures of the military-industrial complex and the like; the lack of trust among governments (and governed); the imperfections of human nature. All these and more have been implicated in the elusiveness of disarmament. Which are more important, and which less, as contributory factors, has long been and seems likely to remain matter for disagreement. I have my hunches, as we all do; but I will leave them aside. By choosing the diplomatic level for this attempt to consider why the prospects for nuclear disarmament are dim and how they might be improved, I am doing little more than following the principle of specialisation. In so far as I am able to lay claim to any specialised understanding of the problems of disarmament and the characteristic patterns of its pusuit, it is principally at this level, concerned with such things as the best use of the United Nations system and other international procedures; the negotiation and review of treaties; the elaboration of policy positions and proposals; the building of consensus; the evolution of appropriate institutions; the discourse of verification, consultation, confidence-building measures and the like: in short, the diplomacy of disarmament.

I said 'I am doing *little* more', rather than '*no* more', because my choice of level is predicated on an assumption which is not universally shared and which therefore may usefully be made explicit, and opened to criticism, from the very start. This is the assumption that diplomacy is significant as an element in the disarmament enterprise, or (to put it another way) that it makes sense to pursue disarmament by diplomatic means. Evidently, I affirm that it *is* and it *does*.

The assumption is one which is typically assailed from three distinct quarters.

Firstly, there are those who assert that political will is all that matters: if diplomats are told firmly enough what is required of them they will find a way to get it done, and until they *are* told their supposed difficulties are of little moment because they only reflect the failure of their political masters to take the necessary decision in favour of disarmament. To this, one reply is that the distinction between diplomatic servants and political masters is not equally recognisable in all governments, and that even where the distinction has some constitutional validity the political will hypothesis grossly underrates the complexity and variety of national foreign policy processes (in the field of disarmament policy as in many others). It is, at one and the same time, unfair to the diplomats *and* to the politicians because it oversimplifies their roles to an unacceptable degree. Another reply could question the validity of the notion that disarmament is achievable by a clearcut, discrete decision (however it may be taken) rather than an incremental policy process involving elements of negotiation along the way. A third type of reply might champion the time-honoured virtues of diplomacy and the skills of the diplomatic profession, extolled in a long tradition from Callières through Nicolson[2] to our own day, albeit more critically in some recent rigorous analyses[3], as indispensable tools of statecraft and essential elements in sustaining a durable international order.

Secondly, there are those who see the diplomatic level as irrelevant to the quest for disarmament because diplomacy is by definition an inter-governmental activity and disarmament will come about, in their view, only through popular struggle against the policies of governments and the institutions of the state. Without, on the whole, going so far as to embrace consciously the political theory of anarchism, which would at least lend this hypothesis some broader intellectual coherence, its supporters have made a powerful impact on the operating style of many disarmament campaigns, if not necessarily with equal effect on their policy stances. The populist element in such campaigns not only blurs the vital distinction — vital at any rate in a democracy — between persuasion and coercion; by concentrating on the means of forcing governments to accede to campaign demands, it encourages the adoption of an essentially intranational and confrontational perspective within which international diplomacy has no place. (One can even see this happening to a certain extent in campaigns which were deliberately started with an international perspective.) This is not to say that national campaigns of this kind never co-operate with one another: of course they do, but still within a conceptual framework heavily influenced by the ideology of 'peoples against governments' which makes it hard for them to take as much interest in the diplomatic discourse of disarmament as do those non-governmental organisations which are part of other, internationalist traditions, where the populist impact has been slight.

Without entering into normative arguments about representative democracy and the proper limits of extra-parliamentary, anti-governmental action, one response to this approach is simply to doubt its practicality. In other words, if nuclear disarmament has to wait upon the successful outcome of a series of 'peoples against governments' struggles, the prospects for its achievement become even dimmer. To say this is not to decry the informative and persuasive roles of disarmament campaigns but rather the occasional overtones (sometimes doubtless unconscious) of populist coercion, which seem to rule out the preferable idea of tolerant co-operation between government and governed with the latter encouraging the diplomatic efforts of the former. And in practice, too, some organisations have managed to combine a high degree of populist rhetoric with more conventional attempts to influence the diplomatic conduct of government by persuasion, holding the different elements of their constituency in an uneasy balance.

Thirdly, it is often said that the necessity of achieving nuclear disarmament is too urgent to be left to the elaborate ways of diplomacy.[4] This argument would indeed be worth taking seriously if an alternative to the diplomatic route were seen to be available. Some may think they see one. I remain to be persuaded. Since it is governments which possess and deploy these weapons, it is governments alone which are in a position to communicate and negotiate with one another over their diminution and eventual abandonment. (Although very useful international communication on disarmament issues has taken place *non-governmentally* for 25 years now through the Pugwash Conferences on Science and World Affairs its significance is still measured in terms of the extent to which its products are used *by governments* to modify or develop their positions. The same will be true of Olaf Palme's Independent Commission on Disarmament and Security Issues.) Communication and negotiation among governments are the very stuff of which diplomacy is made. So although, as was said above, only some of the obstacles to nuclear disarmament arise specifically at the level of diplomacy, nevertheless I see no short cut enabling us to by-pass the diplomatic route as the way to our destination. This is not, of course, to deny the potential utility of certain unilateral actions which (particularly when reciprocated) may have a part to play in the promotion of disarmament, as they habitually do in decisions on armament.

Tedious, time-consuming and frustrating though the diplomatic route may often be, we are stuck with it and we must make the best of it. Those involved in the diplomacy of nuclear disarmament are not necessarily as complacent as their detractors like to make out, nor is the process of negotiation always more leisurely than it need be. Instead of making general criticisms of that kind, if we want (as who does not?) to see results sooner rather than later we would be better advised to encourage those who are professionally engaged in this field to pursue their efforts — and to make those efforts more likely to succeed, when we can suggest specific improvements which might help — in the knowledge of our support as they strive towards the goal of nuclear disarmament.

Tensions in diplomacy for disarmament

Having now established the significance of diplomatic activity, and suggested an appropriate attitude towards it, I want to examine two separate tensions which recur as a persistent pattern in the international diplomacy of nuclear disarmament and which hinder progress in that direction. Indeed, it can be argued that they are more than a hindrance: they add up to deadlock.

One is the tension between those governments which emphasise the absolute priority of dealing with *nuclear* weapons and those which refuse to have them singled out with no parallel restraint on *conventional* armaments. This is a problem in the planning of the disarmament process.

The other is the tension between *multilateral* and *bilateral* (or occasionally trilateral) modes of negotiation. This is a problem in the structure of disarmament diplomacy.

Thus simply stated, both tensions may sound dry and technical. In reality, however, they have provoked a great deal of angry rhetoric and a certain amount of genuine resentment.

Nuclear or non-nuclear disarmament? The first tension dominated the negotiation of the Final Document[5] at the Special Session which the UN General Assembly devoted to disarmament in 1978, and seems likely to dominate the Special Session in 1982 as well. It has slowed down progress in the UN Disarmament Commission (New York) and the Committee on Disarmament (Geneva) on drafting a Comprehensive Programme of Disarmament (CPD) for adoption in 1982. Neither the Final Document of the 1978 Special Session, nor the Draft Elements of a CPD subsequently produced by the Commission, has found a formula which does more than paper over a broad gulf of principle. That task has been entrusted, since March 1980, to one of the four *Ad Hoc* Working Groups of the Committee on Disarmament, under the chairmanship first of Ambassador Olu Adeniji of Nigeria and in 1981 of Ambassador Alfonso García Robles of Mexico. Plenty of ideas have been fed into the CPD Working Group by governments and also from non-governmental sources such as the World Disarmament Campaign. Some of these ideas were brought together in a UK working paper on 25 February 1981 which was one of the precursors leading to the Joint Draft CPD of 31 July 1981.[6] This rather persuasive text stands in the names of Australia, Belgium, Federal Germany, Japan and the United Kingdom. Compared, however, with its three counterpart groups on chemical weapons, radiological weapons and (even) negative security assurances to non-nuclear-weapon states, the CPD Working Group has had to wrestle with a singularly abstract subject, and the nature of its agenda does not make for easy or rapid progress.

The trouble is that the absolute priority of nuclear disarmament over all other categories is as unacceptable to some nuclear-weapon states as it is self-evidently imperative to most non-nuclear-weapon states. Those nuclear-weapon states and their allies which fear their relative inferiority in conventional weapons insist that geographical and military asymmetries in the real world require the nuclear element in their force postures to be evaluated in the context of the whole, not subject to removal irrespective of the effect upon their overall military capabilities. Other states ridicule these fears. Nuclear weapons, they retort, are the peak of the arms race and so must take first place in any disarmament strategy. Their disregard for the sensitivities of nuclear-weapon states leads in turn to the accusation that it is all very well for *them* since *they* have nothing in the nuclear line to give up.

Arguments of this kind rapidly degenerate into sterile polemic, and confine states in a characteristic form of diplomatic deadlock which might be called the *politics of excuse*: '*We* can't give up our nuclear weapons until there is agreement on non-nuclear reductions.' 'But *we* can't start disarming until nuclear weapons disappear.' And so on *ad infinitum*.

It is an all too familiar pattern in the discourse of disarmament. We all know that between the Wars each major state (to put it simply) tended to urge priority for the banning of submarines, or aircraft, or whatever it perceived as offering the greatest threat to its own country's security. Because these perceptions contradicted or ran athwart one another, with one country's specific vulnerability another's gleam in the eye, so to speak, the *phasing* of disarmament resisted agreement. In 1929 Professor Salvador de Madariaga, fresh from heading the Disarmament Section in the League of Nations Secretariat, wrote one of the best studies ever made of the subject. When he first took office, he recalled,

The Council had addressed a circular to all the Members, requesting them to set down the reasons — political, geographical and others — which made it necessary for them to maintain the armed forces at the figure stated in the League statistics. The answers were couched in all styles, forms, lengths and languages. Yet the gist of them all could be interpreted in one and the same sentence — 'I am anxious to disarm, but my armaments are already as small as I can safely afford. I am a peaceful nation, but I am surrounded by bellicose countries.' Thus every nation in its own eyes was a lamb, and every other nation a wolf.[7]

Madariaga's image of this pathetic recital as a procession of *soi-disant* lambs, in terror of the predatory wolves all round them, is vivid (if unoriginal) and it does well to remind us of the Hobbesian state of the nature — the war of all against all an ever-present threat — which provided the 'hidden curriculum' of every high-minded conference then as now.

The 'politics of excuse' had begun; the verb *to disarm* was already defective, with no first person and, in its active voice anyway, only a future conditional tense.

Staying with the zoological imagery, it is hard to improve on that fable of the animals' disarmament conference, so often and so ruefully quoted down the years. In one of its more pointedly political versions, it runs thus[8]:

The eagle, looking at the bull, suggests that all horns be razed. The bull, looking at the tiger, says that all claws should be cut short. The tiger, looking at the elephant, is of the opinion that tusks should be either pulled out or shortened. The elephant, looking at the eagle, thinks that all wings should be clipped. Whereupon the bear, with a circular glance at all his brethren, says in a tone of sweet reasonableness 'Comrades, why all these halfway measures? Let us abolish everything — everything but a fraternal, all-embracing hug'.

Which *do* you choose to ban first? The fifth of the McCloy-Zorin Principles,[9] adopted in 1961 and largely reaffirmed by the 1978 Special Session,[10] sounds good, certainly; but it offers only a yard-stick, not a solution: 'All measures of general and complete disarmament should be balanced so that at no stage of the implementation of the treaty could any state or group of states gain military advantage and that security is ensured equally for all.' Wings or claws? Nuclear or conventional weapons? If a compromise over the shape of the CPD now under negotiation is to be found in time for the UN Special Session of 1982 it will have to take into account the asymmetries in security perceptions, not just between states with nuclear weapons and states without, but also between specific pairs of nuclear-weapon states.[11] Those, like the World Disarmament Campaign, who accord a central place in their hopes to the adoption of a CPD in 1982 must accept that such a compromise will not easily be found; unless, that is, all the nuclear-weapon states are somehow, improbably, moved to undergo a simultaneous change of heart and drop their objections to the notion of absolute priority for nuclear disarmament, rendering a compromise unnecessary.

More likely, I fear, is a repetition of the barren confrontation of 1978, taking us no further forward. I wish I knew how we could help the governments which will be taking part to get round this deadlock. At least we can encourage them to lend a more sympathetic ear to one another's security fears and waste less breath on the pointless rhetoric of accusation and deprecation. They should heed the plea attributed to U Thant to spend less time questioning the good faith of others in regard to disarmament and think rather how they might demonstrate their own.

Bilateral or multilateral negotiations? The second tension concerns the structure of disarmament diplomacy. Is nuclear disarmament properly the concern of nuclear-weapon states only or of the world as a whole? To put it in concrete terms, should the forum for negotiation be bilateral (the USA and the USSR), or limited at most to the other nuclear-weapon states; or should it be multilateral, bringing in the other 35 members of the Committee on Disarmament, or even the other 150 members of the United Nations?

Just as the first of our two tensions is illustrated, at the extreme, in the refusal of President Pompidou to let France have anything to do with the 1971 Sea Bed Treaty, because being limited to nuclear weapons and other weapons of mass destruction it discriminated unfairly (in French eyes) against nuclear-weapon states,[12] so his illustrious predecessor provides an extreme example of the anti-multilateral side of this second tension. One of President de Gaulle's objections in 1962 to the newly-formed Eighteen-Nation Disarmament Committee, which France was to boycott until the *politique de la chaise vide* was finally ended in 1978, was that negotiations over nuclear weapons would henceforth be dominated by states which did not know what they were talking about and which, in his memorable phrase, would have nothing to do but groan like the chorus of elders in a Greek tragedy.[13] (In June 1971, as one might have expected, it was President Pompidou who responded most favourably to President Brezhnev's unsuccessful proposal that the five nuclear-weapon states should start their own talks.[14])

On the other side of the fence we find resentment and suspicion on the part of those who feel excluded. From 1972 to 1976 these emotions found their annual focus in resolutions of the UN General Assembly critical of the way in which the superpowers were conducting their bilateral Strategic Arms Limitation Talks and urging them to take more account of Assembly exhortations to move more purposefully in the direction of disarmament. The USA regularly joined the USSR and its allies in voting against these resolutions, while the member-states of NATO were divided between support for the resolution and (for those more sympathetic to their American ally) abstention.[15] This voting pattern made it tempting to regard attitudes to SALT as a test of states' commitment to the norms of sovereign equality and 'democratic international relations' as against the competing principle of order controlled by great-power accommodation and spheres of influence; but, be that as it may, it undoubtedly measured levels of tolerance to the exclusivity of bilateral negotiation on nuclear weapons. Those whose tolerance of it was low used the classic argument that since nuclear weapons threaten all they are inescapably the legitimate concern of all.

Then, following the election of President Carter in the USA the abrasive tone of UN resolutions on SALT softened[16] and the focus of multilateralist impatience shifted to the trilateral negotiations for a comprehensive test ban (CTB) treaty which opened in Geneva in 1977. Had these reached a successful conclusion as quickly as President Carter apparently thought they would, their private character might have been more readily excused. But as they dragged on year after year, with (until 1980) only the most cursory of agreed reports furnished to the multilateral negotiating body, impatience there and at New York grew apace. The Committee on Disarmament's predecessors, after all, had had CTB as a principal item on their agenda for the best part of two decades; draft treaties had been worked out by one of their most active member-states, Sweden; and three of their non-nuclear-weapon members — Canada, Japan and Sweden — had largely pioneered a global system of seismic information-sharing which was still being refined into an International Exchange of Seismic Data by Dr Ulf Ericsson and his Group of Scientific Experts, inherited from the CCD in 1979.[17] By what prescriptive right could three of its nuclear-weapon members sweep the whole item off the Committee's agenda? The three would insist that they had done nothing of the kind; that they 'recognised the strong and legitimate interest of the Committee on Disarmament in their activities' and 'welcomed [its] continued support and encouragement'[18]; that they were only drafting a CTB with 'additional measures' and 'supplemental data'[19] to assure their own mutual security over and above whatever general scheme of verification the eventual treaty would apply to all states parties.

This defence has been received with some, understandable, scepticism. It has not prevented many CD members from seeking the establishment of an *Ad Hoc* Working Group on CTB, a demand supported by the Soviet Union but until now opposed by the American and British governments. We shall return to this question in a moment.

The tension between multilateralists and bilateralists has been particularly evident in the USA, partly because of the uniquely open processes of government with which it is favoured (or some would say hampered) and partly because of visible pressure from some of its allies, such as Australia, Canada, Italy and the Netherlands, to become better disposed towards multilateral negotiations. I have described elsewhere[20] how this pressure built up over the period 1976–80 in respect of the new bilateral talks on chemical weapons, and the problem of 'parallelism' with the multilateral discussion of that subject, which had been pursued continuously since 1968 in the Geneva negotiating body. I am less familiar with the nuclear domain than with the realm of biological and chemical disarmament, but from what I have seen of it the pressures are similar. Here too the problem of 'parallelism' hinges on superpower readiness to accommodate multilateral discussions (within narrowly defined limits; witness the restricted mandate[21] granted in 1980 to the *Ad Hoc* Working Group on Chemical Weapons) instead of seeing them as an intrusion or a threat to their own tête-à-tête conversations. A small gesture in this direction was made by the USA at the Spring 1981 session of the Committee on Disarmament[22], and it is profoundly to be hoped that when it eventually completes its protracted review of American policies across the board not only will the Reagan Administration have discovered that there are indeed worthy objects of treaty negotiation in this area but also will it prove readier to concede a legitimate multilateral interest in disarmament affairs than did the Carter Administration of 1977–81.

Lest it be thought that only the United States needs to reconsider its role in perpetuating the damaging tension between bilateral and multilateral modes of negotiation, it should be emphasised that when Washington *has* shown some welcome readiness to accommodate multilateralist concerns it has sometimes had to drag a reluctant Moscow along behind. It is, I think, generally admitted that the reform of the Geneva negotiating body in 1978 was delayed by Soviet reluctance to relinquish institutionalised bilateral control of the CCD, in the shape of the anachronistic and unpopular Co-Chairmanship, for some time after the USA had conceded its demise; and that the American delegation at Geneva had to persuade its Soviet counterpart first to make a detailed report on the status of their chemical weapons 'bilaterals', in July 1979, and then to allow the Committee on Disarmament its *Ad Hoc* Working Group eight months later. For a government which makes so much of its supposed anti-imperialism, the Soviet Union's behaviour in the multilateral settings of disarmament diplomacy is sometimes so high-handed and contemptuous of smaller states that – leaving aside the favourite Chinese charge of 'hegemonism' – the adjectives which come to mind as the most apt are Professor Neild's: 'an old-fashioned imperial power'. (I hope he is correct when he goes on: '. . . on the defensive in Europe'.)[23]

There are several things that the superpowers, severally or together, could do to alleviate this tension, by paying more than lip-service to the legitimate interest of other states. For a start, both could win goodwill, and at the same time lay the foundations of a global verification system which would serve their long-term interests as much as anyone's, by embracing the French proposal of 1978 for an International Satellite Monitoring Agency.

This imaginative plan for a whole technology of intelligence-gathering to be placed at the service of all – in the interests of disarmament – rather than remaining the prerogative of a few, gets to the heart of the matter. It was arguably the most far-reaching of all the disarmament proposals which President Giscard d'Estaing took with him to the Special Session. It has since been followed up by a Group of Experts appointed by the UN Secretary-General. We should not fall into the temptation of seeing satellite photo-reconnaissance as a solution to all the problems of ascertaining states' compliance with their obligations under a disarmament régime.[24] Neither should we under-estimate the likely difficulties of negotiating the controlling mechanisms of the putative Agency (e.g. who is to decide what data are to be disseminated and with what degree of interpretation added), its relationship to the United Nations, and appropriate dispute-handling procedures. All these issues present problems comparable with those which UNCLOS III has faced in the course of setting up an International Seabed Authority.

The fact remains that the principle underlying the French proposal deserves emphatic support from the superpowers. Even a mere declaration of intent at this stage would be a start. The negotiations that would follow would certainly test the ingenuity and perseverance of the diplomatic community to the limit: nothing wrong with that. Having listened to Ambassador Jean de la Gorce, the leader of the French delegation to the Committee on Disarmament, expounding the merits of the idea at Geneva, and now that it has been under consideration for three years, I am convinced that the crucial issue remains the far-sightedness of the USA and USSR. Without their participation, the International Satellite Monitoring Agency would stand little chance of success. They should accordingly be given every encouragement to take the long view. Endorsing the French proposal is in their interest, as well as the general international interest, and it would be no bad thing if their friends were to tell them so, courteously but firmly.

There are three other things, less far-reaching but still of some utility, which particular superpowers could do to help improve the situation.

First, the USA (as I have already hinted) should agree to the Committee on Disarmament setting up an *Ad Hoc* Working Group on CTB. A test ban, however comprehensive, is not disarmament; but it has acquired great symbolic value over twenty-three years at Geneva, and as the current focus of bilateral/multilateral tension it is where an accommodation is most urgently needed to improve the diplomatic climate and hence indirectly the prospects for the negotiated abolition of nuclear weapons. To continue to withhold the Working Group from the CD is less defensible than ever in 1981, with the trilateral CTB negotiating teams disbanded while Washington ponders their future. There are now no private negotiations any longer at risk of being jeopardised by whatever may be said in a multilateral setting by the other 37 delegations, even if there was such a risk before.

Even at the level of public relations, the USA and its allies ought to be able to seize a certain advantage by putting the Soviet Union's probably opportunistic support for the Working Group's creation to the test and seeing how it performs. The Soviet Union can hardly have made itself popular with most non-nuclear-weapon states by arguing the American and British governments (to their shame) down to an initial duration for the CTB treaty of only three years, or by its record of having conducted more nuclear test explosions in 1979 than the three Western powers put together.[25] For such resolute crusaders against the Soviet Union as President Reagan and Mrs Thatcher, the tally of lost opportunities to score off Soviet short-comings in the field of arms control and disarmament is growing surprisingly long. May it be that a more robust and decisive approach to diplomacy in this field depends upon the realisation, in Washington as well as London, that to engage in purposeful negotiations is not a favour to be conferred on repentant Russians as a reward for good behaviour but, rather, a means of pursuing an interest which is every bit as solid whether Soviet intentions are regarded as benign or quite the contrary?

Secondly, the USSR should make a gesture to indicate that as regards willingness to accept a genuine mixture of national *and international* means of verification it is not quite the hopeless case, to be given up for lost, which it might appear. If we take a sufficiently long historical perspective we can see that this bleak rejection of international verification has been relieved from time to time by Soviet offers to consider some degree of international accountability. The Russian tradition of official secrecy has combined with Marxist–Leninist doctrines of state responsibility to produce a suspicion of snooping foreigners ('inspection as legalised espionage') which makes Soviet attitudes to verification seem most of the time insuperably remote from those current in the rest of the world; yet, even so, there have on occasion been signs of an apparent willingness to entertain notions of international supervision of disarmament — even in the shape of inspection. Such glimmers of hope should not be dismissed as glibly as is sometimes the case in Western diplomatic circles.

The fact remains, however, that in recent years the only concessions the Soviet Union has seen fit to make from its stereotypically hard line on verification have been concessions offered exclusively to the USA, as in the Peaceful Nuclear Explosions Treaty of 1976, a supplement to the Threshold Test Ban Treaty of 1974 which has never entered into force. This bilateralism may be better than nothing, but if we are to get any further with disarmament proper the Soviet Union will have to accept, sooner or later, the multilateral dimension of verification.

Most states will not be content to rely solely on the superpowers to police each other in a cosy bilateral arrangement, a kind of indefinite prolongation of the SALT I régime set up in 1972. Nor is it reasonable that they should be expected to rest content with procedures suited to bilateralism. Multilateral treaty régimes demand a multilateral dimension to their provisions for verification. On the whole the United States has shown itself a little readier to appreciate this uncomfortable fact than has the Soviet Union — which is not to say that American attitudes are, by and large, anything like as enlightened as one could wish in respect of this very important aspect of disarmament.

If it cannot bring itself to embrace the French proposal for internationalising the technology of satellite photo-reconnaissance, there are several, less demanding gestures the Soviet Union could make for a start. It could, for instance, accept International Atomic Energy Agency safeguards on its civil nuclear facilities comparable with those accepted by non-nuclear-weapon states under the Non-Proliferation Treaty and the Treaty of Tlatelolco. This is what the other two nuclear-weapon state sponsors of the Non-Proliferation Treaty offered as long ago as December 1967, as a solid indication of their willingness to move nearer to 'an acceptable balance of mutual responsibilities and obligations'[26] (the UN criterion of 1965) in the treaty then under negotiation. The USSR belatedly joined its fellow nuclear-weapon states in recognising the denuclearised status of Latin America, through the Second Protocol to the Treaty of Tlatelolco, just in time for the 1978 Special Session; why not now this further step?

Without some evidence of Soviet willingness to accept a truly international (and not just an American) element in the verification process, prospects for nuclear disarmament — as, more immediately, for chemical disarmament — are unlikely to brighten.

Thirdly, the USA and USSR should bring to a speedy conclusion their unprofitable deadlock over CD/4. This is the document tabled by the Soviet Union and its six closest allies (Bulgaria, Czechoslovakia, German Democratic Republic, Hungary, Mongolia and Poland) in the Committee on Disarmament on 1 February 1979, right at the start of its first session. It was entitled 'Negotiations on ending the production of all types of nuclear weapons and gradually reducing their stockpiles until they have been completely destroyed'; which explains why it is more commonly referred to as CD/4. Its content is brief, vague and innocuous: without detriment to any other negotiations (including SALT) there should be multilateral negotiations on all the different aspects of nuclear disarmament, taking these aspects in whatever order may be agreed on, and 'for the purpose of preparing the negotiations, consultations should be held in the framework of the Committee on Disarmament.' The Committee may or may not be the forum chosen for the eventual negotiations themselves.

Since 1980 the USA and *its* allies have been on the defensive, resisting pressure for an *Ad Hoc* Working Group with its mandate drawn from CD/4. They have got themselves into a singularly unrewarding position. While they may well be right in seeing CD/4 as yet another in the long line of essentially vacuous 'peace initiatives' launched from Moscow, they have made uncommonly heavy weather of dealing with this one. They have neither called the Soviet Union's bluff by going into the consultations proposed, in a mode which would find favour with the neutral and non-alligned majority on the Committee, and demonstrating the hollowness (or otherwise) of Soviet professions of interest in serious measures for nuclear disarmament, nor countered CD/4 with a more immediately practical alternative, as was done with unacceptable Soviet resolutions on military budget reductions and on new weapons of mass destruction at the UN in the mid-1970s.

The West has little to lose now by conceding, as gracefully as the lapse of time will allow, the case for the Committee on

Disarmament to move beyond the informal conversations of its most recent (1981) session and consider nuclear disarmament in an *Ad Hoc* Working Group devoted to that subject. But if CD/4 is too much for the West to swallow, having been blown up to symbolic proportions it never deserved, then let the West propose an alternative mandate; one which embodies a reminder of the need for progress in the non-nuclear realm as well, if the fear of nuclear disarmament being accorded absolute priority is a point of special difficulty for the American, British and French governments; one, moreover, which opposes specifics to the unacceptably vague 'broadbrush' treatment we have come to expect from the Russian tradition of disarmament proposals.

So long as nothing is done, CD/4 will remain on the table, the Soviet Union will be left unhindered to pose as the solitary champion of nuclear disarmament among the nuclear-weapon states, and the West will get the blame for preventing the Committee from using the mode of discussion which most of its members prefer to consider, multilaterally, one of the most weighty of all current issues.

There, then, are four suggestions for alleviation of the multilateral/bilateral tension from the side of the nuclear-weapon states. But it would be unreasonable to expect all the ameliorative efforts that are desirable to come from them.

Non-nuclear-weapon states, for their part, have got to accept that bilateral negotiations have their own legitimate place in the overall search for nuclear disarmament. Just now (September 1981) that means exerting every effort to encourage the USA and USSR to bring under control the build-up of their Euro-strategic missiles, or long-range theatre nuclear forces (TNF): whatever we may call them, their build-up is already causing justifiable alarm in many countries and threatens to enter a new dimension in 1983 if it is not restrained first. This paper will not go into the subject of TNF, because that would take us off disarmament proper into arms control (which is a different subject) and in any case that particular sequence of politico-military negotiation or quasi-diplomacy is sufficiently topical to be overtaken rapidly by events. But it seems pretty clear at the time of writing that if the USA and USSR get nowhere in their TNF negotiations — for which preliminary talks were held in Geneva in October and November 1980 and which are currently expected to open in negotiating mode in late 1981 — then they will be in no mood to make progress on the substance of nuclear disarmament proper. So it goes without saying that a high priority for all concerned with nuclear disarmament must be to see that the TNF negotiations do, in fact, get going without further delay and continue as intensively as necessary until they succeed in producing an acceptable measure of reciprocal restraint.

Professional optimism

Our Section President, Frank Barnaby, in his latest book has proposed an additional explanation of the difficulties encountered in the diplomatic pursuit of disarmament. Discussion of the point raised by Dr Barnaby takes us beyond the purely nuclear realm into the issue of disarmament negotiation as such, which is no bad thing, for nuclear disarmament cannot sensibly be considered in isolation beyond a certain point, and that point is reached sooner rather than later.

He suggests that there is an element of self-deception in measurements of achievement taken from within the 'business'. Objectively, he says, this achievement is minimal —

> But perhaps not surprisingly [the political leaders], and those involved in negotiating arms control treaties, take on a 'professional optimism' which apparently causes them to convince themselves that substantial progress is being made. This may be a psychological necessity for those involved but it also hampers progress towards disarmament.[27]

Dr Barnaby is kinder to the negotiators than were two earlier critics, also British, who saw in this 'professional optimism' not so much psychological necessity as deliberate oversell. Dr David Owen in 1972 accused unnamed politicians of misleading the public into believing that something was really being done about disarmament when what was actually taking place (he had in mind the Sea Bed Treaty) was only 'cosmetic'.[28] Mrs Elizabeth Young in the same year had written of superpower collusion in 'presenting to the world a series of insignificant treaties at very considerable expense of international time and trouble and breath'.[29] I have discussed these and similar accusations in *Approaches to Disarmament*, where among other things I raised the possibility that the public might not be as credulous as is sometimes supposed: 'Politicians, after all, like teachers, have a professional interest in believing that their words are heeded by those to whom they are addressed.'[30]

The 'professional interest' of politicians brings us back to the 'professional optimism' attributed to some of those involved in negotiating arms control treaties. It can certainly not be attributed to all. Those veteran leaders of the neutral and non-aligned states at Geneva since 1962, Alfonso García Robles of Mexico and Alva Myrdal and Inga Thorsson of Sweden, could never be accused of fostering delusions of progress; *tout au contraire*, all three have acquired a formidable reputation for delivering swingeing attacks on those (principally the USA and USSR) whom they hold responsible for the relative lack of success in the negotiations of the Eighteen-Nation Disarmament Committee from 1962 to 1969, the Conference of the Committee of Disarmament from 1969 to 1978, and the present Committee since 1979.[31] Their more transient colleagues in the broadly non-aligned Group of 21 and its predecessors (originally the Group numbered only 8, then 12, then 15) have uttered similar if less authoritative sentiments of impatience and frustration. Indeed, a reading of the Committee on Disarmament's proceedings for its first year alone yields a vivid contrast in the end-of-session assessments offered by, at one extreme, the Group of 21,[32] and, at the other, the Group of Socialist States (these latter verging on complacency)[33] as well as by individual ambassadors. I recommend in this connection the contrast — almost a verbal duel — between Ambassadors Benjamin Fonseka of Sri Lanka and Viktor Issraelyan of the Soviet Union.[34]

But how far does this difference in tone correspond to genuine differences in assessment of progress, and how far merely to the variety inherent in rhetorical styles of diplomacy? How can we know?

One element in the 'professional optimism' of disarmament negotiators, where it does exist, may be the sheer difficulty of seeing the wood for the trees, of preserving a broad perspective in the immediate context where much negotiation concerns narrow points, often of language or procedure, and even the smallest decision can take an unconscionable time in the making. It is, then, hardly surprising if an agreement which seems to the outsider not worth writing home about assumes a greater significance to the negotiators responsible for producing it. The diplomatic context of Geneva is almost bound to encourage short-term perceptions of success and failure. This does not, of course, excuse deliberate attempts to paint the scene rosier than it is, but it may explain some of the 'professional optimism' to which Dr Barnaby rightly draws attention as a phenomenon in the diplomacy of disarmament as it unwinds its tortuous course.

Priorities and prospects

It is a slow, thankless, painfully laborious business, the diplomacy of nuclear disarmament. Considering the magnitude of the transformation which it is designed to achieve, could we expect it to be otherwise? I think not. It behoves us to extend to those who carry heavy responsibilities in the conduct of this diplomacy our understanding, our encouragement and — when we can, for criticism may sometimes have to be the order of the day — our gratitude, for the noble enterprise in which they are engaged ultimately serves the interests of us all.

But, it may be objected, this noble enterprise (as I have called it) is not so regarded by those who actually make and implement policy. To them it is simply one posting among many, over the course of a diplomatic or political career, in which a certain conception of the national interest has to be upheld with as little disturbance to established positions as can be managed. So they should not be credited with a spurious idealism.

I accept that this is true of some: I cannot accept that it is true of all. For what it may be worth, my limited experience of disarmament diplomacy has made me aware of gradations of commitment from the very high to the virtually non-existent (and these have nothing to do with nationality) along with wide variations in ability. Both types of variation mirror those to be found among the population at large. Diplomats and politicians are human: they have admittedly to fill roles which constrain them in their official functions, but personal factors (thank goodness) still obtrude so that role-expectations are by no means the whole story.

I do not ask you to believe that every member of every delegation at Geneva and every instructing department in national capitals is a saint. I do ask that they should not be written off *en masse* as cynics or ciphers. Most, I suggest, want to do a decent job, and not a few want to do more than that if they can.

So I do not find it strange that the diplomacy of disarmament should embrace among its practitioners (first as a diplomat, then as a politician and Cabinet Minister) someone of the calibre of Alva Myrdal. Madame Myrdal came upon disarmament relatively late in an already distinguished career and found, in her own words, that 'Once I had begun, I was never able to stop the search for the why's and how's of something so senseless as the arms race.'[35] Twenty years on, many beneficiaries of her new-found enthusiasm for this cause have reason to be thankful that she has, indeed, never stopped the search. She has done more than most in that time to strengthen the disarmament enterprise as 'a strategy of truth . . . facing the arms race as the major intellectual and moral dilemma of our time.'[36]

Even those practitioners of disarmament diplomacy who cannot conceive of their work in such elevated terms as that may nevertheless serve a useful purpose by their tenacity in holding on to a conviction which is frequently under attack. This is the conviction that disarmament can be worthy of effort, something to be taken seriously, even under conditions of imperfect security; that it is a mistake — perhaps a fatal mistake — to suppose that nothing can be done about it until everything else which is wrong with international society has been put right.

Back in 1929 Madariaga was having to affirm this conviction

against powerful voices urging that disarmament must wait upon the 'organisation of peace'. Now Madariaga was no simplistic thinker of the 'Arms cause wars' variety: he was in fact a strong advocate of the 'organisation of peace' (a French phrase which he liked) and appreciated as much as any self-styled realist the obstacles with which the precarious structure of international security and the deficiencies of international institutions hampered progress towards disarming the world. The point he was making was that the world should not wait until all the other laudable processes of international relations (subsumed under the 'organisation of peace') had run their course before starting out on the road to disarmament.[37]

This point of Madariaga's was echoed by another veteran of Geneva's disarmament diplomacy, somewhat later. Sir Michael Wright, whose personal commitment shines through another classic work in this literature, *Disarm and Verify*,[38] put it most succinctly when he wrote, in 1965: 'Disarmament and the solution of political problems can and should go hand in hand. Each can contribute to the other; but if either is made to wait on the other, we may have to wait a long time and end by getting neither.'[39] Sir Michael Wright was one of several British diplomats whose practical and sustained (if typically understated) work for disarmament has encouraged me considerably in my own and deserves to be more warmly appreciated among supporters of disarmament in their own country.

The characteristically wise advice of Sir Michael Wright which I have just quoted, issued shortly after his retirement from HM Foreign Service and in the first of his seven years as chairman of the United Nations Association's Disarmament Committee (on which Dr Barnaby and I had the honour to serve under him), remains as pertinent to the international climate of today as to that of 1965. In one sense it is even more pertinent today, because the conviction out of which it springs is under such fierce attack.

Crude notions of reward and punishment, seldom appropriate to the practice of international relations even if they retain any place in the upbringing of children, have swept back into fashion. The fundamental community of interest in negotiating a safer world is, in some influential quarters, all but denied. Instead, negotiations tend to be treated as a potential reward, to be conferred on evidence of good behaviour or withheld on suspicion of less than benign intent. No matter that a state may have just as good reasons to seek reciprocal disarmament with another state which it fears as with one it considers benign. A notion of 'linkage', which sounds sophisticated and in tune with the inter-dependent complexities of modern life but in practice allows a multitude of misapprehensions to persist under its reassuring cover, pushes such logical truths of inter-national relations right off the agenda.

Once this dangerously simplistic perspective takes hold, and the reward-and-punishment syndrome gets a grip on the policy process, it is all too easy — as we have been seeing of late — for disarmament to find itself, as a policy option, relegated to the very margins of credibility.

When it is fashionable to be a hawk, even the case for 'respectable', moderate *arms control* has to struggle for a fair hearing — let alone *disarmament*. Logic counts for less than toughness, or what passes for toughness. A robust stance is everything: moderation is suspect. (Conversely, one could wish for greater tolerance and reasonableness among the remaining advocates of disarmament, who some-times manifest an arrogant extremism detrimental to their cause.) Can we honestly expect much more from the UN Special Session in 1982 than sheer tenacity, in refusing to withdraw from the positions established in the Final Docu-ment of 1978 despite all that has happened since then?

In these circumstances, merely to reaffirm the conviction that disarmament is still worth pursuing, merely to hold the line against all the pressures for retreat, is in itself going to be something of a diplomatic achievement.

References

1. *Approaches to Disarmament* (London: QPS, 1979) pp. 127–30.
2. François de Callières' treatise *On the Manner of Negotiating with Princes* was first published in 1716; Harold Nicolson, *Diplomacy* (London: OUP, 1939, 1950, 1963, 1969) and *The Evolution of Diplomatic Method* (London: Constable, 1954).

3. Two leading analyses, by the Professors of International Relations at Oxford and Keele respectively, are Hedley Bull, 'Diplomacy and International Order' in his book *The Anarchical Society: A Study of Order in World Politics* (London: Macmillan, 1977) pp. 162–83, and Alan James, 'Diplomacy and International Society', *International Relations* 6, 6 (November 1980) pp. 931–48.

4. The second and third of these lines of attack on the diplomatic handling of disarmament may be seen combined in an eloquent polemic by Mortimer Lipsky, *A Time for Hysteria: The Citizen's Guide to Disarmament* (South Brunswick & New York: A S Barnes; London: Thomas Yoseloff, 1969).

5. The full text of the Final Document has been published by the UN and HMSO, and is reproduced in *Approaches to Disarmament* (see reference 1; 1979 edition) pp. 155–74.

6. The UK working paper is Committee on Disarmament (Geneva) document CD/CPD/WP.19. The Foreign and Commonwealth Office has published the text in its newsletter *Arms Control and Disarmament: Developments in the International Negotiations* No 8 (May 1981) pp. 6–7. The Joint Draft CPD is document CD/205 (CD/CPD/WP.52).

7. Salvador de Madariaga, *Disarmament* (Oxford: OUP, 1929) p. 46.

8. John W. Spanier, *World Politics in an Age of Revolution* (New York: Praeger, 1967) p. 121.

9. The Joint Statement of Agreed Principles for Disarmament Negotiations, published as UN document A/4879 on 20 September 1961, was drawn up by John J. McCloy for the USA and Valerian A. Zorin for the USSR over a series of meetings between June and September 1961 and led to the resumption of negotiations at Geneva six months later in the Eighteen-Nation Disarmament Committee. The McCloy-Zorin Principles have been reproduced in many publications, including *The United Nations and Disarmament 1945-1970* (New York: UN, 1970) pp. 87–8.

10. See paragraph 29 of the Final Document.

11. One reason (*inter alia*) for welcoming the Joint Draft CPD of 31 July 1981 is that its flexibility of approach allows for these awkward facts of life, as a more tightly drawn scheme with rigid phases and target dates could not. A cumulative, but pragmatic, disarmament strategy, with the dovetailing of its sequences entrusted to successive review conferences, indicates a healthy respect for the unpredictability of international relations. It also recalls, whether intentionally or not, the origins of CPD in 1969-70 which owed much to Italian (and earlier French) conceptualisation of the disarmament process. See Nicholas A. Sims, 'General and complete disarmament: the Italian initiative of 1969-70 and

the synoptic approach to the disarmament process', *Reconciliation Quarterly*, new series, 6, 1 (March 1976) pp. 40-6.

12. UN document A/C.1/PV.1754; 9 November 1970.

13. '. . . ne peut rien faire que gémir comme le choeur des vieillards dans la tragédie antique'; press conference of 15 May 1962, quoted by Jean Klein, 'La France et le désarmement', *Projet* (Paris: 1978), p. 611. On the broad lines of French policy, and their application in practice under Presidents de Gaulle and Pompidou, Jean Klein, ' "Désarmement" ou "Arms Control": la position française sous la Ve République', *Etudies Internationales* (Québec) 1972 No 3, pp. 356-89, is particularly illuminating.

14. *World Armaments and Disarmament: SIPRI Yearbook 1972*, (Stockholm: Almqvist and Wiksell, 1972) p. 558.

15. e.g. GA Res 31/189A, adopted 107-10-11 on 21 December 1976; for summary of content see *Approaches to Disarmament* (see reference 1; 1979 edition) pp. 14-15.

16. GA Res 32/87G, adopted 134-2-0 on 12 December 1977.

17. The '*Ad Hoc* Group of Scientific Experts to consider international co-operative measures to detect and to identify seismic events', under the chairmanship of Dr Ulf Ericsson (Sweden), was originally established by a decision of the Conference of the Committee on Disarmament on 22 July 1976, a full year before even the exploratory talks leading to the trilateral CTB negotiations were to open at Geneva.

18. Joint Report to the Committee on Disarmament by the UK, USA and USSR (CD/130: 30 July 1980), paragraph 2.

19. Joint Report paragraphs 20-2.

20. 'Britain, Chemical Weapons and Disarmament', *ADIU Report* II, 3 (University of Sussex Armament and Disarmament Information Unit, July/August 1980).

21. '. . . to define, through substantive examination, issues to be dealt with in the negotiation of such a convention, taking into account all existing proposals and future initiatives' (CD/80: 17 March 1980). Ambassador Okawa of Japan was appointed chairman of the group in April 1980; in 1981 he was succeeded by Ambassador Lidgard of Sweden.

22. I refer to the introduction of informal meetings to consider the modalities of how the Committee might best handle the CTB item; this has been seen as a halfway step towards allowing a Working Group to be set up by the Committee.

23. Robert Neild, *How to make up your mind about the Bomb* (London: André Deutsch, 1981) p. 14.

24. *Approaches to Disarmament* (see reference 1; 1979 edition) p. 39, p. 42.

25. USSR 28, USA 15, France 9, UK 1. The same is true for 1978 (USSR 27, USA 12, France 7, UK 2) but probably not for 1980: SIPRI's *preliminary* data for that year show USSR 20, USA 14, France 11, UK 4. The USA still leads the nuclear testing league taken from 1945 (and, for that matter, taken from 1963). See *World Armaments and Disarmament: SIPRI Yearbook 1981* (London, Taylor & Francis, 1981) p. 381.

26. GA Res 2028 (XX), paragraph 2b: 23 November 1965. This formula reappears as paragraph 30 of the Final Document adopted by the 1978 UN Special Session, which says that the balance in question 'should be strictly observed'.

27. Frank Barnaby, *Prospects for Peace* (Oxford: Pergamon Press, 1980) p. 82.

28. David Owen, *The Politics of Defence* (London: Jonathan Cape, 1972) p. 10.

29. Elizabeth Young, *A Farewell to Arms Control?* (Harmondsworth: Penguin, 1972) p. 135.

30. *Approaches to Disarmament* (see reference 1; 1979 edition) pp. 75–6.

31. The *locus classicus* of this line of criticism is the well-known book of Alva Myrdal. *The Game of Disarmament* (New York: Citadel, 1976; Manchester: Manchester UP, 1977; Nottingham: Spokesman (first British paperback edition), 1980) but many other examples may be found in the speeches of all three, embodied in the verbatim records of the Geneva negotiating body and the First Committee of the UN General Assembly.

32. Committee on Disarmament document CD/50: 9 August 1979.

33. Committee on Disarmament document CD/51: 10 August 1979.

34. Committee on Disarmament document CD/PV.49: 9 August 1979.

35. Alva Myrdal, 'A Personal Note', in *The Game of Disarmament* (Manchester: Manchester UP, 1977) p. xxiii.

36. *The Game of Disarmament*, see reference 35, p. 334.

37. Salvador de Madariaga, *Disarmament* (Oxford: OUP, 1929) p. 200.

38. London: Chatto & Windus, 1964.

39. Sir Michael Wright, 'The View of a British Diplomat', in *The Road to Peace*, edited by Kenneth Johnstone (London: SCM Press, for the Conference on Christian Approaches to Defence and Disarmament, 1965) p. 46.

Acknowledgements

I am grateful to Elizabeth Leslie for typing the first draft of this paper and to Roy Dean and Trevor Jepson for helpful comments on it.

11. AVERTING HOLOCAUST? STRATEGIES OF POPULAR INTERVENTION AND INITIATIVE IN THE THERMONUCLEAR AGE

Nigel Young

Introduction

At the outset it is worth summarising the main thrust of the argument of this chapter and indicating the principal assumptions that lie behind it. My proposition is that, as the dangers of nuclear catastrophe proliferate, the task of pre-empting such a war may have become too urgent to be left to governments and traditional international strategies and methods. Yet public opinion is an amorphous and wayward social abstraction. Only when organized for action and intervention can it have any real hope of changing the course of the arms race. Yet the multiple-stranded peace tradition which I shall try to describe has patently failed to do more than marginally affect the arms spiral — even though its impact on the issues of nuclear weapons, the B1 bomber or the Vietnam war does seem to have changed both public attitudes and state policy (possibly preventing a nuclear exchange, helping reverse US policy in Indo-China, and helping ensure an Atmospheric Test Ban).

But the *historic peace movements*, religious, pacifist, liberal, internationalist, socialist, Gandhian, and war-resistant, have been deeply divided over aims, methods, analysis, and strategy. They have occasionally united to resist specific wars (Vietnam), specific weapons (nuclear weapons) and to oppose militarist attitudes and policies.[1] But their failure to develop a new and adequate model of action relevant to a changing global society, and the intensifying threat of the breakdown of deterrence into nuclear attack, suggests that many of the efforts to mobilize opinion may be diversionary or ineffective.

Yet through the activities of human rights groups like Amnesty International, and the new European Nuclear Disarmament Campaign (END) and some of the innovative anti-war radicalism of the 1960s, as well as the anti-nuclear energy campaigns, I shall argue a *new model* may be emerging that *both* coincides with new social realities observed by a number of distinguished academic researchers, *and* draws on the best of the anti-militarist and transnationalist impulses of an earlier era. This new model is both transnational (a concept I shall briefly define) and extra-governmental: it aspires to defy ideological and military frontiers and works on a populist principle of linking peoples and communities, including occupational communities across the highly danger-ous divides of geo-political boundaries. It is ready to confront national states, even by direct action. It has an essentially secular political strategy but draws on the reservoir of re-ligious and public moral outrage at the potential use of weapons of mass destruction.

This perspective on disarmament is radically different from that advocated by Nicholas Sims in another part of this volume, in the sense that it does not reduce the dis-armament process to state actions and inter-state relations. But the dialectic between non-governmental processes and proposals and government negotiations and agreements is an open one. Non-state actions and initiatives may be parallel or complimentary to state efforts. On the other hand, they may in the longer term, represent a substitute. The world is changing too rapidly to dismiss this possibility[2] in a para-graph. On the other hand, I am not reducing the disarmament issue to popular intervention and non-governmental initiative.

Public opinion: myth and reality

As I have hinted, I was initially asked as a political sociologist to address in this chapter the issue of the role of public opinion in halting or reversing the arms race. But because of my scep-ticism of both the concept of public opinion and the abstract notion of people halting or reversing an arms race, I intend to re-define and narrow the two components. I would like to talk mainly about the history of one section of organized political opinion and behaviour, and its role in, or relationship to, possibly postponing or averting nuclear catastrophe.

To talk about permanently halting or reversing the arms race seems to me to represent an issue of fundamental social change. It would be an equally important topic but would represent a quite different and far more ambitious project.

There is a proposition in social theory — indeed it is the one that is often said to be one of the few real laws of social life — which is the theorem 'that things that are *perceived as real* are real in their social consequences'[2]. Public opinion is such a myth[3], but since it is perceived as real, political leaders, decision makers, states, social groups, even the public themselves, act as if it concretely existed, and therefore the effects are as if it *did* exist. There is not time here to explore the complex vagaries of attitudes, opinions and beliefs; their volatile, contradictory and ever-changing character; their ambiguous and perverse relationship with behaviour — and the resulting impossibility of scientific study of public opinion[4]. What is relevant is that public opinion is a manipulable variable by both states and oppositions that can be used to justify new arms spirals this month, and unilateral initiatives to disarm the next (or sometimes both at the same time).

A famous historical example of the social proposition of the 'reality' of the social myth is that of the general strike. If ten people believed that — in the classic Syndicalist example — a general strike could bring about a revolutionary crisis then it would remain an esoteric, utopian fantasy. If ten million believe it and as a result act in unison, there is a real chance of the prophecy being realized[5]. Indeed, general strikes and lesser strikes have achieved dramatic results. In the period before 1914, Socialist anti-militarists tried to link such a myth to the idea of war prevention: if the organized producers, now numbering tens of millions in Europe, could strike against war in unison across national frontiers, then the militarists and nationalists, the Generals, Tsars and capitalist-backed governments would call a war but no one would come[6].

There is not space here to analyse why the myth of the international general strike of workers of all countries against war failed to materialise, though it is an important and instructive political experience. But the fact that it failed for specific historical reasons, clearly does not necessarily mean that all such dreams of people acting globally — across nation-state boundaries — to prevent war, even nuclear war, must always remain a myth. For example, even though they have not stopped arms races, general strikes have on occasions led to significant social change[7]. If such an ideal, of trans-national, popular action of a non-governmental kind is perceived as real, if it is acted on as if it *is* possible by large enough numbers then, whilst one cannot predict with exactness the consequences (and they may not be without risk), then immense social impact is possible. The tragedy is that the nuclear arms race produces a form of sclerosis of innovative action. Governments may introduce horrendous new weapons systems, but action by peoples is usually seen to be destabilising, whereas the governments own actions are viewed as maintaining a stable arms race. Too much pressure on governments is feared as threatening chaos.

The paradox is however — and President Reagan has recently been echoing the words of President Eisenhower on the subject — that many statesmen appear to take seriously both the existence of and a role for popular views and attitudes. Eisenhower's often-quoted warning that if governments did not deliver peace then they might have to step aside and let people take it for themselves was linked to a populist perception of a deep and widespread public desire for peace. The peace rhetoric of the equally and massively militarist Soviet state also (perhaps more cynically) stresses 'the peace-loving people'; though with a memory of 20 million war dead the evidence of quite genuine Russian peace orientation at the public level seems clear — however manipulated in practice.

Here we come to the paradox of organised peace movements in relation both to states and to that apparently nebulous entity, a public opinion that — at least most of the time — apparently desires peace. In the 160 years or so of their existence, secular peace organisations and anti-militarist movements have had little obvious political impact, despite their recurrent ability to mobilize sections of opinion on particular issues at particular times.

Organised opinion for peace

For this is the subject that I wish to address: not ephemeral congeries of public attitudes, but the organised opinion leading to political action in pressure groups and mass movements; 'publics' against particular weapons, particular wars, particular policies — even against war in general — or the societies that are seen to generate war. For whilst opinion in general is notoriously difficult to measure, the actual efforts of peace organisations *can* be described and analysed. It is here that the issue of organised opinion on peace — perhaps only the top of an iceberg of unorganised opinion— and its impact on arms races and wars in the past, present and perhaps future can at least in a preliminary way be studied, estimated, and judged. The results of their activity are always ambiguous, like other great social change or social protest movements. They have both latent and manifest consequences. Their relative success or failure always depends on other independent factors, not just the degree or level of activity achieved. This has been one of the illusions of the peace movements. The structural or historical context of the abolitionist movement against slavery for example was as, or more, important than the efforts of the abolitionist campaigns themselves. Moreover the abolition of slavery left or even produced new evils.

There is little doubt that any organised movement of opinion against the arms race would need such a favourable context to succeed. Again, the study of that overall context is beyond the scope of this paper, but it has to some extent been dealt with by others. What is clear however, if one takes the impact of public opinion as organised by peace movements in America in the 1960s, is that it does and did have an effect on the course of events; the organisation of movements against nuclear weapons in the five years before the Cuban Missile Crisis created a public moral climate in which the use of nuclear weapons was less 'thinkable' than say in 1957. It has been said that Kennedy implied this was a factor restraining the actors from a nuclear exchange[8].

During the Vietnam War, in the context of a worldwide shift in public opinion, the draft resistance movement at home and the popular resistance to the war in Indo-China itself, helped change domestic opinion at home. Changes in public opinion in the US were not just due to military stalemate, which was linked to this delegitimation process in any case. The resignation of President Lyndon Johnson, the shift from the use of US groundforces, the growth of support for the political doves in 1968, the search for a peace settlement, and the preparation of the Pentagon papers and their release, can all be related to the effective — if transitory — organisation of public opinion, particularly amongst young males of draft age. They were potential recruits to the Dow Chemical Company and other key sectors of society[9]; in other words, strategic groups like scientists, public officials and others.

However in this instance as in so many instances of uni-lateral, or nationally-bounded peace action, there was a fatal ambiguity in the activity of the organised political opinion represented by the American peace movement. Much of it became in a sense 'aligned'[10]: it is arguable that by weakening the American will to fight, it probably strengthened the North Vietnamese determination to continue fighting despite the terrible losses of the Tet period. There is evidence that Hanoi believed that the anti-Vietnam war movement was even stronger than it was. Exaggerating its domestic influence, they believed it would quickly neutralise the US army and the US state, leading to a capitulationist peace settlement. This is not in any way to denigrate the whole movement against one side in a barbaric war, but to stress the limita-tions of national unilateral movements which may arguably prolong a war or an arms race — as is possible in the Viet-namese case (and some of the most appalling blood-letting in Indo-China, it must be remembered, occurred during the Paris peace talks, in the offensives of 1970 and 1972).

It was also argued, with far less evidence, that the some-what belated strength of pacifist feeling in Western Europe and in particular Britain (e.g. the Oxford Oath) encouraged the growth of German militarism and Facism in the 1930s[11].

Yet before 1932 there was also a strong German peace movement. Perhaps the failure was, as in the case of Vietnam, to create a genuinely transnational movement across borders and to intervene actively early enough. But it is not at all clear that initiating an arms race earlier would have checked Nazism.

If we translate this into our current situation, we are faced with the typical establishment charge, that unilateral initiatives will act as an invitation to the Russian war machine to move into action, to nibble away at Western freedoms, to Finlandise us or others, to retrench its hegemony throughout eastern Europe, or even at worst to use nuclear blackmail to terrorise the rest of Europe into Satellite status[12]. Whether any of these risks are as great as those of nuclear war is another issue. What is essential however — and I will return to this at the end of the paper — is that unilateral initiatives are followed up at some level by reciprocal initiatives; that the lifting of the nuclear threat in Europe, even if predominantly by one side, is followed by, for example, a breathing space for those in Poland or Russia who have felt threatened, to take the opportunity to extend their liberties and their demands[13]. Here the need for cross-frontier linkages and strategies appears most essential. Human rights, *including* the right to live without nuclear threat, have undeniably emerged as a transnational issue.

History of peace movements

At this point it is worth looking briefly back at a summary history of peace movements in terms especially of a typology of popular initiatives and proposals and their relevance to our present situation (see Figure 1). The history of anti-war sentiment or peace ideas is much older than the first secular peace groups after 1815, and was actively expressed in the war resistance of various sects and groups from the early Christian period onwards. Typically, war and military service were opposed by the poor, illiterate, and inarticulate; peasants and crafts-people, standing outside the state; persecuted religious sects and communities; emigrants and immigrants[14]. The history of elite plans and proposals for peace and disarmament also preceded the butchery of Napoleon and

1. Religious pacifism   (conscientious objection)
2. Liberal internationalism   ('pacificism')
3. Anti-conscriptionism   (civil liberties)
4. Socialist war-resistance   (anti-militarism)
5. Socialist internationalism   (the Second International)
6. Radical pacifism   (Gandhian nonviolence)
7. 'Nuclear pacifism'   (unilateral nuclear disarmament)

A new model?

Figure 1 The peace traditions: a typology

became widespread in ruling circles first in the seventeenth century during and after the carnage of the Thirty Years War[15]. They are parallelled by the focus of religious nonconformity (especially Quakerism) both on witness against war and on the possibility of a new nonviolent order of international harmony — an idea that coincided with some of the more cosmopolitan and visionary ideas of Enlightenment humanism. But after the French and American revolutions, Europe saw the spread of the new nation state, the new conscripted armies, the new industralised militarism, and imperial expansion. As the public became more involved (through conscription and civilian bombing), so did organised opinion on war grow.

The first modern peace movements of the nineteenth century are an ambiguous mixture of previous elements: sectarian religious pacifism; popular war resistance; international plans; platitudes against war; nonconformist anti-statism or civil libertarianism, and communal resistance to compulsory military service. I call these syntheses modern because they seek to organise public opinion in society either to create new institutions that have a bearing on peace (or to pressurise existing politicians and structures to change their ways or to introduce new policies or institutions) or, in the case of the new socialist peace orientation, to mobilise people to create a new warless world society, even by violently overthrowing the old order. One of the key divisions was between nonconformist, free-trade liberalism on the one hand, that saw global capitalism as creating a new warless world; and socialism on the other that saw instead the creation of the basis of a highly militarised, centralised, exploitative state system of enormous destructive capability.

Six traditions. From these tendencies one can identify six main types of peace tradition and then compare them with their twentieth-century counterparts. As has been seen, the oldest tradition was that of religious pacifism associated with absolutist war resistance and, in relation to the spread of compulsory military service, conscientious objection. The second was that of liberal internationalism, which gave the peace plans of the seventeenth and eighteenth-century statesmen a broader basis in popular opinion and political pressure. It has often been termed 'pacificism' since it aims to avert war but does not renounce its use, or participation in it (as pacifists do). It was associated with the peace conferences at the Hague, the League and the UN. The third tradition was that of anti-conscriptionism, often based on the issue of civil rights or the liberty of the individual, and thus overlapping with war resistance in conscientious objection. The fourth type was socialist war resistance that resisted militarist governments, conscription and war preparations as an integral aspect of capitalism, imperialism and class rule[16]. The fifth, which overlapped with it, was socialist internationalism, which, unlike the fourth tradition, was less rooted in the popular movements and communities and more linked to the sentiments of national leaders of socialist parties and unions; however it often supported, like socialist war resisters, ideas such as a strike against war. Unlike liberal internationalism, however, it had much less faith in agreements between governments. All these five types coexisted and overlapped at the time of the First World War, and survived it.

However this period also saw the birth of a sixth type that drew from all of them: a new, secular, radical pacifism that linked international war resistance, anti-conscriptionism and civil libertarianism with schemes of utopian social (if not always socialist) change to be brought about by the new direct-action techniques of Gandhi rather than by the violent class war endorsed by most socialist anti-militarists[17].

1. Religious pacifism	Quakers, Fellowship of Reconciliation Pax Christi (Peace Pledge Union)
2. Liberal internationalism	United Nations Association, National Peace Council, World Disarmament Campaign.
3. Anti-conscriptionism	No contemporary expression in UK but potentially Peace Pledge Union/National Council for Civil Liberties *Elsewhere*: War Resisters International/Amnesty International Single Issue lobbies: Campaign Against the Arms Trade (Campaign for Nuclear Disarmament?)
4. Socialist war-resistance	No contemporary equivalent in UK but War Resisters International elsewhere. (European Nuclear Disarmament movement?)
5. Socialist internationalism	No contemporary expression: European Nuclear Disarmament movement representing revival?
6. Radical pacifism	Peace News. War Resisters International (anti-nuclear energy movement)
7. 'Nuclear pacifism'	Campaign for Nuclear Disarmament?

Figure 2 The peace traditions and their contemporary organisational equivalents (UK 1980)

By the 1960s, when the (again belated) upsurge of public opinion against nuclear weapons had manifested itself in Europe, North America, and Japan, most of these strands of peace tradition still survived, though it has been argued that 'nuclear pacifism', e.g. the Campaign for Nuclear Disarmament (CND), even though drawing on them, represented a new type, reflecting the drastically altered character of war and weaponry.

Contemporary equivalents. Nevertheless, the six previous types each have their contemporary equivalents and organisational expression. The first (religious) type represented by the FOR, Quakers and Pax Christi overlaps with the more secular Peace Pledge Union which reflects the movement of the mass pacifism of the 1930s. The second liberal stream is represented by the World Disarmament Campaign, the United Nations Association or the National Peace Council. The third anti-militarist tendency is no longer a major focus of organisation in this country because Britain is one of only a handful of countries in the world without conscription; but single-issue campaigns like the Campaign Against the Arms Trade, the National Council for Civil Liberties, or Amnesty International represent this tradition (as also perhaps does CND). The fourth (socialist war resistance) was a tradition that tended to die with the domination of the Russian Communist parties and the rise of Fascism but may be undergoing a revival; in many countries the War Resisters International (WRI) represents a synthesis now overtly both socialist and anti-conscriptionist. The fifth tendency, socialist internationalism, tended to merge either with socialist militarism and the geopolitical interests of the Soviet bloc after 1920, or else with social democracy, and the liberal internationalism of the League. The emergence of the European Nuclear Disarmament movement (END) however has a distinctly independent and cross-national character more reminiscent of pre-1917 internationalism. Its great danger, however, is that it too will be a movement of leaders and parties rather than of community impulses. The sixth type (radical nonviolence) tended to become submerged in the counter-cultural movements of the 1960s but has retained strong links to groups such as the WRI and is expressed in a magazine like the 45-year old *Peace News* ('for nonviolent revolution'). It is also now closely identified with the environmentalist and anti-nuclear power lobby, itself globalist in orientation and with community roots[18].

To summarise: one has seen two main, somewhat contrary, tendencies in the organisation of public opinion on peace since 1918. One is towards alignment with the world system of nation states either for example by seeing peace through a Russian or American hegemony (a Pax Americana) or through a League, or a UN order, or even through a non-aligned third force.

The other has been towards increasing claims against that global state system; extension of rights, of conscience, draft resistance, civil disobedience, direct action against nuclear weapons or the Vietnam war, transnational movement and identification, the strengthening of dissident subcultures (the New Left), and the re-emergence of non-governmentalist and extraparliamentarist strategies for social change[19]. Both these tendencies have become increasingly secular and political in comparison with the peace movement of the early twentieth century.

I believe however that a significant new model of what a peace movement can be, and a new possibility of organising opinion effectively against the arms race and to prevent nuclear war, has emerged (or is emerging); though it is hardly perceived as such by the six peace traditions that I have described, nor by the nuclear pacifists of CND, nor certainly by the politicians that oppose or manipulate these orientations.

Governmental response to peace movements

Before I outline that model and strategy however, it is worth looking briefly at the reaction of governments to the potential organisation of public opinion on issues of war and peace: particularly the response of states to the peace movement in the thermonuclear age. For it is quite clear that the relationship between politicians and this movement is distinctly ambivalent. This is in spite of the lip-service paid to the popular role, and the undoubted impact of public campaigning in creating a context for the Atmospheric Test Ban Treaty of 1963 (itself involving a unilateral element) or of the 'hot line' and other precautionary measures. It is quite clear that those who now organise and claim to control the arms race are in practice, distinctly suspicious of any non-governmental role — even in relation to the UN. They fear that non-governmental initiatives could be destabilising.

Clearly, as their censorious and anxious responses suggest,

liberal establishments have felt themselves threatened by signs of mass participation in peace movements, as such relatively mild challenges as the early anti-nuclear protests illustrated. To the extent that mass intervention characterises the anti-war movement (and in the nature of its goals this is likely either to start outside the frame of institutionalised political activity, or be forced there), then it may appear to conform to a model of extremism. It was perhaps inevitable that the earlier nuclear disarmament campaigns, with their direct action at the centres of power, mobilisation of previously apolitical individuals, and what appeared to be their remote and uncompromising moral appeals directed largely outside the institutionalised order, should be analysed as mass, even extremist, movements[20].

Liberal critics and moderate opinion have particularly baulked at the use of direct action against nuclear installations. The main argument was that it entailed dangers worse than trying to deal with problems within the parliamentary system; moral or ideological solutions were, they argued, irrelevant to the complexities of contemporary situations; Cold War tensions did not permit anything but piecemeal and gradualist approaches; and the West could not afford non-nuclear status, non-alignment, or neutralism. In any case it was held that the political system itself remained open to normal political pressure[21].

In the contemporary, more conservative, model of pluralist political systems, organised interests tend to develop to the degree that they balance one another; where, however, one of the pressure groups becomes a mass movement, and no counterbalancing movement arises, confrontation with the state may ensue. This type of pattern emerged in 1960–1 in the case of the CND. Initially and potentially a pressure group willing to bargain and give its support to existing political groups, the movement developed rapidly beyond a single-issue lobby, acquiring a mass base and confronting an opposition that was based not on mass support but on bureaucratic power. This power was manifest, as far as the state was concerned in the Civil Service, the ruling government party *and* in the leadership of the Labour Party (then in opposition). The CND by now no longer fitted the democratic-elitist model; it was too popular, too moralistic, and too single-minded to operate in coalition politics; so it was left with no other form of immediate leverage on the state than that of mass demonstrations, civil disobedience, or mobilising public opinion. The committee of 100 was inevitable[22].

Yet the work of sociologists tended to justify the peace activists; in their analysis confirmed the widening gap between elites and masses[23]. The irresponsibility, impermeability and secrecy of military and intelligence elites in all the great powers appeared almost impenetrable by popular movements: even basic 'neutral' information about weapons was unavailable. The CND spent much of its time educating public opinion. In many countries, media bias (or silence) accompanied the co-option (or repression) of dissent, both within and outside major political parties.[24]

A new model

As Sean McBride insisted, in criticising the World Communications Order, the free dissemination of information on nuclear weapons was crucial to the mobilisation of public opinion against the arms race and the near certainty of nuclear catastrophe. The role of the Stockholm International Peace Research Institute (SIPRI) as a *nongovernmental* institution has been critical; as has that of Pugwash. New and parallel enterprises are now emerging in many places. Their development and funding can be linked to the Waldheim proposals for a world peace fund, and national peace tax campaigns.

But willingness to engage in extra-parliamentary action reflects a wide range of factors connected with crises of liberal values in the West and disenchantment with bi-partisan party-political rhetoric. Radical social philosophers like C. W. Mills and radical pacifists like A. J. Muste urged the peace movements to treat the mystique of the electoral process with scepticism; the latter warned that if the peace movement was diverted into formal political action, its moral urgency would be lost and 'every problem' would become one of 'strategy rather than ethics'. In Britain it was this aspect that brought disillusion with the Labour Party amongst those — many of them young, idealistic and impatient — who tried to influence it during the CND's development. Similarly disillusioned were those who put their trust in liberal politicians in the USA, or tried to effect a radical re-alignment in the Democratic Party.

One characteristic of these movements, the lack of an enmeshing of ordinary members in the ongoing political order, means that the national leadership, especially in its relations with the state, may often act as a brake, seeking to protect organisational interest and survival. For example the strongest opposition to the trend towards radical democratism, direct actionism and extra-legal activities in the CND came from its own executive, which oriented its strategy even closer to the Labour Party, as against both independent electoral ventures (peace candidates) and extra-parliamentary activity[25]. Indeed its attempt to channel and institutionalise popular protest, tended to compound the felt frustrations of the anti-nuclear campaigners at the community level; it was this that explained the formation of a variety of *ad hoc* groups on both sides of the Atlantic, quite independent of any centralised (national) political leadership.

As some political groups have discovered, as loose, open coalitions, peace *movements* (as opposed to organisations) cannot be highly ideological formations. Because of cross pressures (the multiple affiliations of their members and overlapping memberships with other groups), their manoeuvrability is restricted[26]. Moreover, there have been significant pressures on such groups, both from the external environment (the state) and from internal factors (the membership) to keep movements safely 'segmental' so that they remain non-inclusive, and obsessively concerned with narrow themes or problems. Nevertheless the nuclear issue gave and gives a particular intensity to these campaigns that is hard for established political institutions to harness or channel, and tends to broaden out into a wider social critique.

For example the disenchantment with supra-national organisations during the fifties had been based on their military and narrow character, furthering purely national concerns through regional blocs and alliances, within or outside world organisations. Part of the disillusion with official arms negotiations (as with international organisations) was also caused by the opportunist and cynical usage of them, by great powers as a forum for propaganda; some proposals were geared solely for consumption by public opinion rather than contributing to disarmament agreements.

Few twentieth century nation states have revealed any inclination towards unilateral renunciation of armaments: moreover neutrality as an option has shown little correlation with disarmament. Bilateral or multilateral summits and arms control talks have tended to reinforce the given system and framework of nation states, not only in reality and in the public mind but in that of the new peace movement as well. The fifties and sixties saw many shades of peace and pacifist opinion focused, reluctantly, time and time again on international talks like SALT: attempts to achieve bans, treaties, limitations or reductions relating particularly to the nuclear arms race between major states, but also turning to nuclear proliferation and the control of nuclear energy.

It is in this context of disenchantment that new models which channel the frustrated energies and failed strategies of the previous peace traditions and movements become paramount. In that sense both unilateralism and multi-lateralism represented failed strategies. They focused on state and interstate policy alone, without the ability to channel public opinion directly into action on the issues, and without transcending the established intellectual ideo-logical and military boundaries effectively. Interestingly enough, the innovative organisational archetype was not directly related to the peace movement at all, but to human rights. Amnesty International's work, though still based in national sections, has been both extra- and trans-national, as well as non-governmental. Sean Mcbride who significantly warned of the governmental character of the UN, and the vested interests and expertise working against disarmament has contributed much both to Amnesty and to the principle of 'We the people. . .' (the role of non-governmental organisa-tions in relation to the UN)[27].

This emphasis on nongovernmental intervention in global

affairs (which marks some of the efforts of the new World Disarmament Campaign), appears to make it something more than a rehash of the liberal internationalism of the League and the UN, or the multilateral reformism which accompanied it. If this new movement follows Amnesty's emphasis on independent action (and, if necessary, confrontation with governments) it represents a potent model for popular initiatives to arrest the arms race, and also links it with the model of grassroots, international solidarity of the socialist anti-militarists inherited from before the patriotic mobilisations of 1914.

The END. Another new initiative that conforms clearly to this model is that of the European Nuclear Disarmament (END) movement — a movement of movements in different countries and contexts, as well as communities and localities. It is one which goes beyond either unilateral gestures in one country, or multilateral rhetoric without concrete action or initiative. The problems of the CND in its first phase, were not its moralism — no healthy response to genocidal weapons can or should lack that — but its lack of internationalism and political strategy. It had, and perhaps still has, an element of 'little englandism' that is unrealistic if not isolationist. Moreover its lack of a truly transnational strategy left it open to ideological and political manipulation by sections of the left that in turn alienated public opinion. It had no alternative defence policy; it had no alternative foreign policy. In the end it was stuck with that familiar orientation to governments or political parties, and it lost touch with its rank and file in the communities in the process.

The END, with what E. P. Thompson calls its 'multilateral-unilateralism', its principle of cross-boundary campaigning and reciprocity, its focus on nuclear-free zones wherever and however achieved, its focus on linkages between groups and communities *across* frontiers and divides, rather than *between* states, makes it potentially the most significant and effective of the new peace movements, and one that bridges most of the previous peace traditions, as well as bridging organisations like the CND and the WDC.

The new peace efforts of the past two years also draw on

the mobilisation and organisation of public opinion on the nuclear energy issue, and its community base. This in turn draws on the new radicalism and counter culture of the sixties and seventies. The creation of local nuclear-free zones, and their linkage with the larger concept of nuclear-free plans, are symptomatic of this new alliance.

Although the END's attempts at ideological, and military, even-handedness often appear crude, if not naive, it is genuinely non-aligned in a way that the CND after 1963 was often not. By campaigning in alliance with popular and dissenting groups in *all* European countries (including the neutral, non-nuclear, and Eastern states) it at least offers the possibility of an alternative strategy and alternative foreign policy, and in a sense opens up the debate on alternative defence. Whether a truly transnational momentum of unilateral, graduated, tension-reducing steps can be triggered by this movement is problematic. The obstacles are enormous; the whole momentum of decades of the Cold War and the arms race will have to be reversed. Moreover to some extent the conventions of political life in both East and West will have to be jettisoned. The risks are obvious: instead of confidence-building measures, unilateral initiatives, if not linked or reciprocated, could lead to instability, crisis, a power vacuum and new tensions.

But there is another difference between the current and past contexts in which national pressure groups like the CND work; both media and public opinion are now relatively better informed and more accessible. This is partly due to the work done in the 1960s. Moreover the peace movement is itself much better informed and educated now, and has better resources; the peace research and peace education movements were in their infancy in 1960[28]. They now represent a substantial and growing resource. But the challenge to groups like the CND is whether they can relate themselves adequately to the new peace movement; which is non-aligned, non-governmental, transnational, and drawing on the accumulated knowledge and experience of twenty years work, and centuries of peace tradition. They are challenged in their relation to the next (1982) special session of the UN (particularly the role and participation of the nongovernmental organisations), to the new European movements, to the nuclear free zone campaigns, and to peace research and education. These relations may prove critical.

Conscientious objection. The one other peace tradition not so far directly mentioned in relation to this new model is that of conscientious objection and more personal forms of war resistance. It is arguable that its role is not confined to conscripting societies or non-nuclear forces since it clearly has recently widened both in its scope and in its methods to imply a withdrawal from injustice: social injustice, including the injustice of war, and above all nuclear war. The non-cooperation of scientists or civil servants can be urged more systematically by Pugwash and the newer groupings. Refusal to comply with such a system through work-research or payment of taxes, votes or ideological acquiescence, implies that this tradition can and will be widened to relate to the nuclear threat[29]. Here again the evidence is that such resistance needs a community base and a global vision, a transnational linkage, to be sustained. Non-cooperation can be communal as well as individual.

Summary

In summary and to conclude: if, as I have implied, both multilateralism and unilateralism as concepts and strategies are dead — if they have been tried and in their present forms found wanting — what is needed is the ability to set up reciprocal initiatives through governmental or nongovernmental action, whereby unilateral, confidence-building steps can be placed in a context of a new orientation to defence and foreign (or global) affairs. 'Multilateral-unilateralism' can proceed at the community level (e.g. twinning) as well as in regions, and between countries. The principle of the nuclear free zone ideally fits such a model.

But this new movement also synthesises the right to protest and organise with the right to live free from the threat of nuclear attack. Thus human rights and nuclear disarmament throughout Europe, and the rest of the globe, become linked.

The concepts of species identity, of ecological inter-dependencies, have grown apace against the background of the thermonuclear threat. If the multiple peace traditions in this context can draw their strands together and turn from their status as isolated, sectarian, marginal and often ineffective minorities to establish the basis of a majority movement, then the contributions of publics to averting catastrophe may be critical where governmental efforts clearly have not halted the arms race.

Such a scenario, that links transnational non-governmental popular or communal initiatives, community-to-community, may still be a utopian myth, but it has some firm support in academic research. James Rosenau's study of the growth of global systems of political and social relations, for example, and the implications for national authority structures and boundaries of growing transnational relationships[30], lend credence to the scenario. Other supportive work includes: Chadwick Algers on the relations between communities and the world[31]; Robert Angell's on the role of nongovernmental transnational groups[32]; Charles Osgood's on graduated reciprocal tension-reducing initiatives[33]; Sharp's on the role of popular non-cooperation in new forms of defence[34]. The work of the Japanese peace researcher Sakamoto on the need for a communal basis for a trans-national identity is a crucial finding of 'mondial training' or global education[35]. In my own work on war resisters, I have found that only where a strong communal base exists, and some orientation other than or beyond the nation state, can such non-cooperation with the warmaking state be reinforced[36].

When such work is set side by side, a synthesis emerges; there appears a possibility that the new peace movement does exist in a social and historical context where it can harness public opinion to a global strategy that may convert myth into reality. If these realities are perceived as such then the scenario may be acted on; the vision of a world disarmed by peoples as opposed to states, is realisable if, as I have suggested, history may be on its side. If enough people act as if it can succeed, it will succeed.

This strategy, like public opinion, *is* a myth, but, if made concrete in action, if perceived as possible and acted on by enough people it can become a reality. A sense of global unity has grown under the shadow of the bomb. The nation-state system is not clearly able to cope with key species problems. Non-state categories — such as women as a socio-logical group, are emerging to play more crucial roles. The hope must be that the contributions of communities, non-governmental groups and publics may succeed in realising the species interest in survival, where nation states have so far failed to bring even a measure of nuclear disarmament.

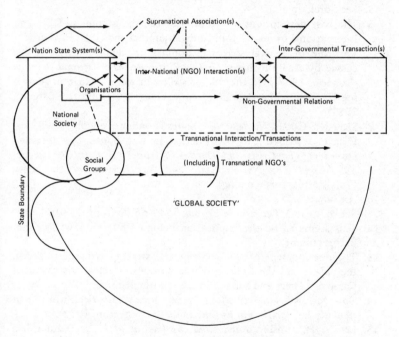

Figure 3 Internationalism and transnationalism (globalism)

References

1. See Bob Overy's classification *How effective are Peace Movements?* (Bradford Peace Studies papers no. 2, University of Bradford, 1981).
2. The proposition is W. I. Thomas's, but it was examined in R. K. Merton's essay on the 'self-fulfilling prophecy' in his *Social Theory and Social Structures* (Glencoe, 1957). It links closely with G. Sorel's formulation of the social 'myth' (see below).
3. The idea of the 'myth' in this sense was first formulated by Georges Sorel in his *Reflections on Violence* (London, 1925).
4. A view confirmed by current critiques of the survey tradition.
5. See Sorel, op cit.
6. The best descriptions are to be found in the accounts of the 2nd International by James Joll, Julius Braunthal and G. D. H. Cole.
7. The role of general strikes in popular or civilian defence is discussed by Adam Roberts, *Civilian Resistance as a National Defence* (London, 1967). On the role of strikes in social change in general see G. Sharp, *The Politics of Nonviolent Action* (Porter Sargent, 1973).
8. See Nigel Calder, *Nuclear Nightmares* (London: Penguin, 1979).
9. I have described this disaffiliation in two books: *An Infantile Disorder? The Crisis and Decline of the New Left* (Routledge, 1977) *and The Nation State and War Resistance* (University of California, forthcoming).
10. *An Infantile Disoder?*, ibid.
11. See M. Ceadel, *Pacifism in Britain, 1948–55* (Oxford, 1980).
12. This seems to be the implication behind Dr David Owen's paper in this volume.
13. The development of this concept and strategy is taking place in the papers and the *Bulletin* of the European Nuclear Disarmament Campaign (Bertrand Russell House, Nottingham).
14. This history is described in Peter Brock's historical work, particularly his *Pacifism in Europe to 1914* (Princeton, 1972).
15. See F. H. Hinsley, *Power and the Pursuit of Peace* (Cambridge, 1963).
16. See Martin Shaw, 'Socialism and Militarism' (Spokesman pamphlet, Nottingham, 1981).
17. This new pacifism is described in P. Brock, *Twentieth Century Pacifism* (van Nostrand, 1970), and for the USA, R. Cooney and H. Michalowski, *The Power of the People* (Peace Press, 1977).
18. Its position is expressed in H. Clark's pamphlet, 'Making Nonviolent Revolution', *Peace News*, 1978.
19. It have analysed this in detail in my description of the New Left (*An Infantile Disorder?*, op. cit.).

20. This is the underlying critique of D. Martin's *Pacifism* (RKP, 1965). Martin follows Bryan Wilson's work and the parallel but earlier analyses by W. Kornhauser, *Politics of the Mass Society* (Free Press, 1959) (criticised by John Rex in *War and Peace* (CND, 1963), vol. 1).

21. See A. Haber's article, 'The End of Ideology as Ideology' reprinted in F. Lindenfeld, *Reader in Political Sociology* (New York, Minerva, 1968).

22. For recent analyses see R. Taylor and C. Pritchard, *The Protest Makers* (Pergamon, 1980), and my own, op. cit.

23. The view first expounded by C. W. Mills, *The Power Elite* (New York: Galaxy Books,) where his notion of 'publics' is discussed.

24. The BBC decision not to show 'War Game' was one indication of this in Britain.

25. It is significant for the present argument that E. P. Thompson was one of those advocating a strategy outside the formal Labour Party procedures.

26. This formulation is articulated in Ralf Dahrendorf's *Class and Class Conflict in Industrial Society* (RKP, 1959), as well as in Kornhauser, op. cit.

27. The 'Bradford Declaration' (International Peace Bureau 1977) on non-governmental representation at the UN and McBride's Bradford lecture, 'Is Nuclear Survival Possible?' (University of Bradford, 1978), are symptomatic of this trend.

28. I have given a brief overview of this history in my 'Problems and Possibilities in the Study of Peace', Ernest Stockdale lecture 1980, University of Bradford *Peace Studies* paper no. 3, 1981. See also P. van den Dungen's 'Bibliography of Peace Research' (no. 1 in the same series).

29. Daniel Ellsberg's revelations of State Department orientations on Indo-China can equally be repeated on nuclear war issues. Professor Humphrey's paper in this volume particularly suggests the potential non-cooperation of scientists and medics on a transnational basis.

30. See, e.g., James Rosenau's address to the International Studies Association of the UK in 1974 and in his various works on International politics over the past decade (Free Press, Glencoe).

31. C. Alger, *Your City in the World: The World in Your City* (Mershon, 1974), a study of Columbus, Ohio.

32. R. Angell, *Peace on the March: Transnational Participation in Politics* (van Nostrand, 1968).

33. Cf. C. Osgood's concept of GRITS (tension-reducing initiatives), developed at the University of Urbana in the early 1960s.

34. G. Sharp, *Politics of Nonviolent Action*, op. cit.
35. The work of Sakamoto and most of the other researchers is summarised in J. Dedring, *Recent Advances in Peace and Conflict Research* (Sage, 1976). Note also the work of Theodore Lentz on global attitudes.
36. My own work is summarised in *The Nation State and War Resistance*, op. cit.

12. THE SCIENTISTS' RESPONSIBILITY

John Humphrey

Scientists and engineers invent the weapons

The presentations which have preceded this final session have made it clear enough that scientists and engineers have been responsible for developing the terrible weapons of destruction with which modern forces are armed. Neither the politicians who decided to order their production nor their military advisers who recommended them to do so could have invented these weapons. I may quote the considered opinion of Lord Zuckerman, Chief Scientific Adviser to a succession of British Prime Ministers, in an address to the American Philosophical Society given in November 1979:

> The scientists and technologists were themselves the ones who initiated new developments, who created new demands, who warned the public about new hazards. They were the ones who, at base, were determining the social, economic and political future of the world. Without any badge of authority conferred on them either by democratic decision or autocratic diktat, without any concern for political values of goals, scientists and engineers had become the begetters of new social demand and the architects of new economic and social situations, over which those who exercised political power had to rule. The nuclear world, with all its hazards, is the scientists' creation; it is certainly not a world which came about in response to any external demand.[1]

Though true this is not totally fair, since it was governments and industry which gave these scientists their jobs and encouraged them to use their ingenuity. I shall return to this later.

How far is scientific knowledge neutral?

My function is to discuss the wider responsibility which scientists and engineers should have, namely a sense of social responsibility for the outcome of their inventiveness. You may wonder why this lecture is given by someone who has never been directly concerned with weapons design or defence against them, apart from the fact that doctors would be deeply involved in trying to pick up and repair the bits if a nuclear war broke out. My explanation allows me to make three points.

One, that my work does not come under the Official Secrets Act, and I am therefore free to speak — even if I have to rely on other people's published data rather than on inside information. The second, that the facts are generally intelligible to anyone who has a reasonable scientific training and whose interests are not narrowed down to his or her particular speciality. The third, that scientific discoveries and scientific knowledge are in themselves socially neither good nor bad, even though intellectually exciting and beautiful and capable of changing man's image of himself. They acquire dimensions of good or evil only when converted into technologies which are applied on a socially significant scale. Once applied, science is no longer neutral. Antibiotics, prophylactic immunization and elementary hygiene, for example, have eradicated many ancient scourges from the developed world, but in the developing countries have led to the population explosion which threatens to produce underfed millions and conflict over resources — a problem emphasized forcibly by Professor A. V. Hill in his Presidential Address to this Association in 1952.

Fundamental research in endocrinology has led to the Pill and other means of fertility control, which have radically changed the relation between the sexes in our society and which could, in principle, contain the world population explosion. Application of genetics has produced improved strains of maize, rice and wheat which have enormously increased yields of staple food but have not solved and may even have increased the problems of its distribution. Even my own subject, immunology, could be applied for biological warfare as readily as for improving health. Thus we must recognize that scientists of all sorts are liable to contribute to developments which have socially important consequences, and we have a right — even a duty — to think about them even when not directly involved in the developments ourselves. The dangers posed by nuclear weapons proliferation are in any case of obvious concern to all of us.

Who does military R & D?

As I stated at the outset, scientists and engineers have been the instruments which have enabled the arms race to escalate. Obviously those involved do not constitute the whole of the scientific community. To judge from the generalist scientific media, such as *Science, Nature*, and *New Scientist*, in which discussion of current issues takes place, they now form an almost silent minority, although during the 1950s and early 1960s their activities were usually admired and applauded. In thinking about responsibility it is important to consider who these scientists and engineers are; how many; and what is their motivation. At the risk of repeating statistics which have already been given I will remind you that they are very many. The 1978 UN Report *Economic and Social Consequences of the Arms Race and of Military Expenditure*[2] suggested that military research and development involved about 400 000 of the world's most highly qualified physical scientists and engineers; or about 40 per cent of the total research personnel. Professor Lloyd J. Dumas, in a paper presented at the Annual Meetings of the AAAS in January 1980[3] stated that in 1974 about 75 per cent of all government-supported research and development funds, and at least one-third of all scientific research and development (R & D) in the USA were for military purposes. He contrasted this with corresponding government expenditure in Japan (3.3 per cent) and Germany (22 per cent) and attributed the greater increase in civilian productivity and innovation in the latter two countries to the fact that they wasted less talent on military projects. In Britain, in 1978, according to the 1980 EEC report *Government Financing of Research and Development 1970-79*[4], 51.5 per cent of government finance of R & D was for defence. The report commented that the UK alone in Europe showed a trend towards an increase in defence appropriations and a reduction in support of the general promotion of knowledge. From the British Government publication *Defence in the 1980's. Statement on the Defence Estimate. Vol. 1*, it can be calculated that at least 40 000 scientists, engineers and technicians in Britain are currently working on defence projects[5]. This is a very large number, even allowing that part of their effort resulted last year in sales of arms worth about £1200 million[6]. I have no corresponding estimates for the USSR, but the magnitude of the Russian military effort implies that they also employ a very large number of trained scientists on military R & D.

Motivation

When it comes to motivation I have few facts to go on, but I doubt whether all these persons have clearly thought through the implications of their work; that they have weighed such facts as those presented during the course of our present discussion and have come to the considered conclusion that true patriotism requires them to develop increasingly sophisticated weaponry to be put at the disposal of their governments. I suspect that the most important factor is that reasonably well-paid jobs are available, in which their scientific training is directly useful. The work will usually not be immediately related to a completed weapon, but to a particular component or to a particular problem — e.g. improving microelectronic circuits, the behaviour of alloys, the thermo-dynamics of gaseous reactions, ultra-sensitive detectors of electromagnetic radiation — and intrinsically interesting. The intellectual environment may be exciting and the problems challenging. The job has official approval, and the spice of secrecy. So why not do it? Once in, specialization, pensions, classification (notably in the USSR), inertia and other reasons make it difficult to get out. There are some added attractions according to Professor Dumas, such as not having to worry too much about the cost of the product — in contrast with something which has to face competition for civilian markets.

In the case of those scientists and engineers employed in military R & D who are not fully convinced of the value of what they are doing — if ever they ask themselves the question — the job is what matters most. The point was well put in an article by the national organiser of the trade union AUEW–TASS: 'As the slogan "Jobs not bombs" resounds through the protests at mass unemployment, it has a hollow ring in the ears of many armaments workers; for here bombs *are* jobs.'[7] In reference to proposals for alternative products made by representatives of the work-force at Lucas Aerospace, at Vickers and at British Aerospace Warton Divison, he quotes the chairman of the Vickers combined shop stewards committee, who said on television, 'While we would always welcome alternative employment, our main concern is work. While some of us have looked at the possibilities of alternatives we don't see anything else at present that could secure full employment. We would welcome five Tridents on our slipways.' In fact one of the members of the Lucas Aerospace Shop Stewards Combine, who was dismissed from his position in the firm for taking too much time off to work on their Alternate Plan, is currently fighting to get back his job as design engineer on the Stingray torpedo project!

When it comes to the motives of senior scientists and engineers who have the power to initiate major projects and to propose new weapons, again I can claim no insight, but Herbert York, the first Director of Defence Research and Engineering in the United States, should be better informed. In *Race to Oblivion* he wrote that their motives are various, but nearly all such individuals — and here he was referring also to politicians, editorial writers, civilian officials and military officers, business executives and labour leaders —

> have had a deep long-term involvement in the arms race. They derive either their incomes, their profits or their consultant fees from it. But much more important than money as a motivating force are the individuals' own psychic and spiritual needs; the majority of the key

individual promoters of the arms race derive a very large part of their self-esteem from their participation in what they believe to be an essential — even a holy — cause . . . They are inspired by ingenious and clever ideas, challenged by bold statements of real and imaginary military requirements, stimulated to match or exceed technological progress by the other side or even by a rival military service here at home, and victimized by rumours and phony intelligence. Some have been lured by the siren call of rapid advancement, personal recognition and umlimited opportunity, and some have been bought by promises of capital gains. Some have sought out and even made up problems to fit the solution they have spent much of their lives discovering and developing. A few have used the arms race to achieve other, often hidden objectives.[8]

Lord Zuckerman's analysis

This passage was quoted by Lord Zuckerman in his evaluation of the role of scientific advisers. He maintains that none of the chief scientific advisers to the Presidents of the United States nor to the British Prime Ministers wishes to see the nuclear arms race continue, and asks, 'Why is it that the scientists at the top, men who had all relevant information at their disposal, have failed to get their views accepted?' He suggests various reasons, including the fact that the decisions of political leaders are based on compromise, which makes it very difficult to halt a process which has behind it strong pressure groups and public opinion (even if manipulated), especially in the case of weapons laboratories which have a continuous existence, whereas presidents and prime ministers and military chiefs are both impermanent and concerned with a host of other problems besides East–West relations and the nuclear arms race. Zuckerman concludes that we need far more open and informed public discussion of the immediate causes that have turned today's advanced industrial societies into the armed camps that they now are; that we need far less of the secrecy that is the environment in which the nuclear arms race pursues its irrational course; that the aims of the Non-Proliferation Treaty would only be furthered if there was a clearer public understanding about the effects of nuclear weapons. And that the kind of issues which are discussed in the Brandt Report (which had not been published when he gave his address) are less urgent but far more important than the arms race. In other words, when the problem is essentially political, only informed political pressure will be effective.

This seems to me good advice. The present meeting of the British Association for the Advancement of Science has indeed been putting some of it into practice.

What the scientific community can do

Are there specific actions which we can take as scientists and engineers to halt and reverse the arms race? The first thing needed is obviously to become better informed ourselves, and to overcome the quite natural inhibition which most of us have about discussing awkward, controversial and emotionally disturbing topics as well as the 'shop' or gossip which make up the usual small talk among scientists. The convention that to discuss party politics is boring has some value, but the problems with which we are concerned transcend party political differences. As Dr Boeker reminded us (Chapter 6), quite a number of bodies exist which can help with this education, such as *The Bulletin of the Atomic Scientists* and the International Pugwash Movement. There are also the well-respected Stockholm International Peace Research Institute, the Institute of Strategic Studies, the Armament and Disarmament Information Unit at Sussex University, and bodies recently established in Britain such as the Medical Campaign against Nuclear Weapons and Scientists against Nuclear Arms. The American Association for the Advancement of Science has for many years provided a forum for information and discussion in its journal *Science*. The primary data, derived from technological literature and official reports, are often harder to find and take more digesting, but some of you may have access to these.

Even if a substantial proportion of scientists have taken the trouble to inform themselves about the arms race and the effects of the weapons involved, by itself this would have no effect on the decisions of the policy-makers. The information may produce approval, disapproval or doubt in the mind of the individual scientist, but it will not threaten politicians with loss of power or industrialists of markets. It is necessary to exert pressure. Sometimes this can be done by argument and advice given at the top level — as I know to have been an important element in achieving the one step which has been taken backwards in the arms race since the Second World War, namely the banning of biological weapons — but, as Lord Zuckerman pointed out, it is popular pressure at the grass roots which ultimately matters. One way to help bring this about is for scientists to explain to the public in plain terms what the use of these weapons implies, by speaking to any groups who will listen and through the media. In doing so it is essential to make clear what are facts and what is surmise, and if we express opinions on policy, as we are bound to do, to claim no special authority by virtue of being scientists — otherwise we lose our credibility. We can also when teaching at undergraduate or graduate level such subjects as radiation physics include, rather than avoid discussing, such matters as nuclear weapons. Grass roots movements which can spring up easily enough in democratic capitalist societies (this is not a complete contradiction in terms, but this is not the place to go into the question) flourish less readily in Communist countries. But we should not accept the idea that people in those countries are not permitted to think for themselves, or that they relish the prospect of nuclear war. The body International Physicians for Prevention of Nuclear War, of which I am a member, contains not only American, Japanese and European doctors but also prominent Soviet physicians who have achieved more publicity for their views in the USSR than was vouchsafed in the USA or in Britain[9].

Another important thing which scientists can do is to maintain and increase personal international contracts, especially with colleagues in countries which are cast as potential enemies. Scientists have bonds of common interests with their colleagues and a tradition of trusting one another. In many instances they depend upon each others' observations for the advancement of their own subjects, and are bound to cooperate, either informally or through international agencies or the International Council of Scientific Unions. I will take as one example the current ten-year intensive study of climate throughout the world, aimed at enabling a sufficiently detailed computer prediction of the weather to make possible growing and harvesting the crops most suited to the particular season. This would have an enormous effect on agricultural productivity. Another might be the effort to achieve controlled nuclear fusion for energy, in which close cooperation between scientists of the Soviet Union, the United States, Great Britain and other countries of Europe has continued despite the ups and downs of political tension. Personal contacts, especially working visits, lead to friendship and remove misapprehensions. We should encourage them to be more frequent and more free — even if it means learning a second language! And if individual scientists in any country get into trouble for legitimately criticizing their government's policies, and arbitrary action is taken against them, their colleagues should be prepared to imagine themselves in a similar situation, and to speak up for them.

I mentioned earlier the importance of jobs — worthwhile gainful employment. It is not much use criticizing, overtly or covertly, our colleagues engaged in military R & D if the result is to will them to join the ranks of the unemployed. Scientists, through the bodies which represent them — trade unions and learned societies — should be giving very serious attention to the problems of where scientific and engineering talent could be usefully, and in the long run profitably, redirected, and to the provision of appropriate retraining. The US National Academy of Science and, to some extent and indirectly, the Royal Society have done some useful work in this direction but the trade unions and those learned societies with which I am acquainted seem to have been content to stand aside. If the scientific community did not have the wit and the imagination to formulate proposals for applying its discoveries — often made with the help of public funds — more productively than in devising new weapons it would cease to merit the support which it enjoys, and could not complain about the anti-scientific trend discernible among many young people in the West. Here I exaggerate of course — individuals and associations of individuals are continuously putting forward good ideas and feasibility studies — but in my view the scientific community as a whole does not take these problems seriously enough.

What else could the professional and learned societies do in this context? It has often been suggested that they might formulate codes of conduct to which their members must subscribe, in a similar manner to the ethical codes which apply to members of the medical profession. The idea of a sort of 'Hippocratic Oath' for scientists has never got very far; partly because of the difficulty of formulating a meaningful code, but mainly because — unlike the medical profession with its General Medical Council — there would be no means of enforcing such a code. The experience which Dr Boeker described with the European Physics Society illustrates some of the difficulties. There is however another way in which scientific societies might play an important part, if they were willing, namely by undertaking part of the responsibility for verification of agreements. A major stumbling block, at least ostensibly, in reaching agreement on measures to limit development and deployment of nuclear, and chemical weapons, has been the problem of verification that the agreement was not being circumvented. The persons who must know whether an agreement was being kept are the scientists and engineers involved. Some of them, I suppose, are bound to belong to their appropriate professional societies, in order to keep in touch with what is going on outside their classified work. If any government had formally and publicly undertaken to take or not to take some particular measure, infringement of this undertaking would be contrary to that government's policy, and it would therefore be proper for those concerned to report suspected infringements. To do so would, of course, require courage; and there would always be the possibility that the suspicion was unfounded, since the proportion of paranoid persons engaged in science is not less than in the population as a whole. Let us suppose, however, that the scientists' professional association had undertaken, as a member of its appropriate International Scientific Union, to receive reports from its members related to verification and to support those who submitted them; also on the one hand to submit all such reports to an elected committee and to pass copies to the International Union, and on the other to investigate whether they were *prima facie* valid. This would be important in two ways: in providing a channel independent of government or employer for reporting suspected infringements through a body which could evaluate them; and in providing a local mechanism for sifting out reports which were clearly unfounded. For such a procedure to work presupposes that in the professional society at least some members of the Committee would be sufficiently independent-minded to disregard pressure to let matters drop, and that the Society understood what verification was about and accepted the responsibility of checking the implementation of its own government's stated policy. Given backing at all levels I believe it could work, but whether governments could ever agree to trust monitoring of scientists by scientists other than their own is another matter.

Much of what I have proposed in this lecture is easier said than done, and requires a willingness to stick out our necks from the cosy and generally appropriate scientific niches in which we normally live our professional lives. But for the sake of the image of science, as well as the survival of our civilization, it is essential that more of us should be emboldened to do so.

References

1. Lord Zuckerman, 'Science Advisers and Scientific Advisers', *Proc. Amer. Philosophical Society*, **124**, 4 (August 1980, reprinted by The Menard Press, London).
2. *Economic and Social Consequences of the Arms Race and of Military Expenditure* (United Nations Publications, Room LX–2300, New York, NY 10017, 1978).
3. Lloyd J. Dumas, 'The Impact of the Military Budget on the Domestic Economy'. Paper presented at the Annual Meeting of the American Association for the Advancement of Science, San Francisco, January 1980.

4. *Government Financing of Research and Development 1970–79* (Luxembourg, Brussels: eurostat 1980).
5. *Defence in the 1980's. Statement on Defence Estimates 1980.* Vol 1. HMSO states that 60 per cent of the output of the aerospace and 20 per cent of electronics industries was defence-related. Application of these percentages to the numbers employed in these industries (Department of Employment *Gazette*) indicates about 280 000 persons employed in defence work. The occupational composition of these industries (D.O.E. *Gazette*, June 1980) suggests that of this 280 000, some 40 000 are scientists, technicians and professional engineers. Central government employment on Defence R & D in 1979 included 7100 scientists and engineers and 5000 technicians (*Economic Trends*, July 1980). I am indebted to Mr Peter Bennett, ASTMS Research Officer, for this analysis.
6. T. Taylor, 'British Arms Exports and R & D Costs' *Survival* (Institute of Strategic Studies, November/December 1980).
7. W. Niven, 'Tridents into Ploughshares', *New Statesman*, 12 June, 1981, p. 12.
8. H. York, *Race to Oblivion*. (New York: Simon & Schuster, 1970).
9. The First Congress of International Physicians for the Prevention of Nuclear War was held at Airlie House, Virginia, USA, 20–25 March 1981. It was attended by 73 senior physicians from North America, Japan and Europe including 13 from the USSR. Its unanimous conclusions concerning the disastrous medical consequences of a nuclear war were reported at length in *Pravda, Izvestia, Komsomolskaya Pravda* and on television by Professor E. I. Chazov, leader of the Russian group.

NOTES ON CONTRIBUTORS

1. *Dr C. F. Barnaby* was Director of the Stockholm International Peace Research Institute (SIPRI) from 1971–81. Before that he was the Executive Secretary of the Pugwash Conferences on Science and World Affairs, a research physicist at University College, London, and employed at the British Atomic Weapons Research Establishment, Aldermaston. He is the author and editor of numerous books and articles on nuclear and disarmament issues and military technology, including *Man and the Atom* (London, Thames and Hudson, 1970), *The Nuclear Age* (London, Taylor and Francis, 1978); and *Prospects for Peace* (Oxford, Pergamon, 1980). Dr Barnaby now lives in Hampshire and is Visiting Professor of Peace Studies at the Free University, Amsterdam. He was President of the British Association's General Section for the 1981 Annual Meeting.

2. *Dr E. Boeker* is Professor of Theoretical Physics at the Free University, Amsterdam. He participates in the working party on peace research at that University and is Chairman of the Netherlands Congress against Nuclear Weapons (comprising most Dutch political parties, churches and trade unions). He is Chairman of the Advisory Commission on Curriculum Innovation in Physics, and publishes on problems of science and society, and co-authored *Physics in Society* Amsterdam (VU bookshop and UK: SISCON, 1981).

3. *Mr S. F. J. Butler* is Deputy Director of the Scientic Advisory Branch of the Home Office where his responsibilities include scientific advice on home defence, criminal justice and prisons. A mathematician with a First Class Honours degree from London University and an M.Sc. in hydrodynamics, Mr Butler has worked at the Royal

Aircraft Establishment and in the Ministry of Defence before moving to the Home Office in 1975.

4. *Dr J. Erickson* is Professor of Politics and Director of Defence Studies at the University of Edinburgh. He has taught various subjects related to Russian history and politics at the Universities of St Andrews, Manchester, Indiana and Cambridge, and has published numerous books and articles on Russian military affairs. His latest book (forthcoming), *The Road to Berlin*, deals with the Soviet–German War.

5. *Dr J. H. Humphrey*, CBE, FI, Biol., FRCP, FRS, is Emeritus Professor of Immunology at the Royal Postgraduate Medical School, Hammersmith Hsopital. He is also currently Chairman of the Medical Campaign against Nuclear Weapons, Secretary of the Committee on Safeguard of Pursuit of Science on the International Council of Scientific Unions, Chairman of the Society for the Protection of Science and Learning and a member of the Executive Committee of the Council for Science and Society. He was Head of the Division of Immunology at the National Institute for Medical Research, and Deputy Director 1961-76, and President of the International Union of Immunological Societies 1974-7.

6. *The Rt Hon Dr D. A. L. Owen* is Member of Parliament for Plymouth, Devenport and one of the leaders of the Social Democratic Party. A physician educated at Sidney Sussex College, Cambridge and St Thomas' Hospital, Dr Owen is a former Minister of Health and Secretary of State for Foreign and Commonwealth Affairs. His publications include *The Politics of Defence* (London: Jonathan Cape, 1972), *Human Rights* (London: Jonathan Cape, 1978), and *Face the Future* (OUP, 1981).

7. *Dr G. Rathjens* is Professor of Political Science at the Massachusetts Institute of Technology and Chairman of committees on arms control and international security of the American Association for the Advancement of Science and the American Academy of Arts and Sciences. During the years 1953-68 he was with the US Department of Defense, the White House Staff and the Institute for Defense Analyses; during 1979-80 Professor Rathjens was with the US Department of State.

8. *Dr J. Rotblat*, CBE, Emeritus Professor of Physics at the University of London, started his scientific career in Poland as a nuclear physicist. During the war he participated in atom bomb work in Los Alamos. As a result of this he turned to medical physics, the treatment of cancer, and radiation biology at St Batholomew's Hospital Medical College, London. He also became active in scientists' movements for peace, and co-founded the Atomic Scientists Association in Great Britain. He is one of the 11 signatories of the Russell–Einstein Manifesto, and founder of the Pugwash Movement, of which he was secretary-general for 17 years; presently he is Chairman of the British Pugwash Group. He has published extensively on nuclear physics, radiation bilogy and Pugwash-related issues.

9. *Mr N. A. Sims* is a Lecturer in International Relations at the London School of Economics and Political Science. His research interests include international organisation, the disarmament policy process, and diplomatic aspects of biological and chemical disarmament. He has written extensively on disarmament since 1961: his books include *Approaches to Disarmament* (London: QPS, 1979).

10. *Dr G. P. Thomas* is Deputy Director of the Department for External Studies at the University of Oxford, and Fellow of Linacre College, Oxford. A former member of the University of Wales and of the Cavendish Laboratory, Cambridge, Dr Thomas is a physicist who has worked for a number of years in adult education. He was Recorder of the General Section of the British Association for its York Meeting.

11. *Mr E. P. Thompson*, writer and historian, was a founder of the movement for European Nuclear Disarmament (6 Endsleigh Street, London WC1H 0DX) and editor (with Dan Smith) of *Protest and Survive* (Harmondsworth Penguin Books 1980). His recent contributions to the debate about disarmament include 'Notes on Exterminism', *New Left Review*, 121, May–June 1980, and 'The End of the Line', *The Bulletin of the Atomic Scientists*, January 1981).

12. *Dr N. J. Young* is Reader in Peace Studies at Bradford University, and a founder member of its School of Peace Studies. He has been active in peace research and education since the 1960s. He has taught at the Universities of California and Northwestern (USA) and at the University of Birmingham. His major books deal with the nation state and war resistance (University of California, forthcoming) and the New Left (*An Infantile Disorder? The Crisis and Decline of the New Left* (London, Routledge, 1977)).